Contents

Alcohol——The AELTC reserves the right to refuse entry to the show court stands to any person carrying alcohol and to request any person drinking alcohol in the stands to leave the stands.

Band Performances——The Band of The Adjutant General's Corps, under the direction of Captain R. Meldrum, will perform on the Aorangi Picnic Terrace between 10.30 a.m. and 12.30 p.m. and on Centre Court between 1.00 p.m. and 1.50 p.m. on Saturday 3rd and Sunday 4th July. On the Bandstand, adjacent to the Champagne & Pimms Bar on the Tea Lawn, a variety of musical entertainment will be provided by the Red Hot & Blue Orchestra (with associated musicians) on each of the first nine days. On the two Finals days, 3rd and 4th July, the winners of the 1999 Perrier Young Jazz Awards will play on the Bandstand. The Merton Music Foundation will perform on the Aorangi Picnic Terrace (Youth Concert Band) from 10.30 a.m. until the start of play on Thursday 1st July and on the Bandstand (Youth Jazz Orchestra) on Friday 2nd July.

Bank——A bank is operated by Barclays Bank at Gate 3.

Catering Arrangements——These are in the hands of FMC Ltd c/o AELTC, Church Road, Wimbledon, SW19 5AE. There are public food outlets in the new No.1 Court, and buffets on the Tea Lawn on the East side of the Centre Court. Spectators are requested *not* to take crockery, cutlery or glasses away from the catering areas. The Wingfield Restaurant, the waitress service restaurant, is in the new No.1 Court stadium where lunch and afternoon tea are served. Reservations for lunch only will be taken on 0181 946 8485. Reservations cannot be accepted from corporate hospitality companies. Bookings are for a maximum of six people.

Chemist Shop——Lloyds Pharmacy provide a chemist shop facility next to the Food Village on the east side of the new No.1 Court stadium.

Cushions——Cushions can be hired daily from the attendants of the British Cushion Supply Company, at a charge of £1.40 per day during The Championships. At the termination of the day's play they should be returned to the company's employees. A souvenir cushion can be purchased at £5.50.

First Aid——There are seven First Aid Posts; three in the Centre Court building, two in the new No.1 Court stadium, one alongside Court 6 and one to the south of Court 13.

Flash Photography——Spectators are advised that the use of flash lights from the stands is strictly forbidden. Automatic flashlights must be suppressed.

Internet Services——Information and latest scores during the Wimbledon Fortnight and all year round are available on the official Wimbledon Internet site hosted by IBM and located at URL **http:\\www.wimbledon.org.** There is an Internet Kiosk on the east side of the new No.1 Court stadium.

Lost Persons——Any spectator who may have lost contact with a relation or friend should make enquiries at the WRVS Information Desk near Court 14 up to 7 p.m. and thereafter at the Church Road Gate 5.

Match Statistics——IBM provides a point by point, results and statistics service for all matches. Touch screen systems located in the Match Statistics Kiosk on the east side of the new No.1 Court stadium also include player biographies, historical Championship statistics and results.

Merchandise——There are two 'Wimbledon Shops' in 1999 both selling products under exclusive licence to the AELTC. The main shop is located on the ground floor of the new No.1 Court stadium opposite courts 16 & 17. A smaller shop is located at the south end of the Grounds behind Court 13. The funds generated from the Wimbledon licence will increase the amount available for the further development of lawn tennis in Great Britain. In addition, there is a souvenir shop on the Tea Lawn by Gate 4. Proceeds from this shop go to The Wimbledon Lawn Tennis Museum.

Newspapers——Newspapers and a selection of magazines are on sale daily in the kiosk on the east side of the new No.1 Court stadium.

Philips Large Screen TV——a giant screen opposite the Aorangi Picnic Terrace provides live relay of matches from both Centre and No.1 Courts and general information throughout the day.

Photographs——Spectators are advised that it is a condition of entry to the Grounds that no unauthorised person shall be entitled to use commercially any still photographs, film, videotape or other audio visual material recorded within the Grounds.

Portable Telephones——Must remain switched off when spectators are on or near a court.

Post Office——Most normal postal, banking and bill-paying facilities are provided from the Post Office kiosk on the east side of the new No.1 Court stadium where Championships' Commemorative covers, with specialised franking, will also be available.

Public Ballot 2000——For details of the 2000 Championships please send a stamped addressed envelope between the beginning of August and the end of December 1999 to: The All England Lawn Tennis & Croquet Club, P.O. Box 98, Church Road, Wimbledon, SW19 5AE. 2000 Championship dates: 26TH June–9th July.

Public Information Points——These are situated in a number of locations throughout the Grounds and provide up to the minute details of the latest scores, results and messages from all courts.

Radio Wimbledon——First introduced in 1992, operating from 8.00 a.m. on the opening Monday throughout the Fortnight on 87.7 FM, this will provide up-to-date information on latest scores, local weather and traffic news up to a four mile radius of Church Road, Wimbledon.

Returned Show Court Tickets——Can be purchased daily, when available, from the kiosk north of Court 18 near the top of St Mary's Walk. The price before 5.00 p.m. is £5 and after 5.00 p.m. £3. All proceeds go to charity.

Survey——An official competitor equipment census is prepared by Sports Marketing Surveys (Telephone: 01932 350600, Facsimile: 01932 350375).

Taxi Service——Taxis are available outside the Grounds on the ranks near Gates 4, 5 on Church Road and at Gate 13 on Somerset Road. Taxi sharing is encouraged during peak periods and a shuttle service is provided to Southfields and Wimbledon stations as well as services to any other destination. Please telephone Licensed Taxi Drivers Association (0171 286 1046) for all taxi enquiries.

Tennis Balls——Balls, posts, nets, etc., are supplied by Slazengers Limited. In all matches used balls will be replaced by new balls at the conclusion of the first seven games and thereafter at the conclusion of every ninth game. Subject to availability, used tennis balls will be sold daily, except Monday 21st June, from the kiosk near No.1 Court.

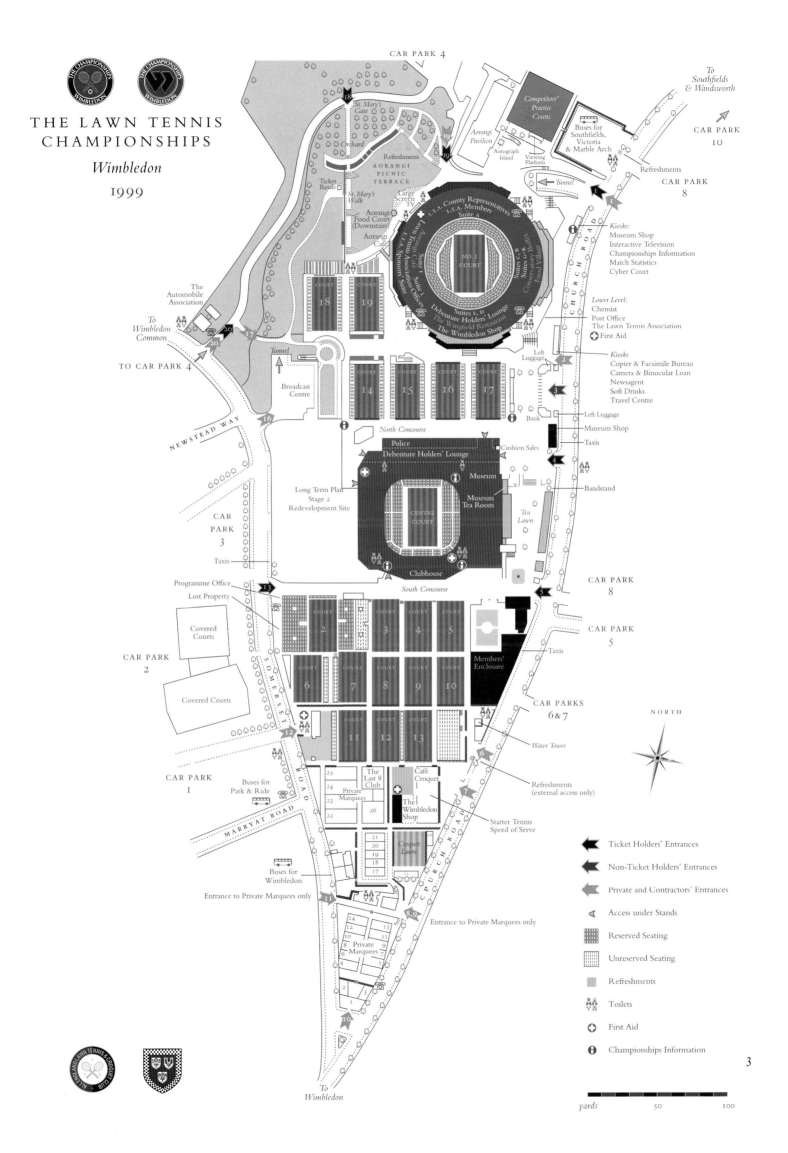

THE LAWN TENNIS
CHAMPIONSHIPS
Wimbledon
1999

CAR PARK 4

To Southfields & Wandsworth

CAR PARK 10

Competitors' Practice Courts

Buses for Southfields, Victoria & Marble Arch

CAR PARK 8

St. Mary's Gate

Orchard

Refreshments

AORANGI PICNIC TERRACE

Ticket Resale

St. Mary's Walk

Aorangi Food Court (Downstairs)

Aorangi Café

Large Screen TV

Aorangi Pavilion

Autograph Island

Viewing Platform

Tunnel

Refreshments

L.T.A. County Representatives
L.T.A. Members Suite A

Lawn Tennis Association Offices
Suites C, B
Suites J, K
Conservatory Buffet
Food Village

NO.1 COURT

Suites E, D
Debenture Holders' Lounge
The Wingfield Restaurant
The Wimbledon Shop

Suites C-K
Sponsors' Suite

Kiosks:
Museum Shop
Interactive Television
Championships Information
Match Statistics
Cyber Court

CHURCH ROAD

Lower Level:
Chemist
Post Office
The Lawn Tennis Association
First Aid

Kiosks:
Copier & Facsimile Bureau
Camera & Binocular Loan
Newsagent
Soft Drinks
Travel Centre

The Automobile Association

To Wimbledon Common

TO CAR PARK 4

Tunnel

Broadcast Centre

NEWSTEAD WAY

COURT 18   COURT 19

COURT 14   COURT 15   COURT 16   COURT 17

Left Luggage

Bank

Left Luggage

Museum Shop

Taxis

North Concourse

Police
Debenture Holders' Lounge

Cushion Sales

Museum

Bandstand

Long Term Plan
Stage 2
Redevelopment Site

CENTRE COURT

Museum Tea Room

Tea Lawn

CAR PARK 3

Taxis

Programme Office

Lost Property

Clubhouse

South Concourse

CAR PARK 8

CAR PARK 5

Covered Courts

CAR PARK 2

Covered Courts

SOMERSET ROAD

COURT 2   COURT 3   COURT 4   COURT 5

COURT 6   COURT 7   COURT 8   COURT 9   COURT 10

Members' Enclosure

Taxis

CAR PARKS 6 & 7

Water Tower

COURT 11   COURT 12   COURT 13

CAR PARK 1

Buses for Park & Ride

25
24   Private Marquees
23
22   26

The Last 8 Club

Café Croquet

The Wimbledon Shop

Refreshments (external access only)

Starter Tennis
Speed of Serve

MARRYAT ROAD

21
20
19
18
17

Croquet Lawn

16

Buses for Wimbledon

Entrance to Private Marquees only

14   13
12   11
10   9
8   7   Private Marquees
6   5
4   3
2   1

CHURCH ROAD

Entrance to Private Marquees only

To Wimbledon

NORTH

Ticket Holders' Entrances

Non-Ticket Holders' Entrances

Private and Contractors' Entrances

Access under Stands

Reserved Seating

Unreserved Seating

Refreshments

Toilets

First Aid

Championships Information

3

yards   50   100

At last. Six finalists and they're all British.

Lemon Barley Water

GREAT BRITAIN
65, 11", 750ml, Wimbledon finalist 1934–99

A Wimbledon legend. Participating in every tournament since 1934, Lemon Barley Water has shared these hallowed grass courts with all the true greats.

Fruit Break Peach

GREAT BRITAIN
2, 7.5", 375ml, Wimbledon finalist 1997–99

Known for an unusual serving technique, this smooth operator's talents combine to make a seductive package. Versatile, portable, and ready for anything.

High Juice Summer Cup

GREAT BRITAIN
1, 11", 1 litre, Wimbledon 1998–99

A relative newcomer on the circuit and known for an exceptionally fruity delivery. With a perfectly balanced combination of apple, raspberry and strawberry, this special edition should give us all a performance to be proud of.

Fruit & Barley
Summer Fruits

GREAT BRITAIN
4, 11", 1 litre, Wimbledon finalist 1995–99

They say some are born to greatness and that couldn't be more correct than with this feisty funster from Norwich. With an exotic complexion, a fruity flair and a smooth delivery, this talented competitor is guaranteed to win everyone's heart on and off the court.

Original
Whole Orange

GREAT BRITAIN
36, 11", 1 litre, Wimbledon finalist 1963–99

Known for an astonishingly fulsome delivery on both first and second servings, this seasoned professional has become a giant of the grass court game, in every sense of the word.

Special R
Apple & Blackcurrant

GREAT BRITAIN
15, 11", 1 litre, Wimbledon finalist 1984–99

This pair's record speaks for itself. Almost an institution on the doubles court at Wimbledon, their different colours and backgrounds complementing each other to deliver one of the most sensational finishes of the game.

The Official Still Soft Drink of The Championships

Eating & Drinking

~ AT THE CHAMPIONSHIPS ~

Aorangi Picnic Terrace
Pimms and Ice Cream

Aorangi Food Court—LEVEL 2
SELF SERVICE
*Salad Bar, Baguettes, Pizza,
and Light Refreshments*

Aorangi Café—LEVEL 3
FAST FOOD SERVICE
*Chicken Sandwich with Fries,
Strawberries & Cream,
Light Refreshments and Bar*

Wingfield Restaurant—LEVEL 2
WAITRESS SERVICE
*booking advisable—0181 946 8485
Luncheon and Afternoon Tea*

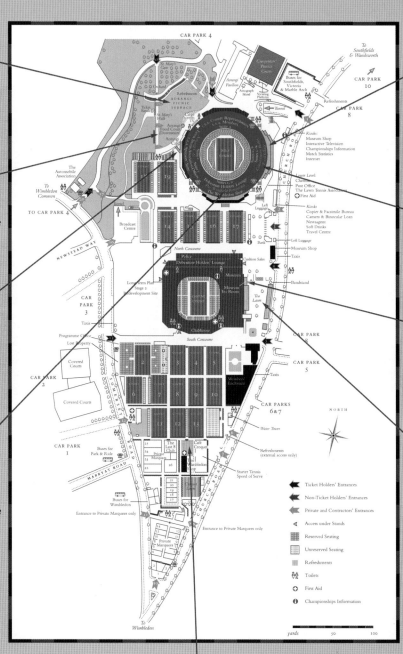

Food Village—LEVEL 1
FAST FOOD SERVICE & BAR
*Offering a Wide Range
of Refreshments including:
Stir-Fry, Fish & Chips, Chargrill,
Pizza, Cookies, Beverages, Ice Cream
and the Village Bar*

Conservatory Buffet—LEVEL 2
SELF-SERVICE
*Lunch Buffet, Afternoon Tea
and Supper*

Museum Tea Room
SELF-SERVICE
*Lunch, Teas
and Light Refreshments*

Tea Lawn & Long Bar
FAST FOOD SERVICE
*Champagne & Pimms,
Light Refreshments including:
Pizza, Dutchees, Sandwiches,
Cookies, Pastries, Baguettes,
Strawberries & Cream,
Ice Cream
and the Long Bar*

Café Croquet
FAST FOOD SERVICE
Crêpes, Ice Cream and Light Refreshments

JEWELLERY

IN FASHION

STRAWBERRIES AND DREAM

The best taste, summer or winter, is a perfect strawberry with lashings of style. Try this generous serving of 18ct rose gold, a pendant seeded with ten delectable diamonds. The leaves and chain contrast in 18ct yellow gold; £995.

Who could resist a second helping – delicious earrings with twelve diamonds, £1,275. And the dreamy brooch with ten diamonds, £1,035. If you want jewellery in fashion, feast your eyes at Boodles.

BOODLE & DUNTHORNE

ESTABLISHED 1798

Telephone 0171 235 0111 www.boodleanddunthorne.com

The only thing we don't guarantee is the weather

Some things at Wimbledon can be relied upon year after year - such as Try Construction meeting its deadlines.

- New No.1 Court Complex and Broadcast Centre, 1997
- Centre Court extension, 1999
- New facilities building, 2000

№ 1 COURT

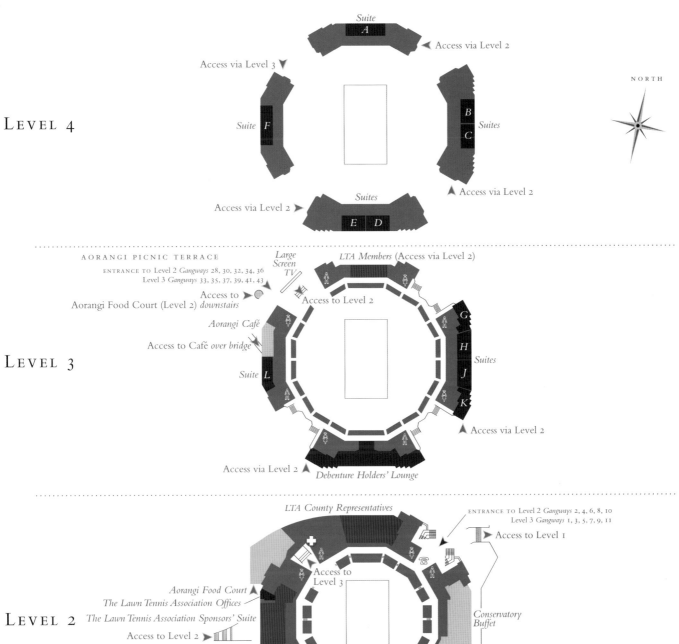

LEVEL 4

Suite
A

Access via Level 2

Access via Level 3

NORTH

Suite F

B
C
Suites

Suites
E   D

Access via Level 2

Access via Level 2

LEVEL 3

AORANGI PICNIC TERRACE
ENTRANCE to Level 2 Gangways 28, 30, 32, 34, 36
Level 3 Gangways 33, 35, 37, 39, 41, 43

Access to
Aorangi Food Court (Level 2) downstairs

Large Screen TV

LTA Members (Access via Level 2)

Access to Level 2

G

H

Aorangi Café

Access to Café over bridge

J
Suites

Suite L

K

Access via Level 2

Access via Level 2

Debenture Holders' Lounge

LEVEL 2

LTA County Representatives

ENTRANCE to Level 2 Gangways 2, 4, 6, 8, 10
Level 3 Gangways 1, 3, 5, 7, 9, 11

Access to Level 1

Access to Level 3

Aorangi Food Court
The Lawn Tennis Association Offices
The Lawn Tennis Association Sponsors' Suite

Access to Level 2

Conservatory Buffet

ENTRANCE to Level 2 Gangways 20, 22, 24, 26, 28
Level 3 Gangways 23, 25, 27, 29, 31, 33

Wingfield Restaurant

ENTRANCE to Level 2 Gangways 10, 12, 14, 16, 18
Level 3 Gangways 11, 13, 15, 17, 19, 21

Access to Level 1

Access to
The Wimbledon Shop & Level 1

LEVEL 1

Tunnel

GATE 1

Food Village

Retail & Information Kiosks:
Museum Shop
Interactive Television
Championships Information
Match Statistics
Cyber Court

CHURCH ROAD

ENTRANCE
B, C

Chemist

Post Office

LTA

Retail & Information Kiosks:
Copier & Facsimile Bureau
Camera & Binocular Loan
Newsagent
Soft Drinks
Travel Information

The Wimbledon Shop

Access to Level 2

GATE 2

9

Tickets

Daily Tickets
for the Centre, No.1 and No.2 Courts

A limited number of seat tickets for these courts can be purchased on the day at the turnstiles from 10.30 a.m. at Gate 3. These tickets cannot be booked in advance of the days for which they are used and can be purchased only at Gate 3.

Centre Court
STANDARD

Monday/Tuesday June 21/22	£24 each
Wednesday/Thursday June 23/24	£30 each
Friday June 25	£36 each
Saturday June 26	£30 each
Monday/Tuesday June 28/29	£42 each
Wednesday June 30	£48 each

No.1 Court
STANDARD

Monday/Tuesday June 21/22	£22 each
Wednesday/Thursday June 23/24	£27 each
Friday June 25	£32 each
Saturday June 26	£25 each
Monday/Tuesday June 28/29	£37 each
Wednesday June 30	£42 each
Thursday July 1	£32 each
Friday/Saturday July 2/3	£18 each
Sunday July 4	£15 each

No.2 Court

Monday/Tuesday June 21/22	£17 each
Wednesday/Thursday June 23/24	£20 each
Friday June 25	£23 each
Saturday June 26	£20 each
Monday June 28	£26 each
Tuesday June 29	£21 each
Wednesday June 30	£19 each

All prices for Centre Court, No.1 and No.2 Courts include admission to the Grounds. All prices inclusive of VAT.

Babes in arms will be allowed into the Grounds free but not into any of the show courts. Children 5 years and over will be charged at full rate. Children under the age of 12 must be accompanied by an adult.

Smoking is prohibited in the stands of Centre, No.1, No.2 Courts and of Courts 13 and 18.

Other Courts

Ground passes will allow access to Courts 3 – 19 in addition to No.2 Court Standing Room.

Ground Opening Times

The Grounds will be open to the public at 10:30 a.m. each day for ticket holders and daily ticket purchasers.

Price of Admission

£10 before 5 p.m.
Monday June 21 to Friday June 25

£7 after 5 p.m.
Monday June 21 to Friday June 25

£5 before 5 p.m.
Saturday June 26

£3 after 5 p.m.
Saturday June 26

£10 before 5 p.m.
Monday June 28

£7 after 5 p.m.
Monday June 28

£8 before 5 p.m.
Tuesday June 29 to Thursday July 1

£6 after 5 p.m.
Tuesday June 29 to Thursday July 1

£7 before 5 p.m.
Friday July 2 to Saturday July 3

£5 after 5 p.m.
Friday July 2 to Saturday July 3

£3 before 5 p.m.
Sunday July 4 (Proceeds to Charity)

£1 after 5 p.m.
Sunday July 4 (Proceeds to Charity)

Please note entrance at any time is subject to Ground capacity.

The Middle Saturday 1999

An additional quantity of Centre Court Open Stand seats and No.1 Court seats will be sold on the day at Gate 3. Centre Court tickets will be sold at the reduced price of £30, and will provide a reserved seat in the East or West Open Stand. No.1 Court tickets will be sold at £25, No.2 Court at £20. Ground admission will be at a reduced price of £5; £3 after 5.00 p.m.

Wimbledon Tickets

Demand for Wimbledon tickets has exceeded supply for most of The Championships' history. Year by year increasing pressure is exerted on the Committee of Management to move tickets out of the public allocation. Wimbledon's policy has always been to protect the number of tickets allocated to the general public because it is the Committee's firm belief that these genuine tennis and Wimbledon fans should have access to their favourite event and that they contribute greatly to the special atmosphere at The Championships. The popularity and public interest surrounding The Championships is such that demand for Wimbledon tickets has reached unprecedented heights. Unfortunately, this means that these tickets can command highly inflated prices on the 'black market'. In an attempt to limit the resale of tickets, the Committee introduced in 1991 new ticket conditions of sale whereby tickets, other than Debenture tickets, cannot be resold or purchased from any person, commercial agent or company other than directly by the applicant from the Club or its authorised agent. Any tickets, apart from Debentures, obtained in breach of these conditions shall be nullified. Any person seeking to use a ticket obtained in breach of these conditions in order to gain or provide entry to or remain at The Championships will be a trespasser and will be ejected and liable to legal action.

Cancellation of Play Due to Rain

Details of the Raincheck policy introduced in 1998 are as follows:

(i) If there is no play because of rain on the court for which tickets have been bought, the *original purchasers* of tickets for that court on that day will be refunded with the amount which they paid for those tickets—the maximum refund payable will be the face value of the tickets for the day concerned.

(ii) Purchasers of Ground Passes will be eligible for a full refund if there is no play on any of Court 2-19 inclusive.

(iii) If there is play only after 6p.m., refunds will be limited to half the amount paid.

(vi) Only the original purchasers are eligible for refunds under this policy.

(v) Refunds will be paid out automatically for tickets bought in advance, but tickets bought at the Club's turnstiles should be sent without delay to: The Ticket Office, The All England Lawn Tennis & Croquet Club, 'Raincheck', P.O. Box 98, Church Road, Wimbledon, London SW19 5AE.

(vi) In view of the numbers that could be involved, please do not call at the Club's Ticket Office.

(vii) Tickets for Sunday 4th July are not included in this scheme since if play continues beyond that date these tickets will be valid for admission on subsequent days. However, holders of these tickets will not be guaranteed a reserved seat except on Sunday 4th July. If there is any play on Monday 5th July and the following days, the Order of Play and entrance conditions will be announced *by the Club at the earliest possible opportunity.*

(viii) Separate terms and conditions apply to Debenture Holders as notified by The All England Lawn Tennis Ground plc.

(ix) The AELTC regrets that it can no longer offer priority for the following year.

Note—*In the event of no play or any curtailment of play, owing to rain or any cause whatsoever, no money can be refunded, except as detailed under the cancellation of play paragraph above.*

CENTRE COURT

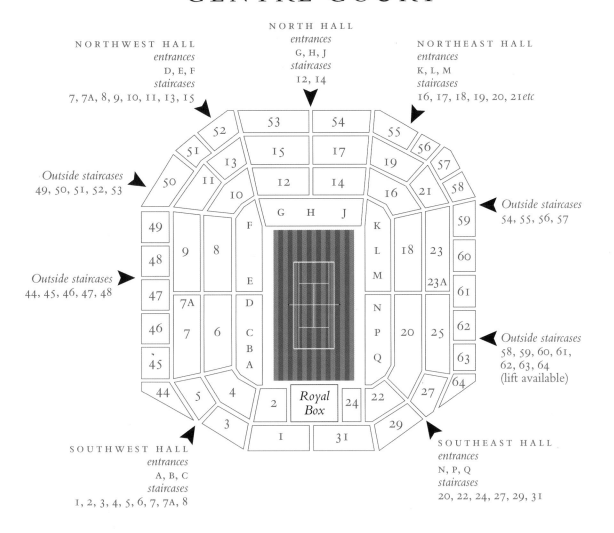

NORTH HALL
entrances
G, H, J
staircases
12, 14

NORTHWEST HALL
entrances
D, E, F
staircases
7, 7A, 8, 9, 10, 11, 13, 15

NORTHEAST HALL
entrances
K, L, M
staircases
16, 17, 18, 19, 20, 21 *etc*

Outside staircases
49, 50, 51, 52, 53

Outside staircases
54, 55, 56, 57

Outside staircases
44, 45, 46, 47, 48

Outside staircases
58, 59, 60, 61,
62, 63, 64
(lift available)

Royal Box

SOUTHWEST HALL
entrances
A, B, C
staircases
1, 2, 3, 4, 5, 6, 7, 7A, 8

SOUTHEAST HALL
entrances
N, P, Q
staircases
20, 22, 24, 27, 29, 31

Nº1 COURT

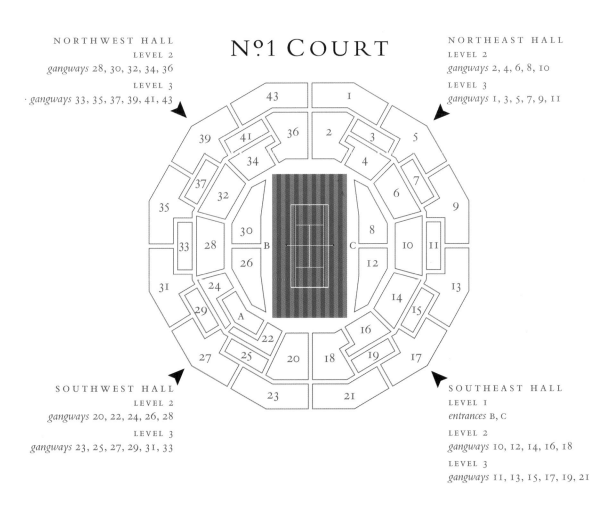

NORTHWEST HALL
LEVEL 2
gangways 28, 30, 32, 34, 36
LEVEL 3
gangways 33, 35, 37, 39, 41, 43

NORTHEAST HALL
LEVEL 2
gangways 2, 4, 6, 8, 10
LEVEL 3
gangways 1, 3, 5, 7, 9, 11

SOUTHWEST HALL
LEVEL 2
gangways 20, 22, 24, 26, 28
LEVEL 3
gangways 23, 25, 27, 29, 31, 33

SOUTHEAST HALL
LEVEL 1
entrances B, C
LEVEL 2
gangways 10, 12, 14, 16, 18
LEVEL 3
gangways 11, 13, 15, 17, 19, 21

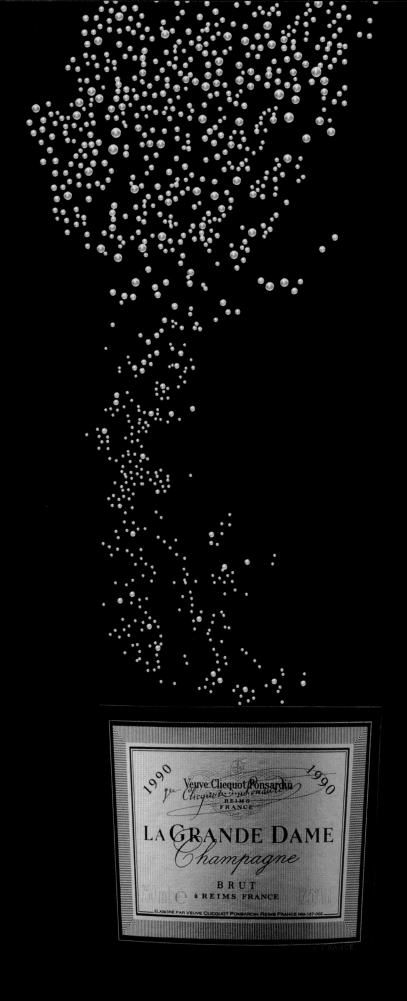

Go on – it's only 0.002% of your racing trainer's fees

The 1998 Wimbledon Champions

MEN'S SINGLES
Champion: P. Sampras (USA)
Runner-up: G. Ivanisevic (Croatia)

LADIES' SINGLES
Champion: Miss J. Novotna (Czech Republic)
Runner-up: Miss N. Tauziat (France)

MEN'S DOUBLES
Champions:
J. Eltingh (Netherlands) & P. Haarhuis (Netherlands)
Runners-up:
T.A. Woodbridge (Australia) & M. Woodforde (Australia)

LADIES' DOUBLES
Champions:
Miss M. Hingis (Switzerland) & Miss J. Novotna (Czech Republic)
Runners-up:
Miss L.A. Davenport (USA) & Miss N. Zvereva (Belarus)

MIXED DOUBLES
Champions:
M. Mirnyi (Belarus) & Miss S. Williams (USA)
Runners-up:
M. Bhupathi (India) & Miss M. Lucic (Croatia)

love-1

ENJOY Diet Coke
THE CHAMPIONSHIP WIMBLEDON

REFRESHING THE CHAMPIONSHIPS

The Chairman's Special Guests

TED SCHROEDER (USA)

At his one and only attempt he became Wimbledon singles champion in 1949, when his coolness and stamina were stretched to the limit as he conceded a record 8 sets. At the same meeting he lost in the final of the doubles with Gardnar Mulloy. He was United States singles champion in 1942 and runner-up in 1949. He won the doubles crown in 1940, 1941 and 1947 and the mixed in 1942.

From 1946 to 1949 his Davis Cup exploits in the Challenge Rounds were legendary, as he was unbeaten in singles. The same years he was ranked No.2 in the world, despite restricted tournament appearances. Born in Newark, USA, 20th July 1921.

ALEX OLMEDO (USA)

Wimbledon singles champion in 1959, at the age of 23. Was the sensation of the earlier Australian season, when he won for the United States, his adopted country, both singles and the doubles in the Davis Cup Challenge Round and went on to win the Australian crown. Later he lost in the final of the United States Championships before turning professional. One of a family of 11 he left Peru at 17 for California, where he learnt the game. Known as 'The Chief', he possessed a strong serve-and-volley attack with outstanding speed of foot. Born in Arequipa, Peru, 24th March 1936.

REX HARTWIG (AUSTRALIA)

An outstanding doubles player who won the Wimbledon title twice, with Mervyn Rose in 1954 and Lew Hoad in 1955. At the Australian Championships he won the doubles crown in 1954 and the mixed title in 1953 and 1954. The United States doubles in 1953 was another of his triumphs. His singles performances peaked in 1954, when he was runner-up at the Australian Championships and also at the United States Championships, losing to Vic Seixas in four sets. The same year he lost in the quarter-finals at Wimbledon to Ken Rosewall. He became a professional in 1955. Played in Davis Cup 1953–55, being ranked No.5 in the world for the last two years. Born in Culcain, Australia, 2nd September 1929.

MARIA BUENO (BRAZIL)

Wimbledon singles champion in 1959, 1960 and 1964 and also captured five doubles titles. Won the United States singles crown in 1959, 1963, 1964 and 1966, together with five doubles titles. Achieved the "Grand Slam" in doubles in 1960. Ranked in the World's top ten from 1958–1968.

A very graceful and artistic player, who hit the ball majestically. Towards the end of her career was plagued by injury. Born in São Paulo, Brazil, 11th October 1939.

JULIAN MUSCAT
The Times

The 1998 Championships

PETE SAMPRAS WINNING THE MEN'S SINGLES TITLE FOR THE FIFTH TIME IN SIX YEARS, JANA NOVOTNA SLAYING HER inner demons to make it third time lucky in the Ladies' Singles final... Tim Henman running Sampras so close in the semi-finals... record crowds over the 13 days. Such memories resonate within most who attended the 112th Wimbledon Championships.

Yet an even greater symbolism was forged from the 1998 renewal. The mood over the fortnight confounded those who maintained that Britain was bewitched by the

World Cup, which unfolded, simultaneously, across the Channel in France. As the nation's football hopes evaporated with that sour defeat by Argentina, Wimbledon reaffirmed itself as the bastion of the sporting summer. The Lady of SW19 was not about to abdicate.

Indeed, Henman, whose semi-final duel with Sampras was defined by a spellbinding third set, almost triggered a wave of national euphoria. Rarely has the outer calm of Sampras, the supreme champion, been reduced to the fraught expression he wore as Henman matched him, blow

17

Wimbledon sunglasses

A collection of 18 sunglass styles for men and women of all ages.

This officially licenced product is now available in the Wimbledon Shop and is offered complete with customised case and cord.

Wimbledon sunglasses can also be made up to your personal prescription.

For your local stockist please call Julie McClory at Rodenstock on 01474 325555.

Rodenstock is the official sponsor of the British Tennis Umpires Association

Jana Novotna with the Plate, at last

for blow, in a match of hypnotic quality. It was little wonder that the American, not one to dispense hollow praise, ventured of Henman after his 6-3 4-6 7-5 6-3 victory: "One day he is going to win this thing."

A year earlier, the Duchess of Kent expressed similar sentiments to Jana Novotna after the Czech girl, playing in her second Wimbledon Singles final, lost out to Martina Hingis. And Novotna made a soothsayer of the Duchess when, in a match brimful with emotion, she prevailed over France's Nathalie Tauziat last year.

Novotna's defeat by Steffi Graf, from a seemingly impregnable position, in the 1993 final thus receded to a dim and distant memory. Her unbridled delight on securing the winning point was something to behold. Where she once spilt tears of anguish, Novotna now shed tears of joy as she bounded round Centre Court like a new-born foal.

No other outcome would suffice after Novotna's comprehensive dismissal of Hingis, the defending champion, in the semi-finals. She recovered from a spluttering start, losing the first nine points to trail 3-0 before successfully adjusting her sights to down Hingis 6-4 6-4 with some vintage grass court tennis.

Novotna's subsequent defeat of Tauziat sated a huge craving for her name to join those already engraved on the Ladies' Singles trophy. For good measure, Novotna then teamed up with Hingis to capture the Ladies' Doubles Championship from Lindsay Davenport and Natasha Zvereva 6-3 3-6 8-6. Zvereva had earlier lost to Tauziat in the second Ladies' semi-final.

Pity poor Tauziat, who threatened to play the part of Wimbledon killjoy. It was she who halted the progress of our own Sam Smith in the fourth round. The Essex girl represented Britain's lone flag-bearer after a heartwarming defeat of eighth-seeded Conchita Martinez, the 1994 champion, in round three. Despite Henman's passage into the second week, it was Smith, world ranked No.94, who cornered the headlines in middle-Sunday's newspapers.

Wimbledon 1998 was thus a tournament in which domestic interest featured prominently. Smith's passage to the fourth round marked a first since Jo Durie achieved the landmark 13 years earlier. And Henman's semi-final

Champagne LANSON Père & Fils (UK Office)
18 Bolton Street, London W1Y 7PA
Telephone: 0171 499 0070 Fax: 0171 408 0841

appearance was last matched by Roger Taylor in 1973. Fittingly, Taylor was present to witness Henman frighten Sampras on the second Friday.

On that day the Centre Court atmosphere, occasionally reminiscent of a Last Night at the Proms, was in marked contrast to much of the first week. Incessant rain breaks saw players marching on and off the courts as though drilled by a belligerent sergeant-major. The crowds appeared to cope better than the men's seeds, six of whom failed to survive the opening round.

Most conspicuous among them was No.2 seed Marcelo Rios, the mercurial Chilean, who fell to Francisco Clavet, of Spain, in five sets. Yet proven Wimbledon campaigners like Sampras, Henman, the 1996 winner Richard Krajicek, and twice finalist Goran Ivanisevic carefully plotted a course through the rubble.

Henman experienced the greatest difficulty. He was not to record a straight-sets verdict until downing No.3 seed Petr Korda in the quarter-final. His play became more assured as the tournament unfolded, in the process enhancing his status as one who excels against the best.

Meanwhile, Ivanisevic advanced with his signature cocktail of erratic brilliance. Correctly promoted, ahead of his world ranking, to No.14 seed, the Croatian confounded his shocking form in advance of The Championships to cross swords with Krajicek, seeded No.9, in the semi-finals.

That was a match of high drama. With two match points, at 5-4 and 40-15 in the fourth set, Ivanisevic dished out a booming ace, Krajicek headed for his chair and that seemed to be that. Not so. A net cord was called, Ivanisevic returned to serve—and his opponent somehow clawed his way back by seizing the ensuing tiebreak.

A titanic fifth set saw Ivanisevic take his chance when decisively breaking an ailing Krajicek to prevail 6-3 6-4 5-7 6-7 15-13 in three hours 21 minutes. Ivanisevic had won through to his third Wimbledon final, but he was to rue the extra 90 minutes he was detained on court.

Sampras required an hour less to overcome Henman and he was the fresher man for the final—itself a repeat of their Centre Court joust four years earlier. If that had

been an eminently forgettable match, this was quite the opposite: a head-on collision between two deadly serve-and-volley merchants.

Ivanisevic was to rue the two set points he squandered in the second-set tiebreak that would have earned him a two-set lead. And squander them he did, both times with errant backhands from a wing that previously flowed like running water. Sampras was back on terms—and apparently cruising to victory after clinching the third set for a 2-1 lead.

Yet back Ivanisevic came, his concentration faultless as he captured set four to herald a deciding set in a Wimbledon final for the first time since he had himself lost to Andre Agassi six years earlier. Sadly, a heartbroken Ivanisevic was to endure a similar fate here as Sampras raised his game for the final drive.

The American now played near flawless tennis, his volleys guided, with laser-like precision, deep into the Croatian's territory. As Ivanisevic noticeably flagged, Sampras had the bit between his teeth. His 6-7 7-6 6-4 3-6 6-2 triumph saw him emulate Bjorn Borg as only the second five-time Singles winner since the Challenge Round's abolition in 1922.

Equally dominant in the Men's Doubles was the Australian combination of Mark Woodforde and Todd Woodbridge, who reached the final in their effort to win the event for a sixth successive year. However, in another gripping encounter, the Dutch pairing of Jacco Eltingh and Paul Haarhuis prevailed 2-6 6-4 7-6 5-7 10-8 in four hours five minutes. Fittingly, it was Eltingh's last appearance at Wimbledon ahead of his retirement.

Two relative newcomers made their first Wimbledon final a winning one when the mixed doubles team of Serena Williams and Max Mirnyi bettered Mahesh Bhupathi and Mirjana Lucic 6-4 6-4. In the junior boys' title, Roger Federer, of Switzerland, overcame Georgian, Irakli Labadze 6-4 6-4. And the junior girls' title went to Slovakia's Katarina Srebotnik, who registered 7-6 6-3 over Belgium's Kim Clijsters.

Wimbledon 1998
sport with a smile

Wimbledon
Centre Court
ROTHERHITHE

This year the BBC will be providing more coverage than ever on TV, Radio and Online.

We are also at the leading edge of Interactive TV, ensuring that for future generations, we will continue to bring Wimbledon alive, wherever you are.

BBC SPORT

PRIZE MONEY
TOTAL £7,595,330

	PLAYER(S) £	TOTAL £
EVENT 1		
GENTLEMEN'S SINGLES CHAMPIONSHIP		
Winner	455,000	
Runner-up	227,500	
Semi-Finalists	113,750	
Quarter-Finalists	59,150	
Losers of the Fourth Round	31,850	
Losers of the Third Round	18,420	
Losers of the Second Round	11,150	
Losers of the First Round	6,830	
		2,490,040
EVENT 2		
GENTLEMEN'S DOUBLES CHAMPIONSHIP *(per pair)*		
Winners	186,420	
Runners-up	93,200	
Semi-Finalists	47,830	
Quarter-Finalists	24,830	
Losers of the Third Round	13,230	
Losers of the Second Round	7,180	
Losers of the First Round	4,210	
		830,040
EVENT 3		
LADIES' SINGLES CHAMPIONSHIP		
Winner	409,500	
Runner-up	204,750	
Semi-Finalists	96,690	
Quarter-Finalists	50,280	
Losers of the Fourth Round	26,280	
Losers of the Third Round	14,270	
Losers of the Second Round	8,640	
Losers of the First Round	5,290	
		2,062,350
EVENT 4		
LADIES' DOUBLES CHAMPIONSHIP *(per pair)*		
Winners	167,770	
Runners-up	83,880	
Semi-Finalists	40,660	
Quarter-Finalists	21,110	
Losers of the Third Round	10,920	
Losers of the Second Round	5,570	
Losers of the First Round	3,260	
		698,210
EVENT 5		
MIXED DOUBLES CHAMPIONSHIP *(per pair)*		
Winners	79,180	
Runners-up	39,590	
Semi-Finalists	19,790	
Quarter-Finalists	9,100	
Losers of the Third Round	4,550	
Losers of the Second Round	2,280	
Losers of the First Round	1,030	
		300,590

	PLAYER(S) £	TOTAL £
EVENT 6		
35 & OVER GENTLEMEN'S INVITATION DOUBLES *(per pair)*		
Winners	15,000	
Runners-up	11,780	
Semi-Finalists	9,300	
Second place in each group	7,470	
Third place in each group	6,810	
Fourth place in each group	6,150	
		127,100
EVENT 7		
45 & OVER GENTLEMEN'S INVITATION DOUBLES *(per pair)*		
Winners	11,780	
Runners-up	9,300	
Semi-Finalists	7,470	
Second round losers	6,150	
First round losers	5,370	
		103,580
EVENT 8		
35 & OVER LADIES' INVITATION DOUBLES *(per pair)*		
Winners	10,700	
Runners-up	8,030	
Second place in each group	6,150	
Third place in each group	5,630	
Fourth place in each group	4,800	
		51,890
QUALIFYING COMPETITION GENTLEMEN'S SINGLES		
Losers of the Third Round	4,330	
Losers of the Second Round	2,170	
Losers of the First Round	1,080	
		207,840
QUALIFYING COMPETITION LADIES' SINGLES		
Losers of the Third Round	3,360	
Losers of the Second Round	1,680	
Losers of the First Round	840	
		80,640
PER DIEM ALLOWANCES—*estimated*		
Championship Events	505,200	
Invitation Doubles	93,600	
Qualifying Competition	44,250	
		643,050
TOTAL PRIZE MONEY		£7,595,330

**ONE SECOND AT WIMBLEDON
CAN LAST A LIFETIME.**

Wimbledon. Centre Court. The finals.

Match point. As the ball hangs in

the air before the racket finds its

target, how much could hang on

the outcome! A lifetime of triumph

for the victor, or endless reflections

on what might have been for the

vanquished. Yet whoever's name

is finally engraved on the trophy,

one name will be there on the

scoreboard to record the

occasion: Rolex of Geneva.

ROLEX
of Geneva

Datejust.
Officially Certified Swiss Chronometer.
For information on the Rolex range write to:
Rolex UK, 3 Stratford Place, London W1N 0ER
or telephone 0171- 629 5071.

1999 WIMBLEDON CHAMPIONSHIPS.

THE CHAMPIONSHIPS
WIMBLEDON

Wimbledon

EVEN OUR BUBBLES
COME FROM THE SOURCE

Perrier
EN BOUTEILLE
A LA SOURCE
FRANCE
S B
POUR LA VIE

Britain's 1979 Davis Cup Team. From the left: Mark Cox, John Lloyd, David Lloyd, Buster Mottram

The Davis Cup

RICHARD EVANS
BBC Radio

IT DID NOT TAKE LONG FOR THE ALL ENGLAND LAWN TENNIS CLUB TO BECOME INVOLVED IN THE NEW INTERNATIONAL TEAM competition devised by a young man from Harvard called Dwight Davis. After the first meeting at the Longwood Cricket Club in 1900—won by Davis and his team mates over the British Isles—the United States held on to the trophy in New York when it was next played in 1902. However the following year the Doherty brothers won a dramatic encounter back in Boston with Laurie and Reggie winning decisive reverse singles side by side in simultaneously played matches.

So, for the first time in its brief history, the Davis Cup, designed by an English immigrant called Rowland Rhodes, hit the high seas and ended up, inevitably, at the venue that was already becoming acknowledged as the home of the game—the All England Lawn Tennis Club at Wimbledon. Not this Wimbledon, of course, but the original site in the town at Worple Road.

Strangely the first Davis Cup tie ever played at Wimbledon—indeed the first ever played outside America—did not feature either Britain or the United States. The USNL-TA, as they were known in those days, were so broke that they could not afford to send a team to challenge for the Cup in 1904, but European nations had quickly woken up to the potential offered by this new format and France and Belgium sent teams to London so that they could meet for the right to play the British Isles in the Challenge Round.

Max Decugis, schooled in England and therefore familiar with grass courts, had already established himself as the first star of French tennis but even he could not prevent the Belgians from creating the competition's first upset when the two nations met at Wimbledon. A gentleman rejoicing in the name of Willie le Maire de Warzée defeated Decugis after trailing by two sets to one and Paul de Borman of Belgium beat P. Ayme of France in the deciding rubber.

On 2 July, 1904 le Maire de Warzée opened the first Challenge Round to be played in Europe against Britain's Frank Riseley, who had stepped into the shoes of the semi-retired Reggie Doherty. Riseley, twice runner-up to Laurie Doherty in The Championships, was too strong on grass and won in straight sets. Laurie then beat Paul de Borman and the next day Reggie emerged to partner his brother in a one-sided doubles that secured tenure of the Cup for Britain.

With the Americans able to send a team and Australasia making its first run at Davis Cup glory, there was much more pre-Challenge Round activity in 1905 but it all took place at the Queen's Club. The Americans, represented by Holcombe Ward and Bill Clothier with Beals Wright helping out in the doubles, dismissed France and Australasia without the loss of a rubber and as Belgium had failed to raise

Britain's 1933 Davis Cup Team fresh from wresting the Cup from France. From the left: Messrs Perry, Austin, Hughes and Lee.

a team, the United States were through to the Challenge Round at Worple Road.

Having led by two sets to love in one rubber and two sets to one in another, the Americans must have wondered how they ended up losing 5-0. But such was their fate after Laurie Doherty had survived an inspired challenge from Ward and a new singles player, Sydney Smith, had increased the British lead by battering Bill Larned with his huge forehand.

The Dohertys, with their unique blend of charm, elegance and ability to win under pressure, had been largely responsible for reviving interest in the game of lawn tennis in the early years of the century, but when they bowed out in 1906 after ensuring that Britain retained the Cup with another victory at Worple Road over the United States, the sport was ready to spread its wings—and would have done so to an even greater extent had wings been available.

However, the need to travel by sea made life very difficult for challenging nations once the intrepid duo of Norman Brookes and Anthony Wilding had disposed of the US at Worple Road in 1907 before taking full advantage of a weakened British team in the Challenge Round. The Australian and the New Zealander made an unlikely pair of team mates for they lived on opposite sides of the world—Wilding having settled in England after coming down from Cambridge—and were opposites, too, in personality and style. Brookes, hugely talented, was a Melbourne socialite of serious demeanour while Wilding was the gallant heart-throb, a fitness fanatic who

rode his motor cycle all over Europe and fell in love with an older woman, the American actress Maxine Elliott.

As a result of these two keeping the Cup in Melbourne—often on Mabel Brookes' dining room sideboard—for the next five years, Wimbledon did not see too much of Davis

Fred Perry v. Frank Shields, Davis Cup, Wimbledon 31st July 1934

Cup play for a while. However, Charles Dixon and James Parke led a remarkable British expedition to Melbourne in 1912 and shocked Brookes, who was without Wilding, by seizing the Cup.

That ensured one more Challenge Round at Worple Road prior to the First World War and, indeed, the move to Church Road soon after hostilities ended. It was not, however, a happy occasion for the British. In July 1913 a young man nicknamed The Comet swept the Cup back into America's keeping. Maurice McLoughlin settled the issue in the fourth rubber by outplaying Dixon and an era ended for the Davis Cup at Worple Road.

The dominance of Bill Tilden and his fellow Americans and, later, France's incomparable Four Musketeers meant that

Britain never got close to staging another major Davis Cup tie until the emergence of Fred Perry in the early thirties. Even then it required heroics on the slow clay of Roland Garros in 1933 before captain H. Roper Barrett, a member of the original British team in 1900, was able to bring his triumphant players back across the Channel clutching the shining silver trophy.

That heralded a period when Wimbledon became a focal point for Davis Cup action. Obviously Britain would be holding Challenge Rounds at the All England Lawn Tennis Club but there was more than that. With air travel in its infancy, it was still deemed necessary to allow overseas teams to play Inter-Zone Finals near the site of the Challenge Round. Frank Shields, grandfather of Brooke, defeated Vivian McGrath in the fifth rubber to give the US a narrow victory over Australia and thus earn the right a few days later for the dubious privilege of meeting a rampant Fred Perry and a team that would retain the Cup for the next three years, beating the US 4-1 in 1934 and 5-0 in 1935. The following year Perry, due to exclude himself by turning professional, was required to beat Jack Crawford in the deciding rubber to ensure a British victory over Australia. Fred did so with a typical touch of arrogance. Irritated by advice on how to play a match that seemed destined to be interrupted for bad light, Perry snapped at anxious officials, "What time is it now? 5.45 pm? Right, we'll be off court and finished by 7.15 pm!"

Poor Crawford never knew what hit him. Coming in on everything Perry stormed to a 6-2 6-3 6-3 victory and, on striding off triumphant at the appointed hour, lingered only for a moment—returning for one last, emotional look at his beloved Centre Court.

Without Perry, Britain lost the Challenge Round in 1937 to an American team strengthened by the blossoming talent of one of the game's greatest players, Don Budge. However, it was in the Inter-Zone Final, also played on the Centre Court, that Budge had produced the defining performance of his career. In the fifth rubber of a contest that is etched into the annals of the game, Baron Gottfried von Cramm, who had received a call from Hitler before walking on court, seemed destined to lead the Fatherland to victory when he led Budge 4-1 in the fifth set.

Instead of buckling under the pressure, Budge told his captain at the change over, "Don't worry, cap. I'll win this one if it kills me!"

Good as his word, the red-headed American charged the net and turned the set around to win it 8-6. The Centre Court rose to both men and the Cup's reputation for producing rare sporting drama was further embellished.

With Harry Hopman taking over the captaincy of Australia and establishing an extraordinary assembly line of champions from Frank Sedgman to John Newcombe with names like Lew Hoad, Ken Rosewall, Neale Fraser, Roy Emerson, Fred Stolle and Rod Laver in between, the Davis Cup become Australian property for no less than fifteen of the eighteen years stretching between 1950 and 1967. Only the United States could compete and even then needed to recruit a Peruvian, Alex Olmedo, to help them do it after

*Britain retains the Cup
on the 28th July 1936 at Wimbledon*

Tony Trabert had turned professional.

During this period Wimbledon obviously faded as a Davis Cup venue and even when Britain did produce some worthwhile teams, the LTA preferred to show the flag at venues like Bristol, Bournemouth and Eastbourne. However, there remains a lasting Davis Cup memory for anyone who watched it—the tie against Italy on the old No.1 Court in 1976. Overall Adriano Panatta and Paolo Bertolucci were too strong but, in the doubles, David and John Lloyd staged an act of defiance that was as thrilling as it was miraculous. Two sets to love down against one of the world's most accomplished pairs, David took his brother by the scruff of the neck and, throwing himself about court in daredevil fashion, orchestrated a stunning victory. Like John McEnroe, who was about to lead the competition into its new association with NEC by virtue of his untiring dedication to the cause, Lloyd could think of no greater honour than representing his country and even the concrete which now stands over the old arena will not suffocate the memory of that little piece of Davis Cup defiance which epitomised so well the essence of a competition entering its second century.

Now the All England Lawn Tennis Club and all supporters of British tennis eagerly await the day when Tim Henman and Greg Rusedski will add further chapters to the unfinished saga of Wimbledon and the Davis Cup.

The Davis Cup may be viewed at the entrance to the Wimbledon Shop behind Court 16, for the duration of The Championships.

If you love tennis...

Enjoy a visit to Wimbledon Lawn Tennis Museum with its bird's eye view over the famous Centre Court. See the displays of historic memorabilia, new costume gallery and video footage of great players past and present. Plus you'll have a wonderful opportunity to view the Championships' Trophies.

We're open daily throughout the year, from 10.30a.m. - 5p.m. Don't worry if you don't have time to visit during The Championships, just bring this advertisement along before 31st May 2000 and save £1 on admission (not valid during The Championships). The time you choose is in your court!

...you'll love WIMBLEDON
Lawn Tennis Museum

The Wimbledon Museum

JOHN BARRETT

Senior Commentator for BBC Television and Tennis Correspondent of the Financial Times

THE CENTRE COURT LIES EMPTY, THE DESERTED TERRACES ECHOING WITH HISTORY. BUT WHAT IS THIS? AS WE stand here on the viewing platform, perched halfway up the north-east quadrant of tiered seating, we can hear a match in progress.

"Forty-thirty" intones the umpire as the applause dies down. Immediately, in our mind's eye, we can see the graceful white-clad figures racing about the court with athletic vigour, see the ball boys swooping like vultures on their prey as they dart across the court to gather stray tennis balls, and recall with affection the smiling Duchess of Kent in the front row of the Royal Box, clapping her hands and bouncing up and down in her seat with the enthusiasm of a teenager.

For the majority of the 50,000 visitors who make their way each year to the Wimbledon Lawn Tennis Museum at the All England Lawn Tennis and Croquet Club it is this intimate view of the Centre Court, awash with memories, that impresses them most.

Next in popularity is the brightly lit trophy cabinet containing all those famous cups that we have seen raised in triumph so many times on television.

Always popular are the films and videos of past Championships which can be seen in the small viewing theatre with its 34 comfortable seats. Further footage at various vantage points reveals the playing styles of former champions—none more popular than the Frenchwoman Suzanne Lenglen whose balletic grace that entranced audiences in the 1920s is captured for posterity on a continuous loop of film, much of it in slow motion.

Designed by Robin Wade and opened in 1977 as part of Wimbledon's centenary celebrations, the Wimbledon Lawn Tennis Museum is open daily throughout the year.

Visitors will find the most comprehensive collection of tennis memorabilia, equipment, costumes, trophies, posters, paintings and photographs in the world. Part of the original men's changing room from the All England Club's original ground in Worple Road is on display, with the original blue and white Doulton wash basins and the familiar ping of ball on racket drifting in through the sunlit, open window.

Another exhibit displays the actual leather "shoes" worn by the pony which pulled the roller used on the original croquet lawns which became tennis courts in 1877. It was to raise money for the repair of the broken roller that the world's first tennis tournament was held that year. With some 200 spectators paying one shilling each, tradition has it that this first Championship meeting realised a profit of £10, ample for the repair of the pony roller—which, incidentally, survives to this day as an impressive display at the entrance to the Museum.

In another corner a complete racket maker's workshop is on display. Chisels, planes and wood shavings are a reminder of the game's origins, before the days of aluminium, graphite and boron.

In a large case opposite there are life-size figures of Victorian tennis players dressed in contemporary attire and a reconstructed Victorian parlour contains an astonishing number of small artefacts, from teapots, teacups and toasters to paper knives, pencils and pocket watches, each with a tennis theme.

Special displays over the years have concentrated on tennis art, the history of the racket, table tennis, tennis humour, tennis stamps, broadcasting, tennis posters and most recently, croquet—in recognition of the All England Club's origins.

A new costume gallery features ladies' tennis fashions through the ages. You can see the tightly laced long dresses of Victorian times and the whalebone corsets beneath (which often drew blood, according to doubles champion Elizabeth Ryan); Gussie Moran's lace-edged panties designed by Teddy Tinling; the beautiful outfits he created for Britain's three post-war champions—Angela Mortimer, Ann Jones and Virginia Wade; Anne White's sensational all-white cat suit of 1985; dresses of the most recent champions—Martina Navratilova, Steffi Graf, Martina Hingis and Jana Novotna.

The Museum's curator, Valerie Warren, who will retire after the 1999 Championships to pursue fresh interests, has been masterminding the displays for the past 21 years. "People who come here are seeking the Wimbledon Experience", she says. "They love browsing around the exhibits just to get the feel of the place and then out they go to see the Centre Court. For many, especially the overseas visitors, it is a sort of pilgrimage. We hope to introduce tours of the Grounds to enhance their experience."

Few visitors leave without purchasing something from the Museum Shop whose wide range of leisure-wear, mementos, books, videos and high quality glass and ceramic merchandise spans a wide spectrum of tastes and prices.

The Kenneth Ritchie Wimbledon Library, named after Lord Ritchie of Dundee who was one of the Club's Vice-Presidents, is believed to be the largest collection of tennis books, magazines, periodicals and historic photographs in the world. The Library is open to the public for study and research by appointment only.

The Museum Tea Room is the perfect place to relax after visiting the exhibits.

From the very first time he was brought to Wimbledon by his mother, Jane, as a five-year-old, Tim Henman has dreamed of the day when he will be centre stage on Centre Court on Men's final day, proudly holding the gleaming trophy, as winner of the most significant lawn tennis title in the world.

"That first visit, which was outside of tournament time, left a deep and lasting impression on me", said the 24-year-old right-hander from Oxfordshire, who now lives in London, barely 15 minutes away on a good driving day from the All England Lawn Tennis Club.

"I was allowed to go on to one of the indoor courts and

If Henman had needed any further inspiration to start crystallising his ambition at such a remarkable early age, it came during that year's tournament. He was able to watch one of Bjorn Borg's matches on his way to becoming champion for a modern record fifth time. "Definitely that and my earlier visit were experiences which I have never forgotten and never will," he says, and the fact that he still has the ticket for the Centre Court seat which was his vantage point that day, underlines the point. It also characterises the sentimental attachment which players, spectators and even hardbitten journalists alike, hold for what Maureen Connolly's coach, "Teach Tennant" once called

hit with Ken Fletcher (an outstanding doubles competitor in the 1960's), which was obviously a big thrill", he recalled recently, as he approached what will be his sixth year as a main draw singles player here. "Then I went and sat on an empty Centre Court, thinking to myself 'this is really what it's all about.'"

"When I got home all I could think about was how one day I was determined to be playing out there myself. I actually set myself three targets, the first was to play at The Championships, the second was to play on Centre Court and the third to become the champion. I've achieved the first two. Now it's down to me to complete the picture by winning the title."

"That little bit of tennis heaven in London s.w.19."

A smile spreads across Henman's face when he relates how, even though he had been playing tennis since the age of two, a lot of people found it hard to take seriously a five-year-old telling them that he already knew his prime ambition in life was to become a professional tennis player. Many youngsters grow out of such early commitments. Not Henman. His determination has just grown and matured with the years and will continue to do so until that ultimate target has been conquered, even though his earliest official appearances on court were not entirely encouraging.

His first was in the juniors in 1992 when he was

drawn to play Enrique Abaroa, a little known Mexican, who has not made any impact since, but although Henman started well and gained an early first set break, he lost the match 6-2 6-2.

When it came to the main events, Henman's debut was in the doubles as he partnered Chris Bailey one year later but they were drawn against the Jensen brothers, Luke and Murphy, who had won the French Open title a month earlier and were very much the flavour of the year. The British pair played and fought well in a match which attracted a near capacity crowd to Court Two but they were still beaten in four sets.

Henman's first appearance in the Men's Singles was in 1994 when, still needing a wild card because his world ranking remained below 200, he was drawn against the durable German, David Prinosil, a qualifier, who had won one round on his initial visit a year earlier. Again Henman started well but he lost his way and was beaten 4-6 6-3 6-2 6-2.

Whatever disappointment others might have been feeling at the time, that in no way dimmed the Oxfordshire player's determination to work on his game and with wise

weeks earlier. It was the first of many Centre Court appearances for Henman, who went on to reach the quarter-final before bowing to the additional service power and experience of the American Todd Martin.

In 1997, Henman not only kept the Centre Court enthralled and excited as he came through to win 14-12 in the fifth against Paul Haarhuis on middle Sunday—inclement weather for much of the first week made the extra day necessary—but prompted BBC Television to let it delay the Sunday evening earlier news as more than 12 million, the highest viewing audience for years, were glued to their sets. He also cherishes this as the most thrilling match he has ever played.

Henman then came back in a match delayed overnight by bad light to beat an even more highly rated Dutchman, Richard Krajicek, before fatigue from two consecutive exhausting matches took its toll when he lost to former champion, Michael Stich, in the quarter-finals.

Last year, though, Henman went one highly significant step further. He began somewhat tentatively, taking five sets to overcome Jiri Novak in round one but then, with increas-

The Final Target

JOHN PARSONS *Daily Telegraph*

counsel from Bill Knight, then manager of men's tennis for the Lawn Tennis Association and David Felgate, who Knight decided was the ideal coach to work with him, it was not long before the obvious upward curve in his game, despite being briefly halted by a broken ankle, was underway.

At Wimbledon in 1995, when he was ranked 174, Henman's potential was enthusiastically noted by Pete Sampras, top-seeded champion at the time, even though the American beat him in straight sets in the second round. Less memorable, though, that year, was the way Henman, of all people—bearing in mind some who might easily have achieved such notoriety earlier—became the first player to be defaulted from The Championships, while playing with Jeremy Bates in a first round doubles against the Americans, Henrik Holm and Jeff Tarango, after he had accidentally struck a ball girl when hitting a ball away in frustration, just as she was crossing in front of him.

One year later, though, Henman's growing romance with Wimbledon got underway, starting with a magnificent five sets win over the Russian Yevgeny Kafelnikov, who had suddenly emerged as a serious player in the chase for world recognition by winning the French Open just over two

ing authority, David Nainkin, Byron Black, Pat Rafter and Petr Korda fell under Henman's spell, as he became the first British man since Roger Taylor for 25 years to reach the semi-finals. And his run only ended there because Pete Sampras, the defending champion, responded to the challenge when forced to produce his very best form.

Henman clearly has lawn tennis, and Wimbledon in particular, in his genes. His grandfather, Henry Billington, a former Davis Cup player, his grandmother and great grandmother, all competed at The Championships. In a sense though, that makes it tougher for him, for expectations are that much greater.

"They were from a different era," he says. "At the same time it adds to the atmosphere of the whole scenario. I'd never say there are any negatives for me at Wimbledon. For sure it's my favourite tournament, even though it is difficult to find peace and quiet. Without doubt it's the event with the most prestige. If you speak to the majority of the players they'll tell you Wimbledon is the tournament they most want to win. That's even more so with me."

35

UNION-CASTLE LINE

CENTENARY VOYAGE

DECEMBER 1999 - FEBRUARY 2000

THE DREAM VOYAGE HAS JUST BECOME A REALITY FOR EVERYONE...

...SHORTER SECTORS NOW AVAILABLE!

	No. of Nights
Atlantic Islands Odyssey **Southampton** - **Madeira** - **Las Palmas**	from 4
Heading South for the Party of a Lifetime **Las Palmas** - Dakar - St. Helena - Walvis Bay - **Cape Town** - Port Elizabeth - East London - **Durban**	from 13
Cape Town's Millennium Celebrations* Four days moored right in the heart of Cape Town's famous **Victoria & Alfred Waterfront**	4

	No. of Nights
Follow in the footsteps of the Spice Traders **Cape Town** - Port Elizabeth - East London - **Durban** - Maputo - Reunion - Mauritius - Madagascar - Nosy Be - Comores Is. - Zanzibar - **Mombasa** - **Seychelles**	from 14
Voyage through the Cradle of Civilisation **Mombasa** - **Seychelles** - Aqaba (for Petra) - Suez (for The Pyramids) - Port Said - Ashdod (for Jerusalem) - **Piraeus** (for Athens)	from 12
Cruise the Mediterranean Union-Castle Style! **Piraeus** - Naples - Barcelona - Gibraltar - **Southampton**	9

For your free brochure detailing our 66 night gala cruise around Africa and the Spice Islands of the Indian Ocean, call

01703 226232

or visit your local Travel Agent

PASSENGER SHIPPING ASSOCIATION MEMBER

www.union-castle-line.com

THE UNION-CASTLE MAIL STEAMSHIP COMPANY LIMITED

LIMITED OFFER restricted to certain cabin grades only. All offers subject to availability.
* NOTE This sector must be purchased as an extension of another sector. It is not available for separate purchase.

Man Power

BIOGRAPHIES OF THIS YEAR'S LEADING MEN

BARRY NEWCOMBE

Pete Sampras

USA

27; 6' 1"; 170lb; RH; Champion: 1993, 94, 95, 97, 98 SF 92, QF 96

The world No.1 ranking might see-saw a little these days but Pete Sampras, without question, starts each Wimbledon he plays as the favourite. Nobody in the current field, and only a handful outside it, can match his record of five Wimbledon titles, the first in 1993, the fifth last year. That put Sampras level on eleven major titles with Rod Laver, his boyhood hero, who won the last of his four Wimbledon titles in 1969, the year of his second Grand Slam, and with Bjorn Borg. Sampras began this year still searching for a 12th Grand Slam title which would give him a share of the record held by Roy Emerson. But Sampras decided not to play in the Australian Open and denied himself the opportunity of catching up with Emerson there. Sampras has completed each of the past six years with the world No.1 ranking in hand, a unique feat. Last year's Wimbledon saw Sampras produce a career high of 117 aces in his Wimbledon campaign and his last three opponents in the final stages of The Championships were grass court specialists in Mark Philippoussis, Tim Henman and Goran Ivanisevic. Sampras has a basic athleticism, strength and racket harmony which makes him a formidable challenger, but having played a reduced schedule this year he may have set himself a harder task than usual.

AUSTRALIA'S TOP DROP.

JACOB'S CREEK: *Official Australian wine supplier to The Championships, Wimbledon.*

Yevgeny Kafelnikov

RUSSIA

25; 6'3"; 179lb; RH; QF 1995

Yevgeny Kafelnikov began 1999 by winning the Australian Open for his second Grand Slam title—the first was the French in 1996—to present himself as an even more credible candidate for Wimbledon. He was more than busy last year with 150 matches played, the most by anyone on the ATP tour, but cannot look back with any pleasure at Wimbledon where he was unseated by Mark Philippoussis in the first round. Kafelnikov had looked a good bet for Wimbledon 1998 having won the title in the grass court tournament at Halle, Germany, a couple of weeks earlier. Wimbledon had Kafelnikov at seventh seed but Philippoussis saw him off in four sets and gave Kafelnikov the role of first seed to be defeated. If Kafelnikov looks back at 1996 and remembers that he beat Pete Sampras and Michael Stich, both Wimbledon champions, to lift the French crown it would serve as a reminder that he has the pedigree to win on any surface. The son of a high school volleyball coach and a basketball player, Kafelnikov was naturally destined for some kind of sporting activity as he matured and he started to play tennis at the age of six. He likes fishing (in the Black Sea), soccer, basketball, and hockey for recreation but how Kafelnikov fits this into his life as a father and a tennis player with a demanding tournament schedule is sometimes bewildering. He is a busy doubles player as well, twice reaching the Wimbledon semi-finals, and has won the French and US Open titles. This is his sixth attempt to win Wimbledon and after two first round defeats in the last three years he will looking for an improvement. Form watchers will know that Kafelnikov beat Tim Henman in the Rotterdam final in February.

Boris Becker

GERMANY

31; 6'3"; 187lb; RH

Champion 1985, 86, 89, F 88, 90, 91,95,
SF 93, 94 QF 92, 97

Boris Becker is, truly, a man of Wimbledon because he encompasses 15 years of competition in The Championships, starting in 1984, and here he is again, challenging once more for the title he has won three times and for which he has finished runner-up four times. Two years ago, after falling to Pete Sampras in the quarter-finals, Becker spoke in terms of that day being his last appearance in a Grand Slam championship but the fact that he is back in the field this time demonstrates his love for the event and gives his considerable army of supporters the opportunity to bid farewell to him properly. When Becker first competed at Wimbledon John McEnroe and Jimmy Connors played in the final, but in 1985, after some impressive performances in winning his first tournament at Queen's Club, Becker went on to win at Wimbledon with a victory over the South African Kevin Curren in the final and become the youngest champion at the age of 17 years and seven months. In 1986 Becker repeated his Wimbledon triumph, defeating Ivan Lendl in the final, and in 1988 began his three year sequence of playing Stefan Edberg in the final, winning his third and last title in 1989. Two years later, Becker was in the final for the seventh time, falling to compatriot Michael Stich, and his last final was in 1995 when he was beaten by Sampras. Injuries have curtailed Becker's tournament plans in the last three summers but he has a tournament final on his record this year—he was runner-up to Andre Agassi in Hong Kong. Becker has only twice been affected by injuries during his Wimbledon appearances which he has always conducted with a fearsome commitment to duty. He has left a considerable mark on the records of The Championships and, one suspects, on the courts as well. Nobody has dived so spectacularly in pursuit of success and there must be a few dents where his body has landed on Wimbledon grass.

Patrick Rafter

AUSTRALIA

26; 6'1"; 175lb; RH

Patrick Rafter is Australia's best player, today's representative of a heritage of worldwide success created by men like Lew Hoad, Rod Laver, Roy Emerson and John Newcombe. Indeed, Rafter is the first Australian to rank in the top five in back-to-back seasons since Newcombe in 1974. In winning six titles last year Rafter also shared another 1974 record with Newcombe as the most successful Australian on the tour. In Grand Slam terms Rafter hustled his way to the top by clinching the US Open over Greg Rusedski in 1997 and retaining the title in 1998, this time halting Mark Philippoussis' challenge in the final. No Australian had won US titles in successive years since the left-hander Neale Fraser in 1959–60. At the US Open last year Rafter was two sets down to the Moroccan Hicham Arazi and in danger of becoming the first defending champion to lose in the first round. He then had to recover from two sets to one down against Pete Sampras in the semi-finals, no mean feat in the frantic atmosphere of Flushing Meadow. In the Australian Open this year Rafter carried a huge amount of expectation as third seed but fell to the Swede Thomas Enqvist, the eventual runner-up, in the third round. Has reached Wimbledon's fourth round three years running—Tim Henman beat him last year—and has also been a semi-finalist at the French Open. He is a Queenslander with a home in Bermuda and is the third youngest of nine children (six boys, three girls). Began playing tennis aged five.

HSBC Tennis

1

2

3

A great service, great returns and winning results

4

5

6

7

Richard Krajicek

NETHERLANDS

27; 6'5'; 190lb; RH;

Champion 1996; SF 98

Only a handful of players can match Richard Krajicek's serving power and the Dutchman has had plenty of opportunities to demonstrate that strength this year, capturing two titles with his win over Greg Rusedski in the Guardian Direct tournament at Battersea and then winning from a bigger field in the Lipton International at Key Biscayne, defeating Sebastien Grosjean in the final. As 1996 Wimbledon champion Krajicek had to beat Pete Sampras in the quarter-finals and then took out Jason Stoltenberg and MaliVai Washington. Tim Henman beat Krajicek in the fourth round in 1997 but last year Krajicek was right back in the frame as he took his ninth-seeded challenge to the semi-finals where he faced Goran Ivanisevic, the first seed he had to play in The Championships. In endurance terms this was one of the classic contests with the fifth set stretching over 28 games before Ivanisevic won it 15-13. They were on court for three hours and 21 minutes and in the fourth set at 5-4 40-15 Ivansevic had his first match point. Krajicek did not hear the let call on the Croatian's serve but took the chance to break back with one of his specialist running forehands. Krajicek hit 42 aces, of which 23 were in the fifth set where he held a break for 3-2. Ivanisevic said of Krajicek: "I have never seen anyone serve like that in my life. It was just 'boom'. I couldn't react." Krajicek, whose daughter Emma was born in March last year, required knee surgery last winter. He ended 1998 ranked tenth in the world and had served 877 aces in the year which put him into the top five for that particular feat.

Carlos Moya

SPAIN

22; 6'3"; 177lb; RH

Seeded fifth at the 1998 Championships, Moya was soon under pressure as he came through a five set first round match against the Indian Davis Cup player Mahesh Bhupathi and then lost in the second round to the Moroccan Hicham Arazi. All that was in direct contrast to events earlier in June when Moya won the French Open for the first time, defeating fellow Spaniard Alex Corretja to become the fourth player from his country to win at Stade Roland Garros. The racket with which Moya won the title was donated subsequently to be auctioned in his home town of Mallorca to raise money for an Aids charity. Moya's pedigree has been obvious since he began playing tennis at the age of six. In Grand Slam terms he made a significant breakthrough in the 1997 Australian Open, taking his challenge to the final with victories over Boris Becker and Michael Chang before Pete Sampras proved too much for him. This year Moya, now fourth seed, suffered a first round defeat in Melbourne to the German Nicolas Kiefer. Moya has graced the courts at Bournemouth with the re-establishment of their clay court tournament, the Samsung Open—he was a finalist in 1997—and no one would have been more delighted in April when his home town football club removed Chelsea from the European Cup Winners' Cup.

Tim Henman

GREAT BRITAIN

24; 6'1"; 155lb; RH;

SF 1998; QF 96, 97

Tim Henman was saying, as the long run-in to Wimbledon began on the European clay courts, that he did not feel he would win the French Open but stood a good chance of capturing the Wimbledon title. After two years in succession as a quarter-finalist Henman went one step further at Wimbledon last year with a place in the last four. But there was one immense problem for Henman—Pete Sampras was on the other side of the net. The record shows that Sampras won 6-3 4-6 7-5 6-3, in two hours and 23 minutes. The second and third sets demonstrated Henman's skills to the full and perhaps a fraction more belief against the man he regards as the best in the world would have given him the chance to tip the balance. Indeed Sampras said of Henman afterwards: "One day he is going to win this thing. There were some really tense moments out there." Sampras would also say that he could not say "enough good things" about Henman's game and added: "He is a very solid player and will eventually win this tournament one year. He is 23 and he is just going to get better and better as the years go on—and he gained some experience today." He moved one step further along the Wimbledon road last year and the months in between have hardly been unproductive as he has played his part in lifting the British Davis Cup team into the World Group as a key member of the team which then fought so hard against the United States in that astonishing first round tie in Birmingham in April. Henman ended 1998 by qualifying for the ATP tour world championships in Hanover and although his challenge in the Australian Open this year ended in the third round against Marc Rosset he was a finalist in Doha in January, losing to Rainer Schuttler in three sets, and again in Rotterdam in February when he lost to Yevgeny Kafelnikov. The statistics tell their own story but what is less obvious is the effect which Henman's carefully structured and largely unseen gymnasium work will have on his overall game.

Go on, *make their day.*

Ring up and say you're at Wimbledon,
having a great time.

From a BT Payphone,
you can reach friends or family, around the corner or around
the world. And you can rely on our service, rain or shine.
So even if play stops, you can have the advantage.

Call them from a BT Payphone here at Wimbledon.
For locations see the map in this programme.

 *It's good to talk*

Marcelo Rios

CHILE

23; 5'9"; 160lb; LH 2HB

The question for Marcelo Rios to answer on grass is "When?" That the man can play is beyond question. He has fast hands and reactions, a left-handed game which is so difficult to tie down especially when he hits his big forehands, and the more you analyse his results it seems to add up that he ought to be doing well at Wimbledon. But so far it has not worked for Rios. In three appearances at Wimbledon he has won three matches, all in 1997 when he was beaten by Boris Becker in the fourth round. Last year, seeded second, he lost in five sets to Francisco Clavet of Spain in the first round, by some distance Clavet's biggest win. He has briefly been ranked No.1 in the world and finished last year in second place. At the start of last month Rios was back at eighth place in the standings, having just completed his best tournament of the year by reaching the Monte Carlo final where he retired injured against the Brazilian Gustavo Kuerten at 6-4 2-1 down. Rios had pulled a thigh muscle in the semi-final and had taken the precaution of giving an explanatory note to the umpire at the final in the event of his being forced to withdraw. "There are times when you have to listen to what your body is telling you," said Rios afterwards as he contemplated a break from the tour to let repairs take place. Rios had been playing tennis since he was 11 and was the top junior in 1993. By March last year Rios had become the first South American to rank No.1 in the world, surpassing such talents as Guillermo Vilas and Jose Luis Clerc of Argentina, neither of whom could quite reach the very top. Rios won enough matches last year to satisfy most players—68 matches in all and seven titles from eight finals—and was No.1 for a total of six weeks. He took key titles in Indian Wells, Key Biscayne, and Rome, and was a quarter-finalist in the French Open. He later took the Grand Slam Cup over Andre Agassi in Munich before playing just one round robin match in the ATP tour world championship, losing to Tim Henman, and pulling out with a back injury.

Mark Philippoussis

AUSTRALIA

22; 6'4"; 202lb; RH; QF 1998

A year ago Mark Philippoussis was in despair about his form on grass but instead of carrying out a threat to come off the tour for a while and re-think his approach he stayed on, dug himself in for Wimbledon, and had his best ever return in The Championships with a quarter-final place. He beat seventh seed Yevgeny Kafelnikov in the first round and then took his unseeded challenge to the last eight where Pete Sampras defeated him in straight sets. The Australian of Greek heritage disappointed himself and all of his supporters in the first half of last year but Wimbledon kick-started a distinct revival with Philippoussis reaching his first Grand Slam final in the US Open, losing to Pat Rafter, and going on to finish the year with a world ranking of 15th, his highest ever. In this year's Australian Open, Philippoussis started at 14th seed and justified that ranking by progressing to the last 16, before losing to the Swede Thomas Enqvist in five sets. Philippoussis was first coached by his father, Nick. He played on grass in Victoria and remembers how much he enjoyed diving around on the game's natural surface. He established a landmark as the first player in the world to serve at 140 m.p.h. and by the time he beat Sampras in the Australian Open in 1996 people were beginning to take notice. John Newcombe, Australia's Davis Cup captain, observed then: "The potential is there to be number one. I do not say that lightly. The thing is, in order to achieve his potential, Mark is going to have to work like hell." This year Philippoussis hit the top ten rankings for the first time, winning the title at the indoor event in San Jose in February and following up outdoors at Indian Wells with a second tour crown. Philippoussis loves cars and motor cycles and keeps a variety of them around the world ranging from a Lamborghini Diablo to a Range Rover 4.6 HSC. But it is on the courts of the world where Philippoussis wants to drive his natural talents and he is working with coach Gavin Hopper for even more progress. Two years ago he was champion on grass in the pre-Wimbledon Stella Artois tournament—and everyone knows how success there can eventually pay dividends at Wimbledon.

Greg Rusedski

GREAT BRITAIN

25; 6'4"; 190lb; LH; QF 1997

Greg Rusedski arrives at Wimbledon knowing that he has an even firmer place in the eyes of his thousands of supporters after his titanic five set finale to the Davis Cup World Group tie against the USA at Birmingham. Rusedski did not win the decisive match against Jim Courier but his efforts, watched by an enthralled crowd and a BBC TV audience of around eight million, brought massive exposure to tennis. Rusedski deserves a run at Wimbledon after his experiences last year when he slipped and fell in the Stella Artois tournament before The Championships and so damaged an ankle ligament that his immediate playing future was in considerable doubt. But Rusedski was determined to try to compete and after intensive treatment he began Wimbledon at fourth seed, hoping that he could play himself in and make a recovery at the same time. But it was a forlorn hope and those who watched Rusedski in action against the Australian qualifier Mark Draper in the first round on No.1 Court unquestionably shared his difficulties with him. It was fortunate for Rusedski that the match was called off overnight but the next day the Canadian born left-hander withdrew from the tournament. This is Rusedski's sixth appearance at Wimbledon. His best Wimbledon so far was in 1997 when he was defeated by Cedric Pioline of France, the eventual runner-up, in four sets at the quarter-final stage. Rusedski next progressed to his first Grand Slam final in the US Open, beating Daniel Vacek, Richard Krajicek, and Jonas Bjorkman in the later rounds to earn the right to face Pat Rafter for the title. Fred Perry was the last British player to win the US title, in 1936, and Rusedski was unable to join him in the record books as Rafter won in four sets. Rusedski's elevation to BBC Sports Personality of the Year in 1997 showed what the world at large thought of his efforts and his continued rise in the world rankings. His rivalry with Tim Henman for the top place in Britain, as well as the strides they have made together in the Davis Cup, combine to make him a player firmly in the spotlight. As an Arsenal fan, Rusedski has not had a bad run for his money in that department either.

43

P A R T N E R S

THE BRITISH TENNIS PARTNERSHIP
Taking British Tennis to the Top

JUNIOR TENNIS INITIATIVE

S U P P O R T E R S

BCA • Evian • Girobank • AT Kearney • John Laing plc •

Mercedes-Benz • Nomura • Northern Electric

 The Lawn Tennis Association

For more information please
telephone: + 44 (0) 171 381 7024
or e-mail: btp@LTA.org.uk

Andre Agassi

USA

29; 5'11"; 165lb; RH 2HB;

Champion 1992, SF 95, QF 91, 93

Andre Agassi is the second most senior former champion in the Wimbledon field—the oldest is Boris Becker—and there are thousands who will remember his 1992 final against Goran Ivanisevic. On the way to that final Agassi had to beat Becker in the quarter-finals and John McEnroe in the semi-finals. Even then, with a first Grand Slam title beckoning for both finalists, Agassi was taken the full five set distance by Ivanisevic. In 1994 Agassi took out five seeded players in seven matches to win the US Open and surged to the No.2 ranking in the world. Agassi started 1995, his best year on the tour, by capturing a third Grand Slam title in Australia. That was one of seven titles which fell to him that year and for a total of 30 weeks he was ranked No.1. But his hopes of adding a second Wimbledon title were ended in the semi-finals with defeat by Becker. Agassi's playing career has had to share equal billing with his life away from the tennis court as the recent ending of his marriage to actress Brooke Shields underlines. But Agassi, the 1996 Olympic champion, remains one of the figurehead players of the game and he started the countdown to Wimbledon a few weeks ago only one place outside the top ten in the world. Agassi's win over Alex Calatrava of Spain in the first round at Wimbledon last year was his 500th career victory but Tommy Haas of Germany was waiting in the next round and Agassi departed. Yet Agassi continued to carve out victories and won 14 matches in a row last summer. He captivated the New York crowds by heading into the fourth round of the US Open where he was two sets down against Karol Kucera of Slovakia before losing in the fifth. All this contributed to Agassi's astonishing jump in the world rankings last year as he moved from 122nd at the end of 1997 to 6th at the end of 1998. In the end of season showdowns he played the Grand Slam Cup in Munich, losing to Marcelo Rios in the final, and in the most astonishing of French Opens, he beat Andrei Medvedev in the Final after five pulsating sets.

Goran Ivanisevic

CROATIA

27; 6'4"; 180lb; LH 2HB;

Finalist 1992, 94, 98, SF 90, 95, QF 96

Goran Ivanisevic is a member of a club that no one wants to join, with three appearances in the Wimbledon final and three defeats. Fred Stolle suffered the same fate for three years running from 1963 and Ken Rosewall was beaten four times in the final, starting in 1954 and ending twenty years later against Jimmy Connors. Ivanisevic played five sets against Andre Agassi in the 1992 final, three sets against Pete Sampras in 1994, and five sets against Sampras last year. There had been no five set finals in between 1992 and 1998 and Ivanisevic played his full part in both, even if he will have to go through life remembering the missed opportunities. Last year he had played a semi-final lasting three hours and 21 minutes against Richard Krajicek and, in the final, missed two chances of establishing a lead of two sets to love. Afterwards Ivanisevic sat on his Centre Court chair with his head slumped, distraught and inconsolable, and would admit: "It hurts the most because this time I had the chance." Perhaps the 14th seeded Ivanisevic paid the bill for that arduous semi-final in the later stages of the final as Sampras pulled through to his fifth title 6-2 in the fifth set. Ivanisevic remained in the top twenty in the world for the ninth year running, sharing that achievement with Sampras alone, but won only one title in 1998 in his hometown of Split, beating Greg Rusedski in the final. Ivanisevic's left-handed serve continues to make him the king of the aces. He served 1065 aces last year, the best in the world, and for five times in eight years has been the best player in that specialised department. Yet Goran knows that aces are not enough if he is to beat his Wimbledon jinx and win the title which he seems so richly equipped to capture.

Todd Martin

USA

28; 6'6"; 190lb; RH;

SF 1994, 96, QF 93

When the United States were finalising their Davis Cup team to play Great Britain in the World Group tie at Birmingham last Easter, Martin was one of the most consistent players in the world and his win over Greg Rusedski on the opening day helped the Americans to their eventual victory. Martin's consistency is reflected in his ranking. He has only been outside the top twenty once in the past six years and that was because he had shin and elbow injuries which put him off the tour for seven months. This year, after winning the Sydney tournament over Alex Corretja, he was 15th seed for the Australian Open and after a protracted struggle over five sets against the defending champion Petr Korda he went to the quarter-finals where he was beaten by the eventual champion Yevgeny Kafelnikov. So Martin was unable to emulate his feat of reaching the final of the Australian championship in 1994 when he was beaten in straight sets by Pete Sampras. Martin is competing at Wimbledon for the seventh time and is particularly well equipped to play on grass as his record underlines—he was a winner at Queen's Club in 1994. In his second championship at Wimbledon in 1993 he made the quarter-finals where he fell to his Davis Cup team mate Jim Courier and the following year went one round further after going the full five set distance to beat Andre Agassi and Wayne Ferreira. With two other five set wins earlier in the tournament Martin became the first player in the Open era to win four five set matches at Wimbledon. A brave effort indeed but in the semi-finals he ran into Sampras and fell in four sets. Another semi-final beckoned Martin in 1996 after he had beaten Tim Henman in the quarter finals. Martin next faced the unseeded MaliVai Washington and was beaten 10-8 in the fifth set. As president of the ATP tour player council Martin has a strong voice in the development of the game while in his home town of Lansing, Michigan, he has set up his own tennis development fund.

45

#1 Titanium

#1 - World #1 uses the Yonex Super RQ Ti-700 Long

#1 - First Titanium Racquet to Win a Grand Slam Tournament

#1 - The 1st Choice in Titanium Mesh Technology

Martina Hingis chooses the power and control
of the Super RQ Ti-700 Long to be the World #1.

YONEX

One hundred and ten percent.

For a copy of our brochure and a list of retail stockists please call quoting WB99/1:   07000 YONEX UK
All facts correct at time of going to print - June 1999   96639 85

Karol Kucera

SLOVAKIA

25; 6'2"; 170lb; RH

Karol Kucera's steady rise up the rankings says that he is a force to be reckoned with and the man who is nicknamed "little cat"—his coach Miloslav Mecir was known as "big cat" as a player—finished last year with his best position of eighth in the world. Kucera made his biggest dent in Grand Slam terms in the Australian championships last year when he put out the defending champion Pete Sampras and his liking for the Australian event was confirmed in January when he justified his seventh seeding with a place in the quarter-finals where he lost to unseeded Nicolas Lapentti of Ecuador. Kucera presents a definite threat on grass because he was runner-up at Nottingham in 1997 when, to be strictly correct, the tournament began on grass and finished indoors because of the weather, and he also won on the Dutch grass courts at Rosmalen in 1995. Kucera's world ranking last year reflected the improvement in his results. He won titles in Sydney and New Haven, out of four finals he played and built up a winning tally of 53 matches. He also had his best US Open with a win over Andre Agassi before falling to Pete Sampras in the quarter-finals. He plays Davis Cup for Slovakia and was also on duty for his country in the Atlanta Olympic Games. Kucera beat Tim Henman in three sets in the quarter-finals of this year's Italian championships. Formerly lived in London.

Thomas Enqvist

SWEDEN

25; 6'3"; 187lb; RH;

After Bjorn Borg in the seventies and Stefan Edberg in the eighties it is always a question of when Sweden will produce another player to threaten to dominate major championships, and although Thomas Enqvist has not yet landed a Grand Slam title the signs are good for the Stockholm-born son of an engineer. A quarter-final place in the Australian Open in 1996 was his best Grand Slam place until this year when in the same championships he came from his ranking of 21st in the world to reach the final. He wielded his racket to great effect against the top Australian challengers, taking out Pat Rafter and Mark Philippoussis in two hard fought and successive rounds, and then two wins in straight sets over Marc Rosset and Nicolas Lapentti took him into the final against Yevgeny Kafelnikov. There the dream ended because after Enqvist had taken the first set Kafelnikov won the second without the loss of a game and ran out the match and the title on a fourth set tie-break where Enqvist won only one point. Enqvist had already done some other damage to Australian reputations as he beat Lleyton Hewitt, then 17, in his home town of Adelaide to win the fourteenth tour title of his career and all of these efforts left him as the highest ranked Swedish player, just ahead of Thomas Johansson, as the run-in to Wimbledon intensified. Enqvist has been as high as seventh in the world rankings, a position he held at the end of 1995, winning five tour titles. Then an ankle injury in 1997 and a foot injury last year forced him to cut back on his planned playing schedule. Enqvist, who was the top junior player in the world in 1991, plays Wimbledon for the fifth time. Last year was his best Wimbledon when he reached the third round. He beat the Canadian Daniel Nestor and the Australian Scott Draper before being beaten by Pete Sampras.

Chris Wilkinson

GREAT BRITAIN

29; 5'11"; 160lb; RH

To those who ask about the British men who are ranked behind Tim Henman and Greg Rusedski, the first in line is Chris Wilkinson, Southampton born, Wimbledon resident, who has reached the third round of Wimbledon four times including three years running from 1993 when he equalled a record established by Mark Cox in 1970. Ten years ago Wilkinson was ranked 668th in the world but he came inside the 200th place in 1992 and that is where he has remained—with a best ranking of 114th in September, 1993. Here at Wimbledon he has made winning in the first week his own speciality and has developed a considerable army of support as a result. His journeys to the third round began in 1993 when he was beaten by former champion Stefan Edberg. In 1994 he was beaten by the South African Wayne Ferreira, Michael Joyce of the USA beat him in 1995, and last year Ferreira was Wilkinson's conqueror for a second time. Ferreira beat Wilkinson in the Guardian Direct tournament in Battersea last year as well. Wilkinson put himself firmly on the map in 1993 when he beat one of the world's great grass court players, Goran Ivanisevic, at Queen's Club and he was a quarter-finalist in doubles with Paul Hand as well. Wilkinson was in the British Davis Cup team for the World group qualifying tie against India at Nottingham last September and had already established another landmark in his career by winning the ATP challenger event in Manchester, his second title there. Challenger tournaments require a special kind of commitment because they are not always on the beaten track and a sense of purpose and self-belief are real requirements for the players involved. Wilkinson has made dents in such diverse locations as the Bronx, Hamburen, Beijing, Singapore, Jakarta and Guam. Chris Wilkinson is indeed a much travelled player—and it is no surprise that he rises to the challenge once he sets foot in Wimbledon.

Wimbledon 1999

by Ronald Atkin

The Thirteenth Day

If we didn't already know that today is the Fourth of July, the penny (or perhaps the cent) has dropped now. Two Americans contesting the men's final, one American going for the women's crown; the United States has picked the perfect moment to remind everyone that their best competitors remain a force to be reckoned with at The Championships. Whether they will march off with both singles titles is open to question, with the question being posed by Steffi Graf. Steffi is going for her eighth Wimbledon, as most people, including her opponent, Lindsay Davenport, are very much aware, and she will take some stopping.

This was a truth which Mirjana Lucic discovered in yesterday's semi-finals, when she dominated the early part of the match only to be run over by the Steffi Express. Steffi then underlined her determination by withdrawing from her mixed doubles fun outing with John McEnroe, pleading a slight thigh strain. The concentration on Grand Slam victory number 23 is absolute. At 30, Steffi knows well enough that the shadows are gathering. After winning the French Open for a sixth time last month, she announced her farewell to the tournament, offering the opinion that there could not be a better way of saying goodbye to the Roland Garros stadium.

So will she also bid adieu to the All England Club premises if she wins today? No comment to that one, says Steffi. She is zeroed in on becoming the first to win the French and Wimbledon in succession since a certain Miss S.Graf in 1996. And if that comes to pass, no doubt Steffi will pronounce on her plans.

Entrusted with the awesome task of stopping all this happening is Davenport, the reigning US Open champion and an easy winner yesterday over her compatriot, Alexandra Stevenson. On their way to the final Graf has dropped three sets, Davenport none. But in their career head-to-head it is Graf who has done better, winning eight of their 13 matches, including a quarter-final at this year's French Open. Those 13 matches do not include a previous meeting at Wimbledon, or indeed any clash on grass.

Andre Agassi will be entitled to an extra strut in his step when he accompanies Pete Sampras onto Centre Court for the Gentlemen's Singles Championship, having replaced Sampras as world number one by virtue of defeating Patrick Rafter in yesterday's semi-finals.

This is the first all-American men's final at Wimbledon since 1993, when Sampras defeated Jim Courier in a contest which one media cynic has categorised as "bored on the Fourth of July." Since then of course, Pete has virtually turned this place into his private fiefdom, winning five times in six years. Another win today would make him the most successful in the modern era, and second only to William Renshaw, who collected seven titles between 1881 and 1889, when the old tournament was not quite so tightly contested and the first prize was probably a sixpenny voucher redeemable at Woolworths.

Big licks now, of course. The men's winner today will pocket £455,000, and the women's champion will be £409,500 the richer. which brings us back to that thorny subject of equal prize money. As Steffi would say in response to questions about her future plans, no comment on that one, especially on this special day.

Sampras is attempting to kick-start a year which started late and went sour quickly. The Stella Artois title at Queen's has helped to cheer the lad up but he badly needs a Grand Slam to lift his hopes of finishing at number one in the rankings for a seventh year. It is Agassi who is chasing the more enticing prize, victory here immediately after capturing the French Open. This has not been achieved since 1980 when Bjorn Borg used to clean up routinely in Paris and London.

Should Sampras emerge triumphant this afternoon he will pull level with Roy Emerson at the head of the Grand Slam singles table with 12 titles. That would surely give Pete enough impetus to go for another best-ever award by winning the US Open this year before declining years (he will soon, after all, be 28)get the better of him. Something like that would help to ease the pain of having lost his number one ranking at the very moment when he tied the all-time longevity merchant, Ivan Lendl, at 270 weeks at the top.

The two American men have been gunning for each other for ten years now, ever since Rome 1989 when Agassi beat Sampras 6-2 6-1 on clay. Pete has won 13 of their 23 matches, including the only previous one on grass, at the 1993 Wimbledon quarter-finals. May the best American win today, though the real winners are the lucky Centre Court ticket holders who find themselves watching two finals for the price of one. So there are some people who will be blessing the British climate.

Head to Head

Pete Sampras v Andre Agassi
SAMPRAS LEADS 13 : 10

Tournament	Surface	Round	Winner	Scores	Tournament	Surface	Round	Winner	Scores
89 Rome	Clay	R32	AGASSI	6-2 6-1	95 Australian Open	Hard	F	AGASSI	4-6 6-1 7-6 6-4
90 Philadelphia	Carpet	R16	SAMPRAS	5-7 7-5 Ret'd	95 Indian Wells	Hard	F	SAMPRAS	7-5 6-3 7-5
90 U.S.Open	Hard	F	SAMPRAS	6-4 6-3 6-2	95 Lipton-Key Biscayn	Hard	F	AGASSI	3-6 6-2 7-6
90 ATP Finals	Carpet	RR	AGASSI	6-4 6-2	95 Canadian Open	Hard	F	AGASSI	3-6 6-2 6-3
91 ATP Finals	Carpet	RR	SAMPRAS	6-3 1-6 6-3	95 U.S.Open	Hard	F	SAMPRAS	6-4 6-3 4-6 7-5
92 Atlanta	Clay	F	AGASSI	7-5 6-4	96 San Jose	Hard	F	SAMPRAS	6-2 6-3
92 French Open	Clay	QF	AGASSI	7-6 6-2 6-1	96 Stuttgart Indoor	Carpet	QF	SAMPRAS	6-4 6-1
93 Wimbledon	Grass	QF	SAMPRAS	6-2 6-2 3-6 3-6 6-4	96 ATP Finals	Carpet	RR	SAMPRAS	6-2 6-1
94 Lipton-Key Biscayn	Hard	F	SAMPRAS	5-7 6-3 6-3	98 San Jose	Hard	F	AGASSI	6-2 6-4
94 Osaka	Hard	SF	SAMPRAS	6-3 6-1	98 Monte Carlo	Clay	R32	SAMPRAS	6-4 7-5
94 Paris Indoor	Carpet	QF	AGASSI	7-6 7-5	98 Canadian Open	Hard	QF	AGASSI	6-7 6-1 6-2
94 ATP Finals	Carpet	SF	SAMPRAS	4-6 7-6 6-3					

Steffi Graf v Lindsay Davenport
GRAF LEADS 8 : 5

Tournament	Surface	Round	Winner	Scores	Tournament	Surface	Round	Winner	Scores
94 Australian Open	Hard	QF	GRAF	6-3 6-2	98 Stanford	Hard	SF	DAVENPORT	6-4 6-7 6-3
94 Lipton	Hard	SF	GRAF	6-0 7-6	98 New Haven	Hard	SF	GRAF	6-3 7-6
96 Indian Wells	Hard	SF	GRAF	6-7 7-6 6-4	98 Philadelphia	Carpet	F	GRAF	4-6 6-3 6-4
96 Lipton	Hard	SF	GRAF	6-4 6-4	98 Chase Championship	Carpet	SF	DAVENPORT	6-1 2-6 6-3
96 Los Angeles	Hard	SF	DAVENPORT	6-3 6-3	99 Sydney	Hard	SF	DAVENPORT	6-2 7-5
96 Chase Championship	Carpet	QF	GRAF	6-4 7-6	99 French Open	Clay	QF	GRAF	6-1 6-7 6-3
98 Indian Wells	Hard	SF	DAVENPORT	6-4 4-6 4-2 Ret'd					

49

Strawberries
& Cream
Hand-Tied

ALPHABETICAL LIST OF COMPETITORS

Bold figures denote position in Singles Draw

LADIES

Abe Miss J. *(Germany)*
Adams Miss K.M. *(USA)*
66 Ahl Miss L.A. *(Great Britain)*
55 Appelmans Miss S. *(Belgium)*
41 Arendt Miss N. *(USA)*
45 Bacheva Miss L. *(Bulgaria)*
24 Barabanschikova Miss O. *(Belarus)*
Barclay Miss C.G. *(Australia)*
Bes Miss E. *(Spain)*
61 Black Miss C. *(Zimbabwe)*
Bollegraf Miss M.M. *(Netherlands)*
77 Boogert Miss K. *(Netherlands)*
13 Brandi Miss K. *(USA)*
39 Callens Miss E.S.H. *(Belgium)*
72 Capriati Miss J. *(USA)*
26 Carlsson Miss A. *(Sweden)*
127 Cervanova Miss L. *(Slovak Republic)*
99 Chi Miss J. *(USA)*
83 Chladkova Miss D. *(Czech Republic)*
118 Clijsters Miss K. *(Belgium)*
40 Cocheteux Miss A. *(France)*
113 Coetzer Miss A.J. *(South Africa)*
124 Courtois Miss L. *(Belgium)*
23 Cristea Miss C. *(Romania)*
Crook Miss H. *(Great Britain)*
120 Cross Miss K.M. *(Great Britain)*
33 Davenport Miss L.A. *(USA)*
Davies Miss V.E. *(Great Britain)*
De Beer Miss S. *(South Africa)*
91 De Lone Miss E.R. *(USA)*
126 de Swardt Miss M. *(South Africa)*
De Villiers Miss N. *(South Africa)*
46 Dechaume-Balleret Mrs A. *(France)*
54 Dechy Miss N. *(France)*
79 Dementieva Miss E. *(Russia)*
Dhenin Miss C. *(France)*
89 Diaz Oliva Miss M. *(Argentina)*
2 Dokic Miss J. *(Australia)*
105 Dragomir Miss R. *(Romania)*
85 Drake Miss M. *(Canada)*
Ellwood Miss A. *(Australia)*
20 Farina Miss S. *(Italy)*
6 Fernandez Miss M.J. *(USA)*
31 Foldenyi Miss A. *(Hungary)*
21 Frazier Miss A. *(USA)*
Freye Miss K. *(Germany)*
34 Fusai Miss A. *(France)*
110 Gagliardi Miss E. *(Switzerland)*
30 Glass Miss A. *(Germany)*
38 Golarsa Miss L. *(Italy)*
107 Gorrochategui Miss I. *(Argentina)*
128 Graf Miss S. *(Germany)*
Graham Miss D.A. *(USA)*
14 Grande Miss R. *(Italy)*
73 Grzybowska Miss M. *(Poland)*
121 Guse Miss K-A. *(Australia)*
35 Habsudova Miss K. *(Slovak Republic)*
17 Halard-Decugis Mrs J. *(France)*
1 Hingis Miss M. *(Switzerland)*
Hiraki Miss R. *(Japan)*
67 Hopmans Miss A. *(Netherlands)*
Horn Miss L. *(South Africa)*
88 Hrdlickova Miss K. *(Czech Republic)*
71 Huber Miss A. *(Germany)*
• Husarova Miss J. *(Slovak Republic)*
59 Jeyaseelan Miss S. *(Canada)*
Jidkova Miss A. *(Russia)*
Kim Miss E. *(Korea Republic)*
68 Kleinova Miss S. *(Czech Republic)*
86 Koulikovskaya Miss E. *(Russia)*
112 Kournikova Miss A. *(Russia)*
5 Kremer Miss A. *(Luxemburg)*
Krizan Miss T. *(Slovenia)*
117 Kruger Miss J. *(South Africa)*
Kunce Mrs K. *(Australia)*
28 Kuti-Kis Miss R. *(Hungary)*
Labat Miss F. *(Argentina)*
Landa Miss M. F. *(Argentina)*
104 Latimer Miss L. *(Great Britain)*
122 Lee Miss J. *(Chinese Taipei)*
47 Leon Garcia Miss G. *(Spain)*
44 Li Miss F. *(China P.R.)*
76 Likhovtseva Miss E. *(Russia)*
4 Loit Miss E. *(France)*
92 Lucic Miss M. *(Croatia)*
Lugina Miss O. *(Ukraine)*
Marosi Miss K. *(Hungary)*
Martincova Miss E. *(Czech Republic)*
27 Martinez Miss C. *(Spain)*
McNeil Miss L.M. *(USA)*
McQuillan Miss R. *(Australia)*
McShea Miss L. *(Australia)*
Melicharova Miss E. *(Czech Republic)*
Menga Miss V. *(Brazil)*
Miyagi Miss N. *(Japan)*
75 Molik Miss A. *(Australia)*
Montalvo Miss L. *(Argentina)*
123 Morariu Miss C. *(USA)*
Muric Miss M. *(Croatia)*
18 Nacuk Miss S. *(Yugoslavia)*
52 Nagyova Miss H. *(Slovak Republic)*
43 Neiland Mrs L. *(Latvia)*
69 Nejedly Miss J. *(Canada)*
Nemeckova Miss L. *(Czech Republic)*
70 Noorlander Miss S. *(Netherlands)*
64 Novotna Miss J. *(Czech Republic)*
Olsza Miss A. *(Poland)*
98 Oremans Miss M. *(Netherlands)*
Ortuno Miss A. *(Spain)*
119 Osterloh Miss L. *(USA)*
51 Panova Miss T. *(Russia)*
115 Papadaki Miss C. *(Greece)*
60 Petrova Miss N. *(Russia)*
16 Pierce Miss M. *(France)*
Pisnik Miss T. *(Slovenia)*
102 Pitkowski Miss S. *(France)*
Pleming Miss L. *(Australia)*
62 Plischke Miss S. *(Austria)*
50 Po Miss K. *(USA)*
114 Pratt Miss N.J. *(Australia)*
Probst Miss W. *(Germany)*
82 Pullin Miss J.M. *(Great Britain)*
29 Raymond Miss L.M. *(USA)*
Reeves Miss S. *(USA)*
8 Rippner Miss B. *(USA)*
84 Rittner Miss B. *(Germany)*
9 Ruano Pascual Miss V. *(Spain)*
78 Rubin Miss C. *(USA)*
116 Saeki Miss M. *(Japan)*
57 Sanchez Lorenzo Miss M.A. *(Spain)*
32 Sanchez Vicario Miss A. *(Spain)*
Schaerer Miss L. *(Paraguay)*
48 Schett Miss B. *(Austria)*
Schlukebir Miss K. *(USA)*
53 Schnyder Miss P. *(Switzerland)*
111 Schwartz Miss B. *(Austria)*
96 Seles Miss M. *(USA)*
Selyutina Miss I. *(Kazakhstan)*
42 Serna Miss M. *(Spain)*
19 Serra-Zanetti Miss A. *(Italy)*
10 Shaughnessy Miss M. *(USA)*
103 Sidot Miss A-G. *(France)*
Singer Miss C. *(Germany)*
90 Smashnova Miss A. *(Israel)*
108 Smith Miss S. *(Great Britain)*
25 Snyder Miss T. *(USA)*
7 Spirlea Miss I. *(Romania)*
101 Srebotnik Miss K. *(Slovenia)*
Steck Miss J. *(South Africa)*
22 Stevenson Miss A. *(USA)*
Stewart Miss B. *(Australia)*
37 Stoyanova Miss P. *(Bulgaria)*
Stubbs Miss R.P. *(Australia)*
3 Studenikova Miss K. *(Slovak Republic)*
106 Suarez Miss P. *(Argentina)*
74 Sugiyama Miss A. *(Japan)*
56 Talaja Miss S. *(Croatia)*
87 Tanasugarn Miss T. *(Thailand)*
Tarabini Miss P. *(Argentina)*
100 Tatarkova Miss E. *(Ukraine)*
65 Tauziat Miss N. *(France)*
81 Testud Miss S. *(France)*
12 Tordoff Miss A. *(Great Britain)*
95 Torrens-Valero Miss C. *(Spain)*
80 Van Roost Mrs D. *(Belgium)*
109 Vento Miss M.A. *(Venezuela)*
Vildova Miss H. *(Czech Republic)*
Vis Miss C.M. *(Netherlands)*
11 Wagner Mrs E. *(Germany)*
63 Wang Miss S-T. *(Chinese Taipei)*
93 Ward Miss J. *(Great Britain)*
Washington Miss M. *(USA)*
125 Watanabe Miss J. *(USA)*
94 Weingartner Miss M. *(Germany)*
58 Wild Miss L. *(USA)*
97 Williams Miss V. *(USA)*
36 Woodroffe Miss L.A. *(Great Britain)*
Yoshida Miss Y. *(Japan)*
15 Zuluaga Miss F. *(Colombia)*
49 Zvereva Miss N. *(Belarus)*

GENTLEMEN

Adams D. *(South Africa)*
96 Agassi A. *(USA)*
119 Alami K. *(Morocco)*
Albano P. *(Argentina)*
7 Alonso J. *(Spain)*
105 Arazi H. *(Morocco)*
Ardinghi M. *(Italy)*
85 Arthurs W. *(Australia)*
Bale L. *(South Africa)*
Barnard M. *(South Africa)*
115 Becker B. *(Germany)*
Bertolini M. *(Italy)*
Bhupathi M. *(India)*
125 Bjorkman J. *(Sweden)*
58 Black B. *(Zimbabwe)*
4 Black W. *(Zimbabwe)*
5 Blanco G. *(Spain)*
Bowen D. *(USA)*
Braasch K. *(Germany)*
Brandi C. *(Italy)*
Broad N. *(Great Britain)*
Bryan B. *(USA)*
Bryan M. *(USA)*
93 Canas G. *(Argentina)*
127 Caratti C. *(Italy)*
Carbonell T. *(Spain)*
Carrasco J. *(Spain)*
Childs L. *(Great Britain)*
28 Clavet F. *(Spain)*
39 Clement A. *(France)*
Coetzee J. *(South Africa)*
19 Costa A. *(Spain)*
Coupe B. *(USA)*
52 Courier J. *(USA)*
51 Cowan B. *(Great Britain)*
37 Damm M. *(Czech Republic)*
De Jager J-L. *(South Africa)*
Del Rio D. *(Argentina)*
Delaitre O. *(France)*
60 Delgado J. *(Great Britain)*
59 Delgado R. *(Paraguay)*
63 Di Pasquale A. *(France)*
Dickson S. *(Great Britain)*
Dilucia D. *(USA)*
Djordjevic N. *(Yugoslavia)*
90 Dosedel S. *(Czech Republic)*
2 Draper S. *(Australia)*
98 Dreekmann H. *(Germany)*
92 El Aynaoui Y. *(Morocco)*
Ellwood B. *(Australia)*
123 Enqvist T. *(Sweden)*
100 Federer R. *(Switzerland)*
Ferreira A. *(Brazil)*
Ferreira E. *(South Africa)*
53 Ferreira W. *(South Africa)*
118 Filippini M. *(Uruguay)*
Flach D. *(USA)*
Florent A. *(Australia)*
83 Fromberg R. *(Australia)*
Galbraith P. *(USA)*
71 Gambill J. *(USA)*
21 Gaudio G. *(Argentina)*
103 Gimelstob J. *(USA)*
Godwin N. *(South Africa)*
Goellner M-K. *(Germany)*
14 Goldstein P. *(USA)*
Grabb J. *(USA)*
Grant G. *(USA)*
Greenhalgh J. *(New Zealand)*
57 Grosjean S. *(France)*
91 Gross O. *(Germany)*
124 Gumy H. *(Argentina)*
84 Gustafsson M. *(Sweden)*
106 Haarhuis P. *(Netherlands)*
81 Haas T. *(Germany)*
Hadad A. *(Israel)*
Haggard C. *(South Africa)*
Haygarth B. *(South Africa)*
64 Henman T. *(Great Britain)*
47 Hernandez A. *(Mexico)*
117 Hewitt L. *(Australia)*
Hill M. *(Australia)*
101 Hipfl M. *(Austria)*
Hood M. *(Argentina)*
30 Hrbaty D. *(Slovak Republic)*
Humphries S. *(USA)*
54 Ilie A. *(Australia)*
112 Ivanisevic G. *(Croatia)*
25 Johansson T. *(Sweden)*
Johnson D. *(USA)*
33 Kafelnikov Y. *(Russia)*
12 Karbacher B. *(Germany)*
Keil M. *(USA)*
Kempers T. *(Netherlands)*
113 Kiefer N. *(Germany)*
Kitinov A. *(Macedonia)*
104 Knippschild J. *(Germany)*
Knowles M. *(Bahamas)*
Koenig R. *(South Africa)*
27 Kohlmann M. *(Germany)*
Kokavec B. *(Canada)*
10 Koubek S. *(Austria)*
Koves G. *(Hungary)*
65 Krajicek R. *(Netherlands)*
Kratzmann A. *(Australia)*
50 Kroslak J. *(Slovak Republic)*
48 Kucera K. *(Slovak Republic)*
80 Kuerten G. *(Brazil)*
Kulti N. *(Sweden)*
88 Lapentti N. *(Ecuador)*
3 Lareau S. *(Canada)*
34 Larsson M. *(Sweden)*
Leach R. *(USA)*
94 Lee M. *(Great Britain)*
Lopez-Moron A. *(Spain)*
116 MacLagan M. *(Great Britain)*
Macpherson D. *(Australia)*
MacPhie B. *(USA)*
31 Malisse X. *(Belgium)*
108 Mamiit C. *(USA)*
69 Manta L. *(Switzerland)*
16 Mantilla F. *(Spain)*
75 Marin J. A. *(Costa Rica)*
121 Marques N. *(Portugal)*
89 Martin A. *(Spain)*
97 Martin T. *(USA)*
McEnroe J.P. *(USA)*
11 Medvedev A. *(Ukraine)*
Merklein M. *(USA)*
Middleton T.J. *(USA)*
23 Milligan L. *(Great Britain)*
Mirnyi M. *(Belarus)*
Montana F. *(USA)*
Motomura G. *(Japan)*
49 Moya C. *(Spain)*
Navarra M. *(Italy)*
9 Nestor D. *(Canada)*
Nicolas E. *(Spain)*
22 Norman M. *(Sweden)*
Norval P. *(South Africa)*
99 Novak J. *(Czech Republic)*
Nyborg P. *(Sweden)*
O'Brien A. *(USA)*
Oncins J. *(Brazil)*
46 Paes L. *(India)*
Palmer J. *(USA)*
20 Parmar A. *(Great Britain)*
95 Pavel A. *(Romania)*
74 Pescariu D. *(Romania)*
Pescosolido S. *(Italy)*
32 Philippoussis M. *(Australia)*
38 Pioline C. *(France)*
40 Portas A. *(Spain)*
43 Pozzi G. *(Italy)*
Prieto S. *(Argentina)*
78 Prinosil D. *(Germany)*
Puentes G. *(Spain)*
128 Rafter P. *(Australia)*
Ran E. *(Israel)*
36 Raoux G. *(France)*
26 Reneberg R.A. *(USA)*
Rikl D. *(Czech Republic)*
Roberts D. *(South Africa)*
Roditi D. *(Mexico)*
77 Rodriguez M. *(Argentina)*
Rosner P. *(South Africa)*
102 Rosset M. *(Switzerland)*
17 Rusedski G. *(Great Britain)*
66 Ruud C. *(Norway)*
45 Sa A. *(Brazil)*
1 Sampras P. *(USA)*
Sanchez J. *(Spain)*
56 Sanguinetti D. *(Italy)*
86 Santopadre V. *(Italy)*
24 Santoro F. *(France)*
8 Sapsford D.E. *(Great Britain)*
62 Sargsian S. *(Armenia)*
55 Schalken S. *(Netherlands)*
122 Schuttler R. *(Germany)*
Sell M. *(USA)*
Sherwood D. *(Great Britain)*
13 Siemerink J. *(Netherlands)*
Silcock G. *(Australia)*
15 Spadea V. *(USA)*
70 Spinks T. *(Great Britain)*
72 Squillari F. *(Argentina)*
35 Srichaphan P. *(Thailand)*
126 Stafford G. *(South Africa)*
67 Stanoytchev O. *(Bulgaria)*
Stark J. *(USA)*
Stepanek R. *(Czech Republic)*
110 Stolle S. *(Australia)*
18 Stoltenberg J. *(Australia)*
Suk C. *(Czech Republic)*
6 Suzuki T. *(Japan)*
76 Tarango J. *(USA)*
Tebbutt M. *(Australia)*
120 Tieleman L. *(Italy)*
111 Tillstrom M. *(Sweden)*
Tramacchi P. *(Australia)*
Trifu G. *(Romania)*
42 Ulihrach B. *(Czech Republic)*
Ullyett K. *(South Africa)*
41 Vacek D. *(Czech Republic)*
109 Van Lottum J. *(Netherlands)*
Vanhoudt T. *(Belgium)*
Velasco J. *(Spain)*
107 Vicente F. *(Spain)*
114 Vinck C. *(Germany)*
Vizner P. *(Czech Republic)*
87 Voinea A. *(Romania)*
44 Voltchkov V. *(Belarus)*
Waite J. *(USA)*
82 Wessels P. *(Netherlands)*
Whitehouse W. *(South Africa)*
79 Wilkinson C. *(Great Britain)*
68 Woodbridge T.A. *(Australia)*
29 Woodforde M. *(Australia)*
61 Woodruff C. *(USA)*
73 Zimonjic N. *(Yugoslavia)*

GIRLS

62 Abram Miss A. *(Poland)*
9 Abramovic Miss I. *(Croatia)*
14 Adamczak Miss M. *(Australia)*
51 Aoyama Miss K. *(Japan)*
3 Babakova Miss M. *(Slovak Republic)*
41 Baker Miss L. *(New Zealand)*
54 Baltacha Miss E. *(Great Britain)*
25 Bao Miss L. *(Switzerland)*
11 Barnes Miss A. *(Great Britain)*
35 Barnes Miss R. *(Great Britain)*
53 Barnikow Miss L. *(USA)*
19 Basu Miss C.A. *(Germany)*
33 Bedanova Miss D. *(Czech Republic)*
21 Benesova Miss I. *(Czech Republic)*
6 Berecz Miss K. *(Hungary)*
5 Birnerova Miss E. *(Czech Republic)*
40 Bovina Miss E. *(Russia)*
26 Camerin Miss M.E. *(Italy)*
24 Cargill Miss A. *(USA)*
18 Carter Miss C. *(Great Britain)*
38 Castro Miss V. *(Chile)*
43 Charbonnier Miss C. *(Switzerland)*
27 Collin Miss H. *(Great Britain)*
29 Culum Miss N. *(Slovenia)*
32 Danilidou Miss E. *(Greece)*
55 Dlhopolcova Miss L. *(Slovak Republic)*
44 Dowse Miss M. *(Australia)*
10 Farr Miss H. *(Great Britain)*
23 Fokina Miss G. *(Russia)*
15 Gerards Miss M. *(Netherlands)*
63 Grandin Miss N. *(South Africa)*
57 Granville Miss L. *(USA)*
Gregg Miss S. *(Great Britain)*
Hawkins Miss A. *(Great Britain)*
31 Hergold Miss T. *(Slovenia)*
48 Kapros Miss A. *(Hungary)*
34 Keothavong Miss A. *(Great Britain)*
49 Krasnoroutskai Miss L. *(Russia)*
52 Krauth Miss E. *(Argentina)*
28 Krauth Miss V. *(Argentina)*
58 Krishnamurthy Miss K. *(Canada)*
36 Krstulovic Miss D. *(Croatia)*
37 Kurhajcova Miss L. *(Slovak Republic)*
59 Luzarova Miss D. *(Czech Republic)*
22 Mojzis Miss A. *(South Africa)*
39 Muller Miss M. *(Germany)*
50 Nikolaeva Miss A. *(Belarus)*
60 Pennetta Miss F. *(Italy)*
8 Perebiynis Miss T. *(Ukraine)*
1 Rafolomana Miss A. *(Madagascar)*
13 Rencken Miss N. *(South Africa)*
30 Resch Miss B. *(Austria)*
45 Reyes Miss Z. *(Mexico)*
12 Reynolds Miss D. *(Mexico)*
16 Salerni Miss M.E. *(Argentina)*
7 Scaringe Miss J. *(USA)*
46 Seal Miss C. *(Great Britain)*
2 Smith Miss J. *(Great Britain)*
Stone Miss S. *(Australia)*
4 Stosur Miss S. *(Australia)*
47 Trinder Miss N. *(Great Britain)*
17 Tulyaganova Miss I. *(Uzbekhistan)*
64 Uda Miss R. *(Japan)*
42 Vinci Miss R. *(Italy)*
20 Vymetal Miss K. *(Great Britain)*
61 Wallace Miss C. *(Great Britain)*
Webley-Smith Miss E. *(Great Britain)*
56 Werner Miss S. *(Germany)*
Wood Miss L. *(Great Britain)*

BOYS

29 Abel M. *(Germany)*
49 Alves T. *(Brazil)*
61 Ancic M. *(Croatia)*
Anderson A. *(South Africa)*
53 Banks A. *(Great Britain)*
19 Beck K. *(Slovak Republic)*
56 Becker B. *(Germany)*
8 Benneteau J. *(France)*
30 Berke S. *(USA)*
36 Bogomolov A. *(USA)*
46 Britzen D. *(Germany)*
10 Brooks R. *(Great Britain)*
60 Childs L. *(Great Britain)*
41 Chramosta L. *(Czech Republic)*
17 Coria G. *(Argentina)*
Davis T. *(USA)*
16 De Armas J. *(Venezuela)*
28 Dickson S. *(Great Britain)*
63 Enev T. *(Bulgaria)*
22 Faurel J-C. *(France)*
40 Fish M. *(USA)*
Francis A. *(USA)*
45 Froberg J. *(Sweden)*
Fruttero J-P. *(USA)*
55 Furukawa H. *(Japan)*
13 Gard C. *(Romania)*
Gray J. *(Great Britain)*
Green R. *(USA)*
18 Greenhouse N. *(Great Britain)*
11 Gremelmayr D. *(Germany)*
39 Hammer P. *(Germany)*
27 Harboe P. *(Chile)*
58 Harper-Griffith L. *(USA)*
14 Hasek J. *(Czech Republic)*
51 Hemmes F. *(Netherlands)*
Higgins T. *(Great Britain)*
42 Hilton M.A. *(Great Britain)*
25 Johansson J. *(Sweden)*
4 Karanusic R. *(Croatia)*
62 Kiendl U. *(Germany)*
43 Kracman A. *(Slovenia)*
2 Lammer M. *(Switzerland)*
20 Langre D. *(Mexico)*
50 Mackin A. *(Great Britain)*
54 Mahut N. *(France)*
5 Martin D. *(USA)*
52 McDade A. *(South Africa)*
59 Meffert D. *(Germany)*
34 Melzer J. *(Austria)*
37 Miyazaki Y. *(Japan)*
64 Nalbandian D. *(Argentina)*
38 Nelson J. *(Great Britain)*
33 Nieminen J. *(Finland)*
6 Nieminen T. *(Finland)*
12 Nugent S. *(Eire)*
44 Ormaza M. *(Argentina)*
47 Pampoulov L. *(Austria)*
1 Pless K. *(Denmark)*
48 Prodon E. *(France)*
31 Riby B. *(Great Britain)*
24 Roddick A. *(USA)*
57 Rojer J-J. *(Netherland Antillies)*
3 Russell R. *(Jamaica)*
15 Stegmann D. *(South Africa)*
7 Thys R. *(Belgium)*
21 Trudgeon M. *(Great Britain)*
9 Villagran C. *(Argentina)*
26 Vlaski A. *(Yugoslavia)*
35 Weaver M. *(Great Britain)*
Weir-Smith B. *(South Africa)*
23 Wong W. *(Hong Kong)*
32 Zovko L. *(Croatia)*

256 TOP PLAYERS HAVE MADE IT TO WIMBLEDON, BUT ONLY ONE STRAWBERRY ICE CREAM.

STRAWBERRY ICE CREAM

CLASSIFIED LIST OF COMPETITORS AND COMPUTER RANKINGS (SINGLES)

Arranged according to Countries

LADIES

ARGENTINA
Diaz Oliva, Mariana (123)
Gorrochategui, Ines (76)
Krauth, Erica
Krauth, Vanessa
Labat, Florencia
Landa, Maria Fernanda
Montalvo, Laura
Salerni, Maria
Suarez, Paola (60)
Tarabini, Patricia

AUSTRALIA
Adamczak, Monique
Barclay, Catherine
Dokic, Jelena (129)
Dowse, Melissa
Ellwood, Annabel
Guse, Kerry-Anne (152)
Kunce, Kristine
Mandlikova, Hana
McQuillan, Rachel
McShea, Lisa
Molik, Alicia (81)
Pleming, Louise
Pratt, Nicole (75)
Smylie, Elizabeth
Stewart, Bryanne
Stone, Sarah
Stosur, Samantha
Stubbs, Rennae
Turnbull, Wendy

AUSTRIA
Plischke, Sylvia (27)
Resch, Bettina
Schett, Barbara (13)
Schwartz, Barbara (50)

BELARUS
Barabanschikova, Olga (57)
Nikolaeva, Alesia
Zvereva, Natasha (12)

BELGIUM
Appelmans, Sabine (80)
Callens, Els (79)
Clijsters, Kim (195)
Courtois, Laurence (71)
Van Roost, Dominique (14)

BRAZIL
Menga, Vanessa

BULGARIA
Bacheva, Lubomira (96)
Stoyanova, Pavlina (101)

CANADA
Drake, Maureen (52)
Jeyaseelan, Sonya (112)
Krishnamurthy, Kavitha
Nejedly, Jana (85)

CHILE
Castro, Valentin

CHINA P.R.
Li, Fang (92)

CHINESE TAIPEI
Lee, Janet (105)
Wang, Shi-Ting (73)

COLOMBIA
Zuluaga, Fabiola (48)

CROATIA
Abramovic, Ivana
Krstulovic, Dora
Lucic, Mirjana (134)
Muric, Maja
Talaja, Silvija (43)

CZECH REPUBLIC
Bedanova, Daniela
Benesova, Iveta
Birnerova, Eva
Chladkova, Denisa (70)
Hrdlickova, Kvetoslava (74)
Kleinova, Sandra (90)
Luzarova, Dominika
Martincova, Eva
Melicharova, Eva
Nemeckova, Lenka
Novotna, Jana (6)
Vildova, Helena

FRANCE
Cocheteux, Amelie (65)
Dechaume-Balleret, Alexia (72)
Dechy, Nathalie (29)
Dhenin, Caroline
Fusai, Alexandra (140)
Halard-Decugis, Julie (18)
Loit, Emilie (83)
Pierce, Mary (7)
Pitkowski, Sarah (36)
Sidot, Anne-Gaelle (45)
Tauziat, Nathalie (8)
Testud, Sandrine (16)

GERMANY
Abe, Julia
Basu, Caroline
Freye, Kirstin
Glass, Andrea (59)
Graf, Steffi (3)
Huber, Anke (30)
Kohde-Kilsch, Claudia
Muller, Martina
Probst, Wiltrud
Rittner, Barbara (47)
Singer, Christina
Wagner, Elena (82)
Weingartner, Marlene (78)
Werner, Scarlett

GREAT BRITAIN
Ahl, Lucie (183)
Baltacha, Elena
Barnes, Alice
Barnes, Ruth
Carter, Claire
Collin, Hannah
Crook, Helen
Cross, Karen (187)
Davies, Victoria
Durie, Jo
Farr, Heidi
Gregg, Sarah
Hawkins, Anna
Hobbs, Anne
Keothavong, Anne
Latimer, Louise (137)
Pullin, Julie (136)
Seal, Claire
Smith, Julia
Smith, Samantha (91)
Tordoff, Abigail (272)
Trinder, Nicola
Vymetal, Katherine
Wade, Virginia
Wallace, Charlotte
Ward, Joanne (192)
Webley-Smith, Emily
Wood, Lucy
Woodroffe, Lorna (222)

GREECE
Danilidou, Eleni
Papadaki, Christina (95)

HUNGARY
Berecz, Kinga
Foldenyi, Annamaria (119)
Kapros, Aniko
Kuti-Kis, Rita (77)
Marosi, Katalin

ISRAEL
Smashnova, Anna (39)

ITALY
Camerin, Maria
Farina, Silvia (24)
Golarsa, Laura (122)
Grande, Rita (56)
Pennetta, Flavia
Serra-Zanetti, Adriana (106)
Vinci, Roberta

JAPAN
Aoyama, Kaori
Hiraki, Rika
Miyagi, Nana
Saeki, Miho (116)
Sugiyama, Ai (31)
Uda, Remi
Yoshida, Yuka

KAZAKHSTAN
Selyutina, Irina

KOREA REPUBLIC
Kim, Eun-Ha

LATVIA
Neiland, Larisa (117)

LUXEMBOURG
Kremer, Anne (35)

MADAGASCAR
Rafolomana, Aina

MEXICO
Reyes, Zerene
Reynolds, Dominique

NETHERLANDS
Bollegraf, Manon
Boogert, Kristie (87)
Gerards, Michelle
Hopmans, Amanda (89)
Noorlander, Seda (126)
Oremans, Miriam (55)
Stove, Betty
Vis, Caroline

NEW ZEALAND
Baker, Leanne

PARAGUAY
Schaerer, Larissa

POLAND
Abram, Agnieska
Grzybowska, Magdalena (131)
Olsza, Aleksandra

ROMANIA
Cristea, Catalina (97)
Dragomir, Ruxandra (26)
Spirlea, Irina (21)

RUSSIA
Bovina, Elena
Dementieva, Elena (108)
Fokina, Galina
Jidkova, Alina
Koulikovskaya, Evgenia (102)
Kournikova, Anna (17)
Krasnoroutskai, Lina
Likhovtseva, Elena (22)
Panova, Tatiana (100)
Petrova, Nadejda (133)

SLOVAK REPUBLIC
Babakova, Martina
Cervanova, Ludmila (99)
Dlhopolcova, Lenka
Habsudova, Karina (68)
Husarova, Janette
Kurhajcova, Lubomira
Nagyova, Henrieta (25)
Studenikova, Katarina (114)

SLOVENIA
Culum, Nives
Hergold, Tina
Jausovec, Mima
Krizan, Tina
Pisnik, Tina
Srebotnik, Katarina (62)

SOUTH AFRICA
Coetzer, Amanda (10)
De Beer, Surina
de Swardt, Mariaan (38)
De Villiers, Nannie
Grandin, Natalie
Horn, Liezel
Kruger, Joannette (94)
Mojzis, Aniela
Nideffer, Rosalyn
Rencken, Nicole
Steck, Jessica
Vermaak, Yvonne

SPAIN
Bes, Eva
Leon Garcia, Gala (40)
Martinez, Conchita (20)
Ortuno, Alicia
Ruano Pascual, Virginia (46)
Sanchez Lorenzo, Maria Antonia (49)
Sanchez Vicario, Arantxa (9)
Serna, Magui (33)
Torrens-Valero, Cristina (53)

SWEDEN
Carlsson, Asa (93)

SWITZERLAND
Bao, Laura
Charbonnier, Caecilia
Gagliardi, Emmanuelle (58)
Hingis, Martina (1)
Schnyder, Patty (19)

THAILAND
Tanasugarn, Tamarine (63)

UKRAINE
Lugina, Olga
Perebiynis, Tetiana
Tatarkova, Elena (64)

UNITED STATES OF AMERICA
Adams, Katrina
Arendt, Nicole (63)
Barnikow, Lauren
Brandi, Kristina (42)
Capriati, Jennifer (44)
Cargill, Ansley
Casals, Rosie
Chi, Jane (69)
Davenport, Lindsay (2)
De Lone, Erika (135)
Fernandez, Gigi
Fernandez, Mary Joe (32)
Frazier, Amy (28)
Graham, Debbie
Granville, Laura
Magers, Gretchen
McNeil, Lori
Morariu, Corina (41)
Nagelsen, Betsy
Osterloh, Lilia (66)
Po, Kimberly (67)
Raymond, Lisa (37)
Reeves, Samantha
Rippner, Brie (64)
Rubin, Chanda (23)
Russell, Joanne
Scaringe, Julia
Schlukebir, Katie
Seles, Monica (4)
Shaughnessy, Meghann (88)
Snyder, Tara (51)
Stevenson, Alexandra (86)
Washington, Mashona
Watanabe, Jolene (110)
Wild, Linda (112)
Williams, Venus (5)

UZBEKHISTAN
Tulyaganova, Iroda

VENEZUELA
Vento, Maria Alejandra (104)

YUGOSLAVIA
Nacuk, Sandra (84)

ZIMBABWE
Black, Cara (34)

SINGLES COMPUTER RANKING IN BRACKETS AFTER NAME – W.T.A. RANKING LIST 21.6.1999

GENTLEMEN

ARGENTINA
Albano, Pablo
Canas, Guillermo (71)
Coria, Guillermo
Del Rio, Diego
Gaudio, Gaston (65)
Gumy, Hernan (99)
Hood, Mariano
Nalbandian, David
Ormaza, Matias
Prieto, Sebastian
Rodriguez, Martin (72)
Squillari, Franco (41)
Villagran, Cristian

ARMENIA
Sargsian, Sargis (64)

AUSTRALIA
Alexander, John
Arthurs, Wayne (163)
Case, Ross
Davidson, Owen
Draper, Scott (75)
Edmondson, Mark
Ellwood, Ben
Fitzgerald, John
Florent, Andrew
Frawley, Rod
Fromberg, Richard (73)
Hewitt, Lleyton (35)
Hill, Michael
Ilie, Andrew (62)
Kratzmann, Andrew
Macpherson, David
Masters, Geoff
Masur, Wally
McNamara, Peter
McNamee, Paul
Newcombe, John
Philippoussis, Mark (11)
Rafter, Patrick (2)
Roche, Tony
Rosewall, Ken
Silcock, Grant
Stolle, Fred
Stolle, Sandon (321)
Stoltenberg, Jason (42)
Stone, Allan
Tebbutt, Michael
Tramacchi, Peter
Woodbridge, Todd (137)
Woodforde, Mark (80)

AUSTRIA
Hipfl, Markus (79)
Koubek, Stefan (55)
Melzer, Jurgen
Pampoulov, Luben

BAHAMAS
Knowles, Mark

BELARUS
Mirnyi, Max
Voltchkov, Vladimir (108)

BELGIUM
Malisse, Xavier (110)
Thys, Renaud
Vanhoudt, Tom

BRAZIL
Alves, Thiago
Ferreira, Adriano
Kuerten, Gustavo (7)
Oncins, Jaime
Sa, Andre (171)

BULGARIA
Enev, Todor
Stanoytchev, Orlin (118)

CANADA
Kokavec, Bobby
Lareau, Sebastien (100)
Nestor, Daniel (87)

CHILE
Fillol, Jaime
Harboe, Phillip

COSTA RICA
Marin, Juan Antonio (97)

CROATIA
Ancic, Mario
Ivanisevic, Goran (15)
Karanusic, Roko
Zovko, Lovro

CZECH REPUBLIC
Chramosta, Ladislav
Damm, Martin (96)
Dosedel, Slava (89)
Hasek, Jakub
Novak, Jiri (59)
Rikl, David
Slozil, Pavel
Smid, Tomas
Stepanek, Radek
Suk, Cyril
Ulihrach, Bohdan (40)
Vacek, Daniel (56)
Vizner, Pavel

DENMARK
Pless, Kristian

ECUADOR
Lapentti, Nicolas (28)

EIRE
Nugent, Stephen

FINLAND
Nieminen, Jarkko
Nieminen, Timo

FRANCE
Benneteau, Julien
Clement, Arnaud (74)
Delaitre, Olivier
Di Pasquale, Arnaud (54)
Faurel, Jean-Christophe
Grosjean, Sebastien (30)
Leconte, Henri
Mahut, Nicolas
Pioline, Cedric (39)
Prodon, Eric
Raoux, Guillaume (70)
Santoro, Fabrice (43)

GERMANY
Abel, Maximilian
Becker, Benjamin
Becker, Boris (77)
Braasch, Karsten
Britzen, Dirk
Dreekmann, Hendrik (90)
Goellner, Marc-Kevin
Gremelmayr, Denis
Gross, Oliver (105)
Haas, Tommy (16)
Hammer, Philipp
Karbacher, Bernd (88)
Kiefer, Nicolas (18)
Kiendl, Uli
Knippschild, Jens (104)
Kohlmann, Michael (115)
Meffert, Dominik
Prinosil, David (57)
Schuttler, Rainer (48)
Vinck, Christian (146)

GREAT BRITAIN
Banks, Andrew
Bates, Jeremy
Broad, Neil
Brooks, Richard
Childs, Lee
Cowan, Barry (276)
Cox, Mark
Delgado, Jamie (376)
Dickson, Simon
Dowdeswell, Colin
Drysdale, Robin
Feaver, John
Gray, Jordan
Greenhouse, Nick
Henman, Tim (6)
Higgins, Tom
Hilton, Mark
Lee, Martin (329)
Mackin, Alan
MacLagan, Miles (298)
Milligan, Luke (272)
Mottram, Buster
Nelson, James
Parmar, Arvind (455)
Riby, Ben
Rusedski, Greg (12)
Sapsford, Danny (595)
Sherwood, David
Spinks, Tom (597)
Taylor, Roger
Trudgeon, Matthew
Weaver, Mark
Wilkinson, Chris (198)

HONG KONG
Wong, Wayne

HUNGARY
Koves, Gabor
Taroczy, Balasz

INDIA
Amritraj, Anand
Amritraj, Vijay
Bhupathi, Mahesh
Krishnan, Ramesh
Paes, Leander (102)

IRAN
Bahrami, Mansour

ISRAEL
Hadad, Amir
Ran, Eyal

ITALY
Ardinghi, Massimo
Bertolini, Massimo
Brandi, Cristian
Caratti, Cristiano (180)
Navarra, Mose
Pescosolido, Stefano
Pozzi, Gianluca (82)
Sanguinetti, Davide (76)
Santopadre, Vincenzo (117)
Tieleman, Laurence (116)

JAMAICA
Russell, Ryan

JAPAN
Furukawa, Hayato
Miyazaki, Yasuo
Motomura, Goichi
Suzuki, Takao (106)

MACEDONIA
Kitinov, Aleksandar

MEXICO
Hernandez, Alejandro (158)
Langre, Daniel
Roditi, David

MOROCCO
Alami, Karim (68)
Arazi, Hicham (37)
El Aynaoui, Younes (34)

NETHERLAND ANTILLIES
Rojer, Jean-Julien

NETHERLANDS
Haarhuis, Paul (93)
Hemmes, Fred
Kempers, Tom
Krajicek, Richard (5)
Okker, Tom
Schalken, Sjeng (50)
Siemerink, Jan (33)
Van Lottum, John (69)
Wessels, Peter (111)

NEW ZEALAND
Greenhalgh, James

NORWAY
Ruud, Christian (51)

PARAGUAY
Delgado, Ramon (85)

PORTUGAL
Marques, Nuno (292)

ROMANIA
Gard, Catalin
Nastase, Ilie
Pavel, Andrei (52)
Pescariu, Dinu (114)
Trifu, Gabriel
Voinea, Adrian (92)

RUSSIA
Kafelnikov, Yevgeny (3)
Metreveli, Alex

SLOVAK REPUBLIC
Beck, Karol
Hrbaty, Dominik (19)
Kroslak, Jan (67)
Kucera, Karol (13)

SLOVENIA
Kracman, Andrej

SOUTH AFRICA
Adams, David
Anderson, Andrew
Bale, Lan
Barnard, Marius
Coetzee, Jeff
De Jager, John-Laffnie
Drysdale, Cliff
Ferreira, Ellis
Ferreira, Wayne (26)
Godwin, Neville
Haggard, Chris
Haygarth, Brent
Koenig, Robbie
McDade, Andrew
McMillan, Frew
Norval, Piet
Roberts, Damien
Rosner, Paul
Stafford, Grant (434)
Stegmann, Dirk
Ullyett, Kevin
Van Rensburg, Christo
Visser, Danie
Weir-Smith, Brandon
Whitehouse, Wesley

SPAIN
Alonso, Julian (176)
Blanco, Galo (101)
Carbonell, Tomas
Carrasco, Juan Ignacio
Clavet, Francisco (22)
Costa, Albert (25)
Lopez-Moron, Alex
Mantilla, Felix (17)
Martin, Alberto (63)
Moya, Carlos (10)
Nicolas, Eduardo
Portas, Albert (84)
Puentes, German
Sanchez, Javier
Santana, Manuel
Velasco, Jairo
Vicente, Fernando (46)

SWEDEN
Bjorkman, Jonas (36)
Enqvist, Thomas (20)
Froberg, Jonas
Gustafsson, Magnus (45)
Jarryd, Anders
Johansson, Joachim
Johansson, Thomas (21)
Kulti, Nicklas
Larsson, Magnus (53)
Norman, Magnus (60)
Nyborg, Peter
Nystrom, Joakim
Pernfors, Mikael
Tillstrom, Mikael (130)

SWITZERLAND
Federer, Roger (103)
Guenthardt, Heinz
Lammer, Michael
Manta, Lorenzo (196)
Rosset, Marc (32)

THAILAND
Srichaphan, Paradorn (254)

UKRAINE
Medvedev, Andrei (31)

URUGUAY
Filippini, Marcelo (81)

UNITED STATES OF AMERICA
Agassi, Andre (4)
Berke, Steve
Bogomolov, Alex
Bowen, Devin
Bryan, Bob
Bryan, Mike
Coupe, Brandon
Courier, Jim (61)
Curren, Kevin
Davis, Tres
Dilucia, David
Donnelly, Gary Wayne
Dupre, Pat
Fish, Mardy
Flach, Doug
Flach, Ken
Fleming, Peter
Francis, Alberto
Fruttero, Jean-Paul
Galbraith, Patrick
Gambill, Jan-Michael (49)
Gimelstob, Justin (66)
Goldstein, Paul (112)
Gottfried, Brian
Grabb, Jim
Grant, Geoff
Green, Robert
Gullikson, Tom
Harper-Griffith, Levar
Humphries, Scott
Johnson, Donald
Keil, Mark
Kriek, Johan
Leach, Rick
Lutz, Bob
MacPhie, Brian
Mamiit, Cecil (78)
Martin, David
Martin, Todd (14)
Mayer, Gene
Mayer, Sandy
McEnroe, John
Merklein, Mark
Middleton, T.J.
Montana, Francisco
O'Brien, Alex
Palmer, Jared
Pugh, Jim
Reneberg, Richey (248)
Riessen, Marty
Roddick, Andy
Sampras, Pete (1)
Seguso, Robert
Sell, Michael
Smith, Stan
Spadea, Vincent (29)
Stark, Jonathan
Stewart, Sherwood
Stockton, Dick
Tanner, Roscoe
Tarango, Jeff (95)
Waite, Jack
Wilkison, Tim
Woodruff, Chris (126)

VENEZUELA
De Armas, Jose

YUGOSLAVIA
Djordjevic, Nebojsa
Vlaski, Aleksandar
Zimonjic, Nenad (266)
Zivojinovic, Slobodan

ZIMBABWE
Black, Byron (47)
Black, Wayne (98)

SINGLES COMPUTER RANKING IN BRACKETS AFTER NAME – A.T.P. RANKING LIST 21.6.1999

ALPHABETICAL LIST OF COMPETITORS ARRANGED ON PAGE 51

MAIDEN NAMES OF LADY COMPETITORS

Mrs A. Dechaume-Balleret – Miss A. Dechaume • *Mrs J. Halard-Decugis* – Miss J. Halard

Mrs K. Kunce – Miss K. Radford • *Mrs G. Magers* – Miss G. Rush

Mrs L. Neiland – Miss L. Savchenko • *Mrs R. Nideffer* – Miss R. Fairbank

Mrs P.D. Smylie – Miss E.M. Sayers • *Mrs D. Van Roost* – Miss D. Monami

Mrs E. Wagner – Miss E. Pampoulova

The Wimbledon Tennis Quiz

1. Which British man reached the third round at Wimbledon for three consecutive years, 1993-95?

2. The first ladies' competitor to come from Madagascar played at Wimbledon in 1996. Who was she?

3. Two players defeated Martina Navratilova in a Wimbledon ladies' singles final. Who were they?

4. Tim Henman's grandfather played Davis Cup. Who was he?

5. Who did Steffi Graf play in her first Wimbledon singles match?

6. Who was the first player to beat her at Wimbledon?

7. Chris Lewis was runner-up in the 1983 Men's Singles. What was his nationality?

8. Which British pair won the Junior Boy's Doubles at Wimbledon in 1994?

9. Carlos Moya comes from which Mediterranean island?

10. What year were service line monitors first used at Wimbledon?

We are grateful to several distinguished members of the Lawn Tennis Writers' Association for compiling the Tennis Quiz. Each day of the Championships poses you different questions. Answers are on page 72.

COUNTRIES IN THIS YEARS CHAMPIONSHIPS – ABBREVIATIONS

ARG	Argentina	COL	Colombia	IND	India	MEX	Mexico	RSA	South Africa
ARM	Armenia	CRC	Costa Rica	IRI	Iran	MAR	Morocco	ESP	Spain
AUS	Australia	CRO	Croatia	IRL	Ireland	NED	Netherlands	SWE	Sweden
AUT	Austria	CZE	Czech Republic	ISR	Israel	AHO	Netherlands Antillies	SUI	Switzerland
BAH	Bahamas	DEN	Denmark	ITA	Italy	NZL	New Zealand	THA	Thailand
BLR	Belarus	ECU	Ecuador	JAM	Jamaica	NOR	Norway	UKR	Ukraine
BEL	Belgium	FIN	Finland	JPN	Japan	PAR	Paraguay	USA	United States of America
BRA	Brazil	FRA	France	KAZ	Kazakhstan	POL	Poland		
BUL	Bulgaria	GER	Germany	KOR	Korea Republic	POR	Portugal	URU	Uruguay
CAN	Canada	GBR	Great Britain	LAT	Latvia	ROM	Romania	UZB	Uzbekistan
CHI	Chile	GRE	Greece	LUX	Luxembourg	RUS	Russia	VEN	Venezuela
CHN	China Peoples Republic	HUN	Hungary	MKD	Macedonia	SVK	Slovak Republic	YUG	Yugoslavia
TPE	Chinese Taipei	HKG	Hong Kong	MAD	Madagascar	SLO	Slovenia	ZIM	Zimbabwe

---

Qualifying Competition – Gentlemen's Singles

Qualifying Competitions are held in the week preceding The Championships at The Bank of England Sports Club. Unless the Committee shall decide otherwise, the last sixteen players in the Gentlemen's Singles will be included in the draw for The Championships. Details of Prize Money will be found on page 25.

First Round	Second Round	Third Round	Qualifiers
1. P.Korda [1] ....(CZE)	P.Korda [1] 7/5 6/2		
2. O.Burrieza ....(ESP)		D.E.Sapsford	
3. R.Schlachter ....(BRA)	D.E.Sapsford ....6/4 6/7(5) 6/1	.....................3/6 7/6(4) 6/4	
(W) 4. D.E.Sapsford ....(GBR)			D.E.Sapsford
5. A.Ferreira ....(BRA)	C.Saulnier 4/6 6/3 6/2		.....................6/4 3/6 4/6 6/4 8/6
6. C.Saulnier ....(FRA)		M.Joyce [32]	
7. G.Solves ....(FRA)	M.Joyce [32] 4/6 7/5 6/2	.....................6/4 6/4	
8. M.Joyce [32] ....(USA)			
9. M.Kohlmann [2] ....(GER)	M.Kohlmann [2] 6/2 6/4		
10. C.Groer ....(USA)		M.Kohlmann [2]	
11. M.Sell ....(USA)	M.Sell 6/1 6/3	.....................2/6 6/3 6/4	
12. I.Rodrigo ....(ESP)			P.Srichaphan
13. D.Dilucia ....(USA)	D.Dilucia 6/0 6/3		
14. N.Welgreen ....(ISR)		P.Srichaphan	.....................1/6 7/6(2) 6/2 6/3
15. P.Srichaphan ....(THA)	P.Srichaphan 1/6 6/1 6/2	.....................7/5 6/1	
16. G.Motomura [31] ....(JPN)			
17. M.Navarra [3] ....(ITA)	S.Dickson 6/4 4/6 13/11		
(W) 18. S.Dickson ....(GBR)		M.Merklein	
19. B.Kokavec ....(CAN)	M.Merklein ....7/6(3) 6/3	.....................6/2 5/7 6/3	
20. M.Merklein ....(USA)			N.Marques
21. N.Marques ....(POR)	N.Marques 6/4 6/4		
22. S.Humphries ....(USA)		N.Marques	.....................7/6(4) 1/6 6/3 6/4
23. J.Palmer ....(USA)	J.Palmer 2/6 6/1 7/5	.....................4/6 6/3 10/8	
24. E.Ran [30] ....(ISR)			
25. A.Pretzsch [4] ....(GER)	A.Pretzsch [4] 6/3 6/3		
26. T.Larkham ....(AUS)		J.Delgado	
27. J.Delgado ....(GBR)	J.Delgado ....6/7(4) 6/2 6/2	.....................7/6(1) 1/6 6/3	
28. T.Mitchell ....(AUS)			J.Delgado
(W) 29. R.Hanger ....(GBR)	F.Stauder 6/2 6/0		
30. F.Stauder ....(GER)		F.Stauder	.....................3/6 6/7(4) 6/3 6/3 7/5
31. M.Knowles ....(BAH)	M.Knowles ....4/6 7/6(5) 6/4	.....................6/7(7) 6/4 6/2	
32. R.Gilbert [29] ....(FRA)			
33. G.Grant [5] ....(USA)	G.Trifu ....6/7(9) 6/4 10/8		
34. G.Trifu ....(ROM)		G.Trifu	
35. J.Sirianni ....(AUS)	S.Iwabuchi 6/2 6/3	.....................4/6 6/1 11/9	
36. S.Iwabuchi ....(JPN)			L.Manta [27]
37. H.Armando ....(USA)	D.Wheaton 7/5 6/3		
38. D.Wheaton ....(USA)		L.Manta [27]	.....................6/3 7/5 7/6(6)
39. I.Gaudi ....(ITA)	L.Manta [27] 7/5 2/6 6/4	.....................7/5 7/6(2)	
40. L.Manta [27] ....(SUI)			
41. M.Mirnyi [6] ....(BLR)	M.Mirnyi [6] ....6/3 7/6(5)		
42. A.Hunt ....(NZL)		M.Mirnyi [6]	
43. F.Niemeyer ....(CAN)	F.Niemeyer 6/2 6/1	.....................6/7(5) 6/4 6/4	
44. R.Svetlik ....(CZE)			A.Parmar
45. M.Washington ....(USA)	A.Parmar 6/1 6/4		
46. A.Parmar ....(GBR)		A.Parmar	.....................7/6(3) 4/6 6/3 6/4
47. D.Bracciali ....(ITA)	S.Pescosolido [28] ...6/7(4) 6/2 1/0 Ret'd	.....................4/6 7/6(5) 6/3	
48. S.Pescosolido [28] ......(ITA)			
49. M.Tillstrom [7] ....(SWE)	M.Tillstrom [7] 6/1 6/3		
50. G.Doyle ....(AUS)		M.Tillstrom [7]	
51. Y.Ishii ....(JPN)	Y.Ishii 1/6 6/1 6/4	.....................6/2 6/3	
52. M.Charpentier ....(ARG)			M.Tillstrom [7]
53. A.Hadad ....(ISR)	D.Musa ....7/6(5) 7/6(3)		
54. D.Musa ....(ITA)		M.Hill [26]	.....................6/4 6/4 3/6 6/4
55. T.Vasiliadis ....(GRE)	M.Hill [26] 6/2 6/3	.....................6/1 6/1	
56. M.Hill [26] ....(AUS)			
57. C.Vinck [8] ....(GER)	C.Vinck [8] 6/3 6/2		
58. R.Givone ....(USA)		C.Vinck [8]	
59. G.Elseneer ....(BEL)	G.Elseneer ....6/7(5) 6/2 6/4	.....................6/3 6/4	
60. I.Kornienko ....(RUS)			C.Vinck [8]
61. J.Sekulov ....(AUS)	J.Sekulov ....7/6(7) 6/3		
62. M.Stepanek ....(CZE)		J.Sekulov	.....................6/3 6/4 6/3
63. I.Labadze ....(GEO)	B.Bryan [25] 7/5 6/1	.....................6/4 6/4	
64. B.Bryan [25] ....(USA)			
65. R.Stepanek [9] ....(CZE)	R.Stepanek [9] 6/2 4/6 6/3		
66. O.Motevassel ....(ISR)		M.Bryan	
67. M.Bryan ....(USA)	M.Bryan 6/4 6/4	.....................w/o	
68. R.Alvarez ....(ARG)			N.Zimonjic
69. M.Visconti ....(ITA)	J.Erlich ....6/7(6) 6/1 6/4		
70. J.Erlich ....(ISR)		N.Zimonjic	.....................6/4 7/6(2) 6/3
71. N.Zimonjic ....(YUG)	N.Zimonjic 6/3 6/2	.....................6/3 6/4	
72. B.MacPhie [24] ....(USA)			
73. S.Prieto [10] ....(ARG)	J.Thomas 6/4 4/6 23/21		
(W) 74. J.Thomas ....(USA)		R.A.Reneberg	
75. R.A.Reneberg ....(USA)	R.A.Reneberg ....6/3 7/6(3)	.....................6/1 6/1	
(W) 76. N.Weal ....(GBR)			R.A.Reneberg
77. J.Stark ....(USA)	J.Stark ....6/3 7/6(3)		
78. T.Guardiola ....(FRA)		J.Stark	.....................6/4 6/3 6/4
79. J.Crabb ....(AUS)	J.Crabb 4/6 6/1 6/3	.....................6/3 6/0	
80. M.Tebbutt [23] ....(AUS)			
81. D.Nargiso [11] ....(ITA)	D.Nargiso [11] 6/2 6/1		
82. S.Aspelin ....(SWE)		B.Ellwood	
83. O.Sela ....(ISR)	B.Ellwood ....7/6(7) 7/5	.....................6/4 6/1	
84. B.Ellwood ....(AUS)			C.Caratti [21]
(W) 85. A.Reichel ....(USA)	J.Varlet 3/6 6/1 6/3		
86. J.Varlet ....(FRA)		C.Caratti [21]	.....................6/2 2/6 6/2 3/6 6/1
87. D.Roberts ....(RSA)	C.Caratti [21] 6/1 6/4	.....................6/3 6/0	
88. C.Caratti [21] ....(ITA)			
89. S.Huet [12] ....(FRA)	D.Miketa ....6/7(3) 6/4 6/1		
90. D.Miketa ....(CZE)		D.Miketa	
91. V.Sendin ....(ESP)	M.Breen 4/6 6/1 6/2	.....................3/6 6/3 7/5	
92. M.Breen ....(AUS)			W.Arthurs [22]
93. N.Thomann ....(FRA)	N.Thomann 4/6 6/3 6/3		
94. S.Randjelovic ....(AUS)		W.Arthurs [22]	.....................7/6(2) 7/6(3) 6/3
95. E.Artoni ....(ARG)	W.Arthurs [22] ....7/6(2) 6/2	.....................6/4 7/6(4)	
96. W.Arthurs [22] ....(AUS)			
97. A.Hernandez [13] ....(MEX)	A.Hernandez [13] 6/2 6/4		
98. M.Hellstrom ....(SWE)		A.Hernandez [13]	
99. Y.Allegro ....(SUI)	D.Petrovic 7/5 6/2	.....................6/4 6/1	
100. D.Petrovic ....(AUS)			A.Hernandez [13]
101. M.Joachim ....(GER)	A.Zingman ....7/6(5) 6/2		
102. A.Zingman ....(ARG)		W.Whitehouse	.....................3/6 6/4 6/4 6/3
103. W.Whitehouse ....(RSA)	W.Whitehouse 6/3 6/3	.....................6/2 6/2	
104. N.Godwin [20] ....(RSA)			
105. T.Ketola [14] ....(FIN)	T.Ketola [14] 6/4 6/0		
(W)106. D.Sherwood ....(GBR)		G.Stafford	
107. E.Erlich ....(ISR)	G.Stafford 6/4 6/2	.....................6/2 7/5	
108. G.Stafford ....(RSA)			G.Stafford
109. C.Auffray ....(FRA)	N.Gould ....7/6(1) 6/2		
110. N.Gould ....(GBR)		M.Draper [19]	.....................7/5 6/7(2) 6/1 6/3
111. J.Layne ....(GBR)	M.Draper [19] 4/6 6/1 6/4	.....................6/3 6/2.	
112. M.Draper [19] ....(AUS)			
113. A.O'Brien [15] ....(USA)	A.O'Brien [15] 6/2 6/4		
(W)114. P.Hand ....(GBR)		A.O'Brien [15]	
(W)115. J.Davidson ....(GBR)	J.Davidson 6/4 7/5	.....................7/5 6/1	
116. P.Pasquier ....(FRA)			A.Sa [17]
117. M.Belgraver ....(NED)	R.Sabau ....6/4 7/6(7)		
118. R.Sabau ....(ROM)		A.Sa [17]	.....................7/5 6/7(5) 6/3 6/3
119. J.Hermansson ....(SWE)	A.Sa [17] ....7/6(3) 3/4 6/4	.....................6/3 2/6 6/3	
120. A.Sa [17] ....(BRA)			
121. I.Heuberger [16] ....(SUI)	M.Bhupathi 6/2 6/2		
122. M.Bhupathi ....(IND)		J.Coetzee	
123. J.Coetzee ....(RSA)	J.Coetzee 6/3 6/1	.....................6/4 6/4	
124. J.Pequery ....(FRA)			S.Stolle
125. S.Duran ....(ESP)	S.Stolle 4/6 6/4 6/1		
126. S.Stolle ....(AUS)		S.Stolle	.....................6/4 6/1 7/6(1)
127. P.Tramacchi ....(AUS)	M.Ruah [18] ....7/6(6) 7/6(4)	.....................6/2 6/3	
128. M.Ruah [18] ....(VEN)			

56

Qualifying Competitions are held in the week preceding The Championships at The Bank of England Sports Club. Unless the Committee shall decide otherwise, the last eight players in the Ladies' Singles will be included in the draw for The Championships. Details of Prize Money will be found on page 25.

First Round

1. **Miss A.Stevenson [1]** ....(USA)
2. Miss S.Cacic ....(USA)
3. Miss L.Horn ....(RSA)
4. Miss A.Ellwood ....(AUS)
5. Miss H.Inoue ....(JPN)
6. Miss C.Watson ....(AUS)
7. Miss H.Rosen ....(ISR)
8. **Miss S.De Beer [10]** ....(RSA)
9. **Miss T.Pisnik [11]** ....(SLO)
10. Miss S.Asagoe ....(JPN)
11. Miss S-H.Park ....(KOR)
12. Miss M.Vavrinec ....(SUI)
(W) 13. Miss N.Payne ....(GBR)
(W) 14. Miss H.Matthews ....(GBR)
15. Miss E.R.De Lone ....(USA)
16. **Miss P.Wartusch [5]** ....(AUT)
17. **Miss M.Schnitzer [3]** ....(GER)
18. Miss M.Washington............(USA)
(W) 19. Miss E.E.Jelfs ....(GBR)
20. Miss F.Lubiani ....(ITA)
(W) 21. Miss V.E.Davies ....(GBR)
(W) 22. Miss K.Warne-Holland ....(GBR)
23. Miss K.Clijsters ....(BEL)
24. **Miss A.Gersi [16]** ....(CZE)
25. **Miss J.Dokic [14]**............(AUS)
26. Miss P.Van Acker ....(BEL)
27. Miss J.Craybas ....(USA)
28. Miss E.Fauth ....(AUT)
29. Miss R.P.Stubbs..................(AUS)
(W) 30. Miss H.Crook ....(GBR)
31. Miss S.Reeves ....(USA)
32. **Miss A.Barna [7]** ....(GER)
33. **Miss T.Garbin [8]** ....(ITA)
34. Miss L.McShea ....(AUS)
35. Miss E.Dominikovic ....(AUS)
36. Miss L.Wild ....(USA)
37. Miss Y.Yoshida ....(JPN)
38. Miss R.Andres....................(ESP)
(W) 39. Miss H.Collin ....(GBR)
40. **Miss E.Makarova [9]** ....(RUS)
41. **Miss N.Petrova [15]**...........(RUS)
42. Miss N.Vaidyanathan..........(IND)
43. Miss C.G.Barclay................(AUS)
44. Miss J.Kostanic ....(CRO)
45. Miss K.Marosi ....(HUN)
(W) 46. Miss L.Herbert....................(GBR)
47. Miss E.Bes..........................(ESP)
48. **Miss N.Miyagi [4]** ....(JPN)
49. **Miss A.Foldenyi [6]**............(HUN)
50. Miss L.Schaerer ....(PAR)
51. Miss T.Krizan ....(SLO)
52. Miss A.Olsza ....(POL)
53. Miss J.Kandarr ....(GER)
54. Miss An.Serra-Zanetti ....(ITA)
55. Miss A.Jidkova ....(RUS)
56. **Miss F.Labat [12]**...............(ARG)
57. **Miss S.Noorlander [13]**......(NED)
58. Miss J.Abe ....(GER)
59. Miss J.Steck ....(RSA)
60. Miss I.Selyutina ....(KAZ)
61. Miss K.Miller.....................(USA)
62. Miss N.Koves ....(HUN)
63. Miss V.Menga ....(BRA)
64. **Miss E.Dementieva [2]**........(RUS)

Second Round

- **Miss A.Stevenson [1]** 6/3 7/5
- Miss A.Ellwood 4/6 6/1 6/4
- Miss H.Inoue 3/6 6/2 8/6
- **Miss S.De Beer [10]**...............6/4 7/6(4)
- Miss S.Asagoe 6/4 5/7 7/5
- Miss M.Vavrinec 7/5 5/7 7/5
- Miss N.Payne 7/5 5/7 6/2
- Miss E.R.De Lone 7/5 6/3
- Miss M.Washington............6/3 6/2
- Miss F.Lubiani ....7/6(4) 6/4
- Miss V.E.Davies ....7/6(4) 6/4
- Miss K.Clijsters 6/2 6/2
- **Miss J.Dokic [14]**................6/4 6/4
- Miss E.Fauth 6/4 6/2
- Miss R.P.Stubbs....................6/2 6/4
- Miss S.Reeves 6/4 6/1
- **Miss T.Garbin [8]** 6/3 4/6 6/3
- Miss L.Wild 6/2 6/1
- Miss Y.Yoshida 6/3 6/0
- **Miss E.Makarova [9]** ....5/3 Ret'd.
- **Miss N.Petrova [15]** 6/4 6/4
- Miss J.Kostanic 6/3 6/2
- Miss K.Marosi 6/0 6/4
- **Miss N.Miyagi [4]** 6/3 6/2
- **Miss A.Foldenyi [6]** 6/1 6/4
- Miss A.Olsza 6/3 6/2
- Miss J.Kandarr 2/6 6/4 6/1
- Miss A.Jidkova 6/3 7/5
- **Miss S.Noorlander [13]** ....7/6(2) 7/5
- Miss I.Selyutina 5/7 7/5 6/2
- Miss K.Miller......................6/2 7/5
- **Miss E.Dementieva [2]** 6/0 6/1

Third Round

- **Miss A.Stevenson [1]** 6/3 6/4
- Miss H.Inoue 6/3 3/6 6/4
- Miss S.Asagoe 6/4 6/1
- Miss E.R.De Lone 6/2 6/4
- Miss F.Lubiani 6/4 6/2
- Miss K.Clijsters 6/1 6/1
- **Miss J.Dokic [14]**................6/0 6/1
- Miss R.P.Stubbs....................7/6(8) 6/3
- Miss L.Wild 6/4 6/4
- Miss Y.Yoshida 6/3 6/3
- **Miss N.Petrova [15]** 6/3 6/0
- Miss K.Marosi ....7/6(9) 3/6 6/4
- **Miss A.Foldenyi [6]** .....7/6(3) 4/6 6/4
- Miss J.Kandarr ....5/7 7/6(1) 6/2
- **Miss S.Noorlander [13]** 6/3 7/5
- **Miss E.Dementieva [2]** 6/1 6/2

Qualifiers

- **Miss A.Stevenson [1]** 6/1 6/4
- Miss E.R.De Lone 6/4 6/4
- Miss K.Clijsters 6/0 6/4
- **Miss J.Dokic [14]**............6/2 7/6(2)
- Miss L.Wild 0/6 6/3 7/5
- **Miss N.Petrova [15]** 7/5 6/3
- **Miss A.Foldenyi [6]** .....7/6(6) 3/6 6/4
- **Miss S.Noorlander [13]** 7/5 5/7 6/4

RANKINGS

World rankings in lawn tennis are updated weekly throughout the year, except during the middle of the four two-week Grand Slam tournaments and 10 day Championship events, by the ATP Tour on behalf of the men and the WTA Tour for the women. Rankings on the men's tour are based on a "Best 14" tournaments system. In other words, if a player has competed in more than 14 events on the tour in the preceding 52 weeks, only performances in his most successful 14 tournaments will be taken into consideration. Rankings on the womens' tour are based on their "Best 18". In both the men's and women's programme, points in each tournament are awarded on a round by round basis with various bonuses on a sliding scale, for beating higher ranked opponents. Womens' rankings are based on the total number of points accumulated by a player over the preceding 52 weeks.

QUALIFIERS, WILD CARD, LUCKY LOSER—AN EXPLANATION

Q—*Qualifier*—winners from the final round of qualifying Competitions staged at Roehampton the week before The Championships.

W—*Wild Card*—Players without high enough world ranking to go straight into the draw but specially nominated by the Committee, usually because of past performances at Wimbledon or to increase British interest.

L—*Lucky Loser*—Losers in the last round of qualifying competitions, chosen in order of world rankings to fill any vacancy which occurs in the draw before the first round has been completed.

CODE OF CONDUCT

Players in the Gentlemen's Singles, Gentlemen's Doubles and the 35 and 45 and Over Gentlemen's Invitation Doubles are subject to the provisions of the Code of Conduct issued by the Grand Slam Committee. The Ladies' Singles, Ladies' Doubles and the 35 and Over Ladies' Invitation Doubles are subject to the provisions of the Code of Conduct issued by the Women's Tennis Council. The Junior Events are subject to the I.T.F. Junior Code of Conduct. Under the Code, violations are punishable by point penalties awarded by the Umpire. At the first offence, the player is given an official warning, the second offence results in a point being awarded to the offender's opponent, the third offence results in the offender being defaulted. The sequence of penalties awarded are for either delay or game violations, abuse of officials and equipment or for unsportsman-like conduct.

WET WEATHER PROCEDURES— COVERING OF THE COURTS

The courts are covered on the decision given by the Referee. The sooner the courts are covered, the less time is needed for them to dry out and for play to resume. Occasionally, if the advice from the London Weather Centre is such, the courts might be covered before the rain arrives.

RESUMPTION OF PLAY

In the interests of the public, play is resumed as soon as possible. Players are officially entitled to 15 minutes from the time the match is called to the time they are due on court. According to the Rules, no warm-up is allowed if the delay is 10 minutes or less; 11–20 minutes, a 3 minute warm-up is allowed, and if the delay is 20 minutes or more, a 5 minute warm-up is allowed. The Committee of Management of The Championships endeavours to be fair to both the public and the players and so, in the event of rain interruptions, everyone's patience is requested.

EMERGENCY EVACUATION

In the event of an *emergency evacuation* spectators are requested to leave the court as quickly and quietly as possible, taking all personal belongings and following the directions of the uniformed stewarding staff.

In order to ensure the effectiveness of any emergency evacuation the All England Club regrets that spectators using *wheelchairs* are only permitted access to designated areas within the stands. For the same reason *picnic hampers, coolboxes* and other *large items* will not be allowed into the stands and should be deposited in one of the left luggage offices.

BRITAIN'S BEST, NOW SERVING AT WIMBLEDON.

OFFICIAL SUPPLIER OF COFFEE

COURT PLACINGS
Sunday 4th July, 1999

GENTLEMEN

Name	Court	Match	Event
Agassi, A.	CC	2	Gentlemen's Singles
Bhupathi, M.	1	1	Gentlemen's Doubles
Bjorkman, J.	TBA	-	Mixed Doubles
Case, R.L.	4	1	Over 45 Gentlemen's Doubles
Childs, L.	5	1	Junior Boys' Doubles
_____	5	3	Junior Boys' Doubles
Coria, G.	5	1	Junior Boys' Doubles
_____	5	3	Junior Boys' Doubles
De Armas, J.	3	2	Junior Boys' Doubles
Dickson, S.	5	1	Junior Boys' Doubles
_____	5	3	Junior Boys' Doubles
Enev, T.	3	2	Junior Boys' Doubles
Flach, K.	13	1	Over 35 Gentlemen's Doubles
_____	1	3	Over 35 Gentlemen's Doubles
Gottfried, B.E.	4	1	Over 45 Gentlemen's Doubles
Gullikson, T.R.	4	1	Over 45 Gentlemen's Doubles
Haarhuis, P.	1	1	Gentlemen's Doubles
Hilton, M.A.	5	3	Junior Boys' Doubles
Jarryd, A.	13	1	Over 35 Gentlemen's Doubles
_____	1	3	Over 35 Gentlemen's Doubles
Knowles, M.	2	3	Mixed Doubles
_____	TBA	-	Mixed Doubles
Langre, D.	3	2	Junior Boys' Doubles
Masters, G.	4	1	Over 45 Gentlemen's Doubles
McNamara, P.B.	1	3	Over 35 Gentlemen's Doubles
McNamee, P.F.	1	3	Over 35 Gentlemen's Doubles
Melzer, J.	2	1	Junior Boys' Singles
Nalbandian, D.	5	1	Junior Boys' Doubles
_____	5	3	Junior Boys' Doubles
Nelson, J.	5	3	Junior Boys' Doubles
Nieminen, J.	3	2	Junior Boys' Doubles
Nystrom, J.	13	1	Over 35 Gentlemen's Doubles
_____	1	3	Over 35 Gentlemen's Doubles
Paes, L.	1	1	Gentlemen's Doubles
_____	2	3	Mixed Doubles
_____	TBA	-	Mixed Doubles
Palmer, J.	1	1	Gentlemen's Doubles
Pless, K.	2	1	Junior Boys' Singles
Sampras, P.	CC	2	Gentlemen's Singles
Seguso, R.	13	1	Over 35 Gentlemen's Doubles
_____	1	3	Over 35 Gentlemen's Doubles

LADIES

Name	Court	Match	Event
Bedanova, Miss D.	2	2	Junior Girls' Doubles
_____	2	4	Junior Girls' Doubles
Berecz, Miss K.	4	3	Junior Girls' Doubles
Cargill, Miss A.	2	4	Junior Girls' Doubles
Davenport, Miss L.A.	CC	1	Ladies' Singles
_____	1	2	Ladies' Doubles
de Swardt, Miss M.	1	2	Ladies' Doubles
Fokina, Miss G.	3	3	Junior Girls' Doubles
Graf, Miss S.	CC	1	Ladies' Singles
Grandin, Miss N.	2	2	Junior Girls' Doubles
_____	2	4	Junior Girls' Doubles
Granville, Miss L.	2	4	Junior Girls' Doubles
Kournikova, Miss A.	TBA	-	Mixed Doubles
Krasnoroutskai, Miss L.	3	1	Junior Girls' Singles
_____	3	3	Junior Girls' Doubles
Likhovtseva, Miss E.	2	3	Mixed Doubles
_____	TBA	-	Mixed Doubles
Magers, Mrs G.	13	3	Over 35 Ladies' Doubles (PM)
Morariu, Miss C.	1	2	Ladies' Doubles
Pennetta, Miss F.	3	3	Junior Girls' Doubles
Perebiynis, Miss T.	4	3	Junior Girls' Doubles
Raymond, Miss L.M.	2	3	Mixed Doubles
_____	TBA	-	Mixed Doubles
Rencken, Miss N.	2	2	Junior Girls' Doubles
_____	2	4	Junior Girls' Doubles
Salerni, Miss M.E.	2	2	Junior Girls' Doubles
_____	2	4	Junior Girls' Doubles
Smylie, Mrs P.D.	13	3	Over 35 Ladies' Doubles (PM)
Stove, Miss B.F.	13	3	Over 35 Ladies' Doubles (PM)
Tatarkova, Miss E.	1	2	Ladies' Doubles
Tulyaganova, Miss I.	3	1	Junior Girls' Singles
_____	4	3	Junior Girls' Doubles
Turnbull, Miss W.M.	13	3	Over 35 Ladies' Doubles (PM)
Vinci, Miss R.	3	3	Junior Girls' Doubles

SEEDED PLAYERS

GENTLEMEN'S SINGLES

1. P. Sampras (USA)	9. G. Rusedski (GBR)
2. P. Rafter (AUS)	10. G. Ivanisevic (CRO)
3. Y. Kafelnikov (RUS)	11. G. Kuerten (BRA)
4. A. Agassi (USA)	12. C. Moya (ESP)
5. R. Krajicek (NED)	13. K. Kucera (SVK)
6. T. Henman (GBR)	14. T. Haas (GER)
7. M. Philippoussis (AUS)	15. N. Kiefer (GER)
8. T. Martin (USA)	16. F. Mantilla (ESP)

LADIES' SINGLES

1. Miss M. Hingis (SUI)	10.
2. Miss S. Graf (GER)	11. Mrs J. Halard-Decugis (FRA)
3. Miss L.A. Davenport (USA)	12. Miss A.J. Coetzer (RSA)
4. Miss M. Seles (USA)	13. Miss S. Testud (FRA)
5. Miss J. Novotna (CZE)	14. Miss B. Schett (AUT)
6. Miss V. Williams (USA)	15. Mrs D. Van Roost (BEL)
7. Miss A. Sanchez Vicario (ESP)	16. Miss N. Zvereva (BLR)
8. Miss N. Tauziat (FRA)	17. Miss A. Kournikova (RUS)
9. Miss M. Pierce (FRA)	

59

SUNDAY 4th July, 1999
INTENDED ORDER OF PLAY

Starting times indicated on each court.

CENTRE COURT   12.00 noon

1. The Final of the Ladies' Singles

Miss L.A. Davenport (USA) [3] *(33)*

v.

Miss S. Graf (GER) [2] *(128)*

Umpire: Miss F.J. Edwards

Not before 2.00 pm

2. The Final of the Gentlemen's Singles

P. Sampras (USA) [1] *(1)*

v.

A. Agassi (USA) [4] *(96)*

Umpire: Mr J.G. Frame

COURT 1   12.00 noon

1. The Final of the Gentlemen's Doubles

M. Bhupathi (IND) and **L. Paes (IND)** [1] *(1)* v.
P. Haarhuis (NED) and **J. Palmer (USA)** [8] *(49)*

Umpire: Mr K.A.M. Craven

2. The Final of the Ladies' Doubles

Miss M. de Swardt (RSA) and **Miss E. Tatarkova (UKR)** [9] *(32)* v.
Miss L.A. Davenport (USA) and **Miss C. Morariu (USA)** [7] *(33)*

Umpire: Mrs J. Harvey

3. The Final of the Over 35 Gentlemen's Invitation Doubles

P.B. McNamara **(AUS)** and P.F. McNamee **(AUS)** *(2)* v.
A. Jarryd **(SWE)** and J. Nystrom **(SWE)** *(3)* OR
K. Flach **(USA)** and R. Seguso **(USA)** *(4)*

COURT 2 - SHOW COURT   12.00 noon

1. The Final of the Junior Boys' Singles

K. Pless (DEN) [1] *(1)* v.
J. Melzer **(AUT)** *(34)*

2. **Miss N. Grandin (RSA)** and **Miss N. Rencken (RSA)** [5] *(25)* v.
Miss D. Bedanova (CZE) and **Miss M.E. Salerni (ARG)** [2] *(32)*
(Junior Girls' Doubles)

3. **L. Paes (IND)** and **Miss L.M. Raymond (USA)** [1] *(1)* v.
M. Knowles (BAH) and **Miss E. Likhovtseva (RUS)** [4] *(17)*

4. **Miss A. Cargill (USA)** and **Miss L. Granville (USA)** [6] *(17)* v.
Miss N. Grandin (RSA) and **Miss N. Rencken (RSA)** [5] *(25)* OR
Miss D. Bedanova (CZE) and **Miss M.E. Salerni (ARG)** [2] *(32)*
(Junior Girls' Doubles)

COURT 3 - SHOW COURT   12.00 noon

1. The Final of the Junior Girls' Singles

Miss I. Tulyaganova (UZB) [4] *(17)* v.
Miss L. Krasnoroutskai (RUS) [7] *(49)*

2. T. Enev **(BUL)** and J. Nieminen **(FIN)** *(20)* v.
J. De Armas (VEN) and **D. Langre (MEX)** [2] *(32)*
(Junior Boys' Doubles)

3. **Miss F. Pennetta (ITA)** and **Miss R. Vinci (ITA)** [1] *(1)* v.
Miss G. Fokina **(RUS)** and Miss L. Krasnoroutskai **(RUS)** *(6)*
(Junior Girls' Doubles)

COURT 13 - SHOW COURT   12.00 noon

1. A. Jarryd **(SWE)** and J. Nystrom **(SWE)** *(3)* v.
K. Flach **(USA)** and R. Seguso **(USA)** *(4)*
(Over 35 Gentlemen's Doubles)

3. The Final of the Over 35 Ladies' Invitation Doubles

Mrs G. Magers **(USA)** and Miss B.F. Stove **(NED)** *(2)* v.
Mrs P.D. Smylie (AUS) and **Miss W.M. Turnbull (AUS)** *(5)*

COURT 4   12.00 noon

1. The Final of the Over 45 Gentlemens' Invitation Doubles

R.L. Case **(AUS)** and G. Masters **(AUS)** *(6)* v.
B.E. Gottfried (USA) and **T.R. Gullikson (USA)** [2] *(16)*

3. Miss L. Baker **(NZL)** and Miss K. Berecz **(HUN)** *(11)* v.
Miss T. Perebiynis (UKR) and **Miss I. Tulyaganova (UZB)** [7] *(16)*
(Junior Girls' Doubles)

COURT 5   12.00 noon

1. **G. Coria (ARG)** and **D. Nalbandian (ARG)** [1] *(1)* v.
L. Childs (GBR) and **S. Dickson (GBR)** [5] *(8)*
(Junior Boys' Doubles)

3. **G. Coria (ARG)** and **D. Nalbandian (ARG)** [1] *(1)* OR
L. Childs (GBR) and **S. Dickson (GBR)** [5] *(8)* v.
M.A. Hilton (GBR) and **J. Nelson (GBR)** *(13)*
(Junior Boys' Doubles)

The Following Matches Will Be Played On Courts To Be Arranged

The Final of the Mixed Doubles

L. Paes (IND) and **Miss L.M. Raymond (USA)** [1] *(1)* OR
M. Knowles (BAH) and **Miss E. Likhovtseva (RUS)** [4] *(17)* v.
J. Bjorkman (SWE) and **Miss A. Kournikova (RUS)** [3] *(48)*
Umpire: Miss H.R. Hunter

**Girls Doubles Semi Finals and Final
Boys Doubles Final**

The Committee, while adhering as closely as possible to the order of play given, are unable to guarantee that it will be maintained in its entirety. This may result in matches being moved from one court to another.

Event I— The Gentlemen's Singles Championship 1999
Holder: P. Sampras

The Winner will become the holder, for the year only, of the CHALLENGE CUP presented by The All England Lawn Tennis and Croquet Club. The Winner will receive a silver replica of the Challenge Cup. A Silver Salver will be presented to the Runner-up and a Bronze Medal to each defeated Semi-finalist. Details of Prize Money will be found on page 25. The matches will be the best of five sets.

First Round

	1.	**P.Sampras [1]**	(USA)
	2.	S.Draper	(AUS)
	3.	S.Lareau	(CAN)
	4.	W.Black	(ZIM)
	5.	G.Blanco	(ESP)
	6.	T.Suzuki	(JPN)
	7.	J.Alonso	(ESP)
(Q)	8.	D.E.Sapsford	(GBR)
	9.	D.Nestor	(CAN)
	10.	S.Koubek	(AUT)
	11.	A.Medvedev	(UKR)
	12.	B.Karbacher	(GER)
	13.	J.Siemerink	(NED)
	14.	P.Goldstein	(USA)
	15.	V.Spadea	(USA)
	16.	**F.Mantilla [16]**	(ESP)
	17.	**G.Rusedski [9]**	(GBR)
	18.	J.Stoltenberg	(AUS)
	19.	A.Costa	(ESP)
(Q)	20.	A.Parmar	(GBR)
	21.	G.Gaudio	(ARG)
	22.	M.Norman	(SWE)
(W)	23.	L.Milligan	(GBR)
	24.	F.Santoro	(FRA)
	25.	T.Johansson	(SWE)
(Q)	26.	R.A.Reneberg	(USA)
(L)	27.	M.Kohlmann	(GER)
	28.	F.Clavet	(ESP)
	29.	M.Woodforde	(AUS)
	30.	D.Hrbaty	(SVK)
	31.	X.Malisse	(BEL)
	32.	**M.Philippoussis [7]**	(AUS)
	33.	**Y.Kafelnikov [3]**	(RUS)
	34.	M.Larsson	(SWE)
(Q)	35.	P.Srichaphan	(THA)
	36.	G.Raoux	(FRA)
	37.	M.Damm	(CZE)
	38.	C.Pioline	(FRA)
	39.	A.Clement	(FRA)
	40.	A.Portas	(ESP)
	41.	D.Vacek	(CZE)
	42.	B.Ulihrach	(CZE)
	43.	G.Pozzi	(ITA)
	44.	V.Voltchkov	(BLR)
(Q)	45.	A.Sa	(BRA)
	46.	L.Paes	(IND)
(Q)	47.	A.Hernandez	(MEX)
	48.	**K.Kucera [13]**	(SVK)
	49.	**C.Moya [12]**	(ESP)
	50.	J.Kroslak	(SVK)
(W)	51.	B.Cowan	(GBR)
	52.	J.Courier	(USA)
	53.	W.Ferreira	(RSA)
	54.	A.Ilie	(AUS)
	55.	S.Schalken	(NED)
	56.	D.Sanguinetti	(ITA)
	57.	S.Grosjean	(FRA)
	58.	B.Black	(ZIM)
	59.	R.Delgado	(PAR)
(Q)	60.	J.Delgado	(GBR)
	61.	C.Woodruff	(USA)
	62.	S.Sargsian	(ARM)
	63.	A.Di Pasquale	(FRA)
	64.	**T.Henman [6]**	(GBR)
	65.	**R.Krajicek [5]**	(NED)
	66.	C.Ruud	(NOR)
	67.	O.Stanoytchev	(BUL)
	68.	T.A.Woodbridge	(AUS)
(Q)	69.	L.Manta	(SUI)
(W)	70.	T.Spinks	(GBR)
	71.	J.Gambill	(USA)
	72.	F.Squillari	(ARG)
(Q)	73.	N.Zimonjic	(YUG)
	74.	D.Pescariu	(ROM)
	75.	J.A.Marin	(CRC)
	76.	J.Tarango	(USA)
	77.	M.Rodriguez	(ARG)
	78.	D.Prinosil	(GER)
(W)	79.	C.Wilkinson	(GBR)
	80.	**G.Kuerten [11]**	(BRA)
	81.	**T.Haas [14]**	(GER)
	82.	P.Wessels	(NED)
	83.	R.Fromberg	(AUS)
	84.	M.Gustafsson	(SWE)
(Q)	85.	W.Arthurs	(AUS)
	86.	V.Santopadre	(IIA)
	87.	A.Voinea	(ROM)
	88.	N.Lapentti	(ECU)
	89.	A.Martin	(ESP)
	90.	S.Dosedel	(CZE)
	91.	O.Gross	(GER)
	92.	Y.El Aynaoui	(MAR)
	93.	G.Canas	(ARG)
(W)	94.	M.Lee	(GBR)
	95.	A.Pavel	(ROM)
	96.	**A.Agassi [4]**	(USA)
	97.	**T.Martin [8]**	(USA)
	98.	H.Dreekmann	(GER)
	99.	J.Novak	(CZE)
(W)	100.	R.Federer	(SUI)
	101.	M.Hipfl	(AUT)
	102.	M.Rosset	(SUI)
	103.	J.Gimelstob	(USA)
	104.	J.Knippschild	(GER)
	105.	H.Arazi	(MAR)
	106.	P.Haarhuis	(NED)
	107.	F.Vicente	(ESP)
	108.	C.Mamiit	(USA)
	109.	J.Van Lottum	(NED)
(Q)	110.	S.Stolle	(AUS)
(Q)	111.	M.Tillstrom	(SWE)
	112.	**G.Ivanisevic [10]**	(CRO)
	113.	**N.Kiefer [15]**	(GER)
(Q)	114.	C.Vinck	(GER)
	115.	B.Becker	(GER)
(W)	116.	M.MacLagan	(GBR)
	117.	L.Hewitt	(AUS)
(W)	118.	M.Filippini	(URU)
	119.	K.Alami	(MAR)
	120.	L.Tieleman	(ITA)
(Q)	121.	N.Marques	(POR)
	122.	R.Schuttler	(GER)
	123.	T.Enqvist	(SWE)
	124.	H.Gumy	(ARG)
	125.	J.Bjorkman	(SWE)
(Q)	126.	G.Stafford	(RSA)
(Q)	127.	C.Caratti	(ITA)
	128.	**P.Rafter [2]**	(AUS)

Second Round

- P.Sampras [1] — 6/3 6/4 6/4
- S.Lareau — 6/1 3/6 6/3 6/3
- G.Blanco — 6/4 3/6 7/6(4) 7/6(7)
- D.E.Sapsford — 6/2 6/2 7/5
- D.Nestor — 6/2 6/3 6/4
- A.Medvedev — 7/6(1) 7/6(3) 6/4
- P.Goldstein — 6/4 5/7 4/6 6/2 6/1
- F.Mantilla [16] — 7/6(2) 7/6(4) 4/6 7/6(7)
- G.Rusedski [9] — 6/1 6/4 6/2
- A.Parmar — 0/6 7/6(5) 6/3 6/3
- M.Norman — 6/4 7/5 7/5
- F.Santoro — 6/4 7/5 7/6(0)
- T.Johansson — 5/7 7/6(5) 6/3 4/6 6/1
- F.Clavet — 6/2 1/6 3/6 7/5 6/4
- M.Woodforde — 6/4 6/2 6/2
- M.Philippoussis [7] — 6/7(4) 6/4 6/3 6/4
- Y.Kafelnikov [3] — 6/7(4) 7/5 7/6(6) 4/6 7/5
- P.Srichaphan — 6/2 6/4 7/6(7)
- C.Pioline — 7/6(7) 6/4 6/2
- A.Clement — 6/3 6/2 6/4
- D.Vacek — 6/1 6/2 6/4
- G.Pozzi — 7/6(6) 6/2 6/2
- A.Sa — 6/4 6/4 7/6(4)
- K.Kucera [13] — 6/2 6/1 6/2
- C.Moya [12] — 6/4 7/5 6/2
- J.Courier — 6/3 6/4 6/4
- A.Ilie — 7/6(13) 7/5 6/7(10) 6/1
- S.Schalken — 5/7 6/4 6/7(5) 7/5 6/3
- S.Grosjean — 5/7 6/0 7/5 7/5
- J.Delgado — 6/2 6/1 7/5
- C.Woodruff — 6/3 3/6 6/3 6/7(7) 6/2
- T.Henman [6] — 6/4 6/0 3/6 7/6(1)
- R.Krajicek [5] — 6/2 6/3 6/1
- T.A.Woodbridge — 6/3 6/7(4) 6/4 6/7(5) 10/8
- L.Manta — 6/7(5) 7/6(3) 7/6(2) 6/2
- J.Gambill — 6/1 6/3 7/6(5)
- N.Zimonjic — 7/6(4) 7/6(3) 6/7(6) 6/4
- J.Tarango — 6/4 6/1 7/5
- D.Prinosil — 7/5 6/4 7/6(5)
- G.Kuerten [11] — 6/4 6/4 6/4
- T.Haas [14] — 3/6 6/4 4/6 6/3 6/4
- R.Fromberg — 6/4 7/6(1) 6/3
- W.Arthurs — 7/6(7) 6/7(5) 7/6(10) 7/6(1)
- N.Lapentti — 7/6(8) 6/3 4/6 2/6 8/6
- A.Martin — 7/6(8) 4/6 7/6(3) 10/8
- Y.El Aynaoui — 6/1 4/6 7/6(3) 6/4
- G.Canas — 4/6 6/3 6/2 1/6 9/7
- A.Agassi [4] — 6/1 6/2 6/3
- T.Martin [8] — 6/7(6) 6/7(5) 6/3 6/2 6/4
- J.Novak — 6/3 3/6 4/6 6/3 6/4
- M.Rosset — 6/4 5/7 3/6 6/3 6/2
- J.Knippschild — 6/3 2/6 5/7 6/2 9/7
- P.Haarhuis — 7/6(4) 6/3 6/2
- F.Vicente — 3/6 6/2 2/6 7/5 6/3
- S.Stolle — 7/6(8) 6/3 6/1
- G.Ivanisevic [10] — 6/4 6/3 6/4
- N.Kiefer [15] — 2/6 6/4 6/3 7/6(4)
- B.Becker — 5/7 6/7(4) 6/4 7/5 6/2
- L.Hewitt — 6/2 6/2 6/1
- K.Alami — 6/4 6/2 6/4
- R.Schuttler — 6/1 6/4 6/4
- T.Enqvist — 6/1 6/4 7/6(2)
- J.Bjorkman — 6/4 6/1 6/4
- P.Rafter [2] — 6/3 6/2 6/2

Third Round

- P.Sampras [1] — 6/4 6/2 6/3
- D.E.Sapsford — 6/3 3/6 6/4 6/2
- D.Nestor — 6/1 7/5 6/3
- P.Goldstein — 6/2 6/4 6/7(5) 6/2
- G.Rusedski [9] — 6/3 6/4 7/6(3)
- M.Norman — 6/2 6/3 7/6(5)
- F.Clavet — 4/6 1/6 6/1 6/3 6/4
- M.Philippoussis [7] — 6/7(4) 7/6(6) 7/6(5) 6/4
- Y.Kafelnikov [3] — 6/7(4) 4/6 7/6(4) 6/4
- C.Pioline — 6/3 6/1 6/3
- D.Vacek — 4/6 6/3 7/6(6) 5/7 6/3
- K.Kucera [13] — 7/6(4) 6/3 6/2
- J.Courier — 6/3 3/6 7/6(1) 3/6 6/2
- S.Schalken — 6/4 6/1 2/6 6/3
- S.Grosjean — 6/2 6/2 7/6(2)
- T.Henman [6] — 6/4 6/3 7/6(4)
- R.Krajicek [5] — 7/5 6/4 6/4
- L.Manta — 6/4 6/4 3/6 7/6(4) 6/3
- N.Zimonjic — 7/6(5) 1/6 6/3 7/6(6)
- G.Kuerten [11] — 6/3 6/3 6/2
- T.Haas [14] — 6/7(4) 4/6 6/4 6/3 6/2
- W.Arthurs — 7/5 7/6(7) 7/5
- A.Martin — 6/2 3/6 7/5 6/3
- A.Agassi [4] — 6/3 6/4 6/3
- T.Martin [8] — 7/6(5) 6/4 6/4
- J.Knippschild — 6/3 6/4 6/4
- P.Haarhuis — 6/2 6/2 6/2
- G.Ivanisevic [10] — 7/6(8) 6/4 4/6 6/4
- B.Becker — 6/4 6/2 6/4
- L.Hewitt — 6/1 4/6 4/6 6/4
- T.Enqvist — 6/2 6/4 7/5
- P.Rafter [2] — 6/2 7/6(3) 6/7(7) 6/2

Fourth Round

- P.Sampras [1] — 6/3 6/4 7/5
- D.Nestor — 6/3 6/7(3) 6/0 6/7(4) 6/4
- G.Rusedski [9] — 6/3 6/4 7/5
- M.Philippoussis [7] — 7/5 6/4 6/4
- C.Pioline — 3/6 6/4 1/0 Ret'd
- K.Kucera [13] — 6/1 6/3 7/6(4)
- J.Courier — 7/6(2) 3/6 3/6 7/5 13/11
- T.Henman [6] — 6/1 6/7(8) 6/3 6/2
- L.Manta — 6/3 7/6(5) 4/6 4/6 6/4
- G.Kuerten [11] — 6/4 6/4 6/2
- W.Arthurs — 7/6(6) 7/6(3) 7/6(2)
- A.Agassi [4] — 6/2 6/0 2/6 6/3
- T.Martin [8] — 6/7(5) 6/1 7/6(6) 7/5
- B.Becker — 6/1 6/4 7/6(5)
- P.Rafter [2] — 7/6(5) 6/2 6/2

Quarter-Finals

- P.Sampras [1] — 6/3 6/4 6/2
- M.Philippoussis [7] — 2/6 7/6(4) 6/3 6/1
- C.Pioline — 6/4 5/7 7/6(5) 4/6 6/3
- T.Henman [6] — 4/6 7/5 7/5 6/7(5) 9/7
- G.Kuerten [11] — 7/5 6/4 5/7 6/3
- A.Agassi [4] — 6/7(5) 7/6(5) 6/1 6/4
- T.Martin [8] — 7/6(3) 6/3 6/4
- P.Rafter [2] — 6/3 6/2 6/3

Semi-Finals

- P.Sampras [1] — 4/6 2/1 Ret'd
- T.Henman [6] — 6/4 6/2 4/6 6/3
- A.Agassi [4] — 6/3 6/4 6/4
- P.Rafter [2] — 6/3 6/7(5) 7/6(5) 7/6(3)

Final

- P.Sampras [1] — 3/6 6/4 6/3 6/4
- A.Agassi [4] — 7/5 7/6(5) 6/2

Winner: P.Sampras [1]

Heavy type denotes seeded players. The figure in brackets against names denotes the order in which they have been seeded. (W)=Wild card. (Q)=Qualifier. (L)=Lucky loser.

For particulars of Abbreviations see page 54

QUIET PLEASE

Forty years in the making

Event II— The Gentlemen's Doubles Championship 1999

Holders: J. Eltingh & P. Haarhuis

The Winners will become the holders, for the year only, of the CHALLENGE CUPS presented by the OXFORD UNIVERSITY LAWN TENNIS CLUB and the late SIR HERBERT WILBERFORCE respectively.
The Winners will receive silver replicas of the two Challenge Cups. A Silver Salver will be presented to each of the Runners-up, and a Bronze Medal to each defeated Semi-finalist.
Details of Prize Money will be found on page 25. The matches will be the best of five sets.

First Round	Second Round	Third Round	Quarter-Finals	Semi-Finals	Final
1. **M.Bhupathi** (IND) & **L.Paes** (IND) ....[1]	M.Bhupathi & L.Paes [1]				
2. T.Kempers (NED) & M.Kohlmann (GER)	..6/4 6/2 7/6(3)	M.Bhupathi & L.Paes [1]			
(Q) 3. B.Kokavec (CAN) & G.Trifu (ROM)	B.Kokavec & G.Trifu		M.Bhupathi & L.Paes [1]		
4. A.Martin (ESP) & E.Ran (ISR)	..6/3 6/4 7/6(5)	....7/5 7/6(3) 6/3			
5. J.Grabb (USA) & D.Johnson (USA)	J.Grabb & D.Johnson		....6/4 4/6 6/4 6/4		
6. M.Hill (AUS) & P.Nyborg (SWE)	..6/4 7/6(4) 7/6(2)	P.Galbraith & J.Gimelstob [16]			
7. M.Ardinghi (ITA) & A.Lopez-Moron (ESP)	P.Galbraith & J.Gimelstob [16]				
8. **P.Galbraith** (USA) & **J.Gimelstob** (USA) ....[16]	..6/0 6/2 6/4	..7/6(12) 6/7(4) 6/3 6/2		M.Bhupathi & L.Paes [1]	
9. **S.Lareau** (CAN) & **A.O'Brien** (USA) ....[9]	S.Lareau & A.O'Brien [9]			3/6 4/6 7/6(5) 6/4 6/4	
10. M.Hood (ARG) & S.Prieto (ARG)	..6/1 6/4 1/6 6/3	S.Lareau & A.O'Brien [9]			
11. G.Koves (HUN) & R.Stepanek (CZE)	D.Bowen & M.Sell		S.Lareau & A.O'Brien [9]		
12. D.Bowen (USA) & M.Sell (USA)	..6/4 2/4 Ret'd	..2/6 6/1 6/3 7/6(3)			
(W) 13. L.Childs (GBR) & S.Dickson (GBR)	B.Bryan & M.Bryan		..4/6 6/4 6/2 4/6 10/8		
14. B.Bryan (USA) & M.Bryan (USA)	..6/3 7/5 7/6(6)	B.Bryan & M.Bryan			
15. G.Grant (USA) & T.J.Middleton (USA)	E.Ferreira & R.Leach [7]				
16. **E.Ferreira** (RSA) & **R.Leach** (USA) ....[7]	..7/5 7/6(5) 7/6(1)	..6/3 5/7 7/6(3) 6/3			M.Bhupathi & L.Paes [1]
17. **W.Black** (ZIM) & **S.Stolle** (AUS) ....[4]	W.Black & S.Stolle [4]				2/6 6/3 7/6(5) 4/6 7/5
18. S.Humphries (USA) & J.Waite (USA)	..6/4 6/4 6/7(6) 6/1	W.Black & S.Stolle [4]			
19. N.Godwin (RSA) & M.Keil (USA)	M.Navarra & S.Pescosolido		W.Black & S.Stolle [4]		
(Q) 20. M.Navarra (ITA) & S.Pescosolido (ITA)	..6/3 6/4 7/6(0)	..7/5 6/3 6/3			
(W) 21. M.MacLagan (GBR) & A.Parmar (GBR)	B.Cowan & W.Whitehouse		..6/4 7/6(3) 6/3		
(W) 22. B.Cowan (GBR) & W.Whitehouse (RSA)	..6/4 6/3 6/3	B.Cowan & W.Whitehouse			
23. B.MacPhie (USA) & J.Tarango (USA)	B.MacPhie & J.Tarango				
24. **D.Prinosil** (GER) & **D.Vacek** (CZE) ....[14]	..6/4 5/7 3/6 7/6(5) 6/4	..6/7(3) 6/3 7/6(4) 7/6(5)		O.Delaitre & F.Santoro [5]	
25. **M.Damm** (CZE) & **C.Suk** (CZE) ....[11]	D.Rikl & S.Schalken			5/7 6/4 6/2 7/5	
26. D.Rikl (CZE) & S.Schalken (NED)	..6/3 6/4 6/7(2) 5/7 6/4	N.Broad & R.Koenig			
27. N.Broad (GBR) & R.Koenig (RSA)	N.Broad & R.Koenig		O.Delaitre & F.Santoro [5]		
28. D.Flach (USA) & M-K.Goellner (GER)	..4/6 6/3 7/5 6/4	..6/4 4/6 5/7 6/2 6/3			
29. P.Tramacchi (AUS) & P.Vizner (CZE)	P.Tramacchi & P.Vizner		..6/4 4/6 6/4 7/5		
(Q) 30. A.Ferreira (BRA) & G.Motomura (JPN)	..4/6 6/4 7/5 6/3	O.Delaitre & F.Santoro [5]			
31. E.Nicolas (ESP) & G.Puentes (ESP)	O.Delaitre & F.Santoro [5]				
32. **O.Delaitre** (FRA) & **F.Santoro** (FRA) ....[5]	..6/1 6/3 6/1	..6/4 3/6 6/3 1/6 6/3			
33. **M.Knowles** (BAH) & **D.Nestor** (CAN) ....[6]	M.Knowles & D.Nestor [6]				
34. N.Marques (POR) & T.Vanhoudt (BEL)	..6/3 7/5 6/1	M.Knowles & D.Nestor [6]			
35. K.Braasch (GER) & C.Haggard (RSA)	K.Braasch & C.Haggard		M.Knowles & D.Nestor [6]		
36. D.Del Rio (ARG) & M.Rodriguez (ARG)	..7/6(2) 7/5 6/3	..3/6 7/6(5) 6/4 7/5			
(W) 37. D.Sherwood (GBR) & T.Spinks (GBR)	R.A.Reneberg & J.Stark		..7/6(7) 6/3 6/4		
38. R.A.Reneberg (USA) & J.Stark (USA)	..6/2 6/1 6/7(8) 7/6(3)	R.A.Reneberg & J.Stark			
39. M.Bertolini (ITA) & C.Brandi (ITA)	W.Arthurs & A.Kratzmann [12]				
40. **W.Arthurs** (AUS) & **A.Kratzmann** (AUS) ....[12]	..4/6 7/6(6) 6/4 7/5	..6/3 7/5 3/6 4/6 7/5		M.Knowles & D.Nestor [6]	
41. **N.Kulti** (SWE) & **M.Tillstrom** (SWE) ....[13]	R.Federer & L.Hewitt			w/o	
(W) 42. R.Federer (SUI) & L.Hewitt (AUS)	..4/6 6/3 7/6(3) 6/7(4) 6/4	R.Federer & L.Hewitt			
43. B.Coupe (USA) & M.Merklein (USA)	B.Coupe & M.Merklein		J.Bjorkman & P.Rafter [3]		
(W) 44. D.E.Sapsford (GBR) & C.Wilkinson (GBR)	..6/3 7/6(4) 6/3	..6/4 7/6(1) 6/3			
45. P.Albano (ARG) & T.Carbonell (ESP)	P.Albano & T.Carbonell		..7/6(1) 5/7 3/6 7/6(3) 6/4		
46. B.Black (ZIM) & W.Ferreira (RSA)	..7/5 4/6 7/5 5/7 8/6	J.Bjorkman & P.Rafter [3]			
47. M.Barnard (RSA) & B.Haygarth (RSA)	J.Bjorkman & P.Rafter [3]				P.Haarhuis & J.Palmer [8]
48. **J.Bjorkman** (SWE) & **P.Rafter** (AUS) ....[3]	..6/1 4/6 4/6 6/3 6/3	..7/5 6/3 6/4			3/6 7/5 7/6(4) 4/6 8/6
49. **P.Haarhuis** (NED) & **J.Palmer** (USA) ....[8]	P.Haarhuis & J.Palmer [8]				
50. J.Greenhalgh (NZL) & G.Silcock (AUS)	..7/5 6/1 6/4	P.Haarhuis & J.Palmer [8]			
51. A.Florent (AUS) & D.Macpherson (AUS)	A.Florent & D.Macpherson		P.Haarhuis & J.Palmer [8]		
52. A.Kitinov (MKD) & F.Montana (USA)	..7/6(4) 4/6 6/4 6/3	..3/6 7/6(6) 7/6(3) 7/6(3)			
53. N.Lapentti (ECU) & J.Sanchez (ESP)	D.Dilucia & P.Rosner		..7/6(3) 6/2 6/1		
54. D.Dilucia (USA) & P.Rosner (RSA)	..6/3 7/6(8) 6/7(4) 6/2	D.Adams & J-L.De Jager [10]			
(L) 55. A.Hadad (ISR) & D.Roberts (RSA)	D.Adams & J-L.De Jager [10]			P.Haarhuis & J.Palmer [8]	
56. **D.Adams** (RSA) & **J-L.De Jager** (RSA) ....[10]	..6/3 6/2 6/4	..6/3 6/2 6/4		6/4 5/7 7/6(7) 6/4	
57. **P.Norval** (RSA) & **K.Ullyett** (RSA) ....[15]	P.Norval & K.Ullyett [15]				
58. N.Djordjevic (YUG) & N.Zimonjic (YUG)	..4/6 6/1 6/3 3/6 10/8	P.Norval & K.Ullyett [15]			
59. P.Goldstein (USA) & D.Roditi (MEX)	L.Bale & G.Stafford		T.A.Woodbridge & M.Woodforde [2]		
60. L.Bale (RSA) & G.Stafford (RSA)	..6/4 6/4 6/3	..7/5 6/7(7) 6/2 7/6(4)			
61. G.Kuerten (BRA) & J.Oncins (BRA)	Y.Kafelnikov & M.Mirnyi		..4/6 6/4 6/3 6/3		
62. Y.Kafelnikov (RUS) & M.Mirnyi (BLR)	..2/6 6/4 6/4 2/6 14/12	T.A.Woodbridge & M.Woodforde [2]			
63. J.Carrasco (ESP) & J.Velasco (ESP)	T.A.Woodbridge & M.Woodforde [2]				
64. **T.A.Woodbridge** (AUS) & **M.Woodforde** (AUS) ....[2]	..7/6(5) 6/2 6/4	..w/o			

Heavy type denotes seeded players. The figure in brackets against names denotes the order in which they have been seeded. (W)=Wild card. (Q)=Qualifier. (L)=Lucky loser.

For particulars of Abbreviations see page 54

63

THE HONDA CHALLENGE

the last official
tennis
tournament

of the...
millennium

The

HONDA
Challenge
for the
▲ **Delta Air Lines**
ATP Senior Tour of Champions

Join us at the Royal Albert Hall from **1st-5th Dec 1999** to see tennis legends such as Jimmy Connors, John McEnroe, Bjorn Borg, Yannick Noah, Henri Leconte and Pat Cash in action.

For corporate hospitality bookings call 0171 351 7499 and for tickets call the Royal Albert Hall Box Office on 0171 589 8212.

The Lawn Tennis Association

ROYAL ALBERT HALL

Event III— The Ladies' Singles Championship 1999

Holder: Miss J. Novotna

The Winner will become the holder, for the year only, of the CHALLENGE TROPHY presented by The All England Lawn Tennis and Croquet Club. The Winner will receive a silver replica of the Trophy. A Silver Salver will be presented to the Runner-up and a Bronze Medal to each defeated Semi-finalist. Details of Prize Money will be found on page 25. The matches will be the best of three sets.

First Round

1. **Miss M.Hingis [1]** (SUI)
2. (Q) Miss J.Dokic (AUS)
3. Miss K.Studenikova (SVK)
4. Miss E.Loit (FRA)
5. Miss A.Kremer (LUX)
6. Miss M.J.Fernandez (USA)
7. Miss I.Spirlea (ROM)
8. Miss B.Rippner (USA)
9. Miss V.Ruano Pascual (ESP)
10. Miss M.Shaughnessy (USA)
11. Mrs E.Wagner (GER)
12. (W) Miss A.Tordoff (GBR)
13. Miss K.Brandi (USA)
14. Miss R.Grande (ITA)
15. Miss F.Zuluaga (COL)
16. **Miss M.Pierce [9]** (FRA)
17. **Mrs J.Halard-Decugis [11]** (FRA)
18. Miss S.Nacuk (YUG)
19. Miss A.Serra-Zanetti (ITA)
20. Miss S.Farina (ITA)
21. Miss A.Frazier (USA)
22. (Q) Miss A.Stevenson (USA)
23. Miss C.Cristea (ROM)
24. Miss O.Barabanschikova (BLR)
25. Miss T.Snyder (USA)
26. Miss A.Carlsson (SWE)
27. Miss C.Martinez (ESP)
28. Miss R.Kuti-Kis (HUN)
29. Miss L.M.Raymond (USA)
30. Miss A.Glass (GER)
31. (Q) Miss A.Foldenyi (HUN)
32. **Miss A.Sanchez Vicario [7]** (ESP)
33. **Miss L.A.Davenport [3]** (USA)
34. Miss A.Fusai (FRA)
35. Miss K.Habsudova (SVK)
36. (W) Miss L.A.Woodroffe (GBR)
37. Miss P.Stoyanova (BUL)
38. Miss L.Golarsa (ITA)
39. Miss E.S.H.Callens (BEL)
40. Miss A.Cocheteux (FRA)
41. Miss N.Arendt (USA)
42. Miss M.Serna (ESP)
43. Mrs L.Neiland (LAT)
44. Miss F.Li (CHN)
45. Miss L.Bacheva (BUL)
46. Mrs A.Dechaume-Balleret (FRA)
47. Miss G.Leon Garcia (ESP)
48. **Miss B.Schett [14]** (AUT)
49. **Miss N.Zvereva [16]** (BLR)
50. Miss K.Po (USA)
51. Miss T.Panova (RUS)
52. Miss H.Nagyova (SVK)
53. Miss P.Schnyder (SUI)
54. Miss N.Dechy (FRA)
55. Miss S.Appelmans (BEL)
56. Miss S.Talaja (CRO)
57. Miss M.A.Sanchez Lorenzo (ESP)
58. (Q) Miss L.Wild (USA)
59. Miss S.Jeyaseelan (CAN)
60. (Q) Miss N.Petrova (RUS)
61. Miss C.Black (ZIM)
62. Miss S.Plischke (AUT)
63. Miss S-T.Wang (TPE)
64. **Miss J.Novotna [5]** (CZE)
65. **Miss N.Tauziat [8]** (FRA)
66. (W) Miss L.A.Ahl (GBR)
67. Miss A.Hopmans (NED)
68. Miss S.Kleinova (CZE)
69. Miss J.Nejedly (CAN)
70. (Q) Miss S.Noorlander (NED)
71. Miss A.Huber (GER)
72. Miss J.Capriati (USA)
73. Miss M.Grzybowska (POL)
74. Miss A.Sugiyama (JPN)
75. Miss A.Molik (AUS)
76. Miss E.Likhovtseva (RUS)
77. Miss K.Boogert (NED)
78. Miss C.Rubin (USA)
79. (L) Miss E.Dementieva (RUS)
80. **Mrs D.Van Roost [15]** (BEL)
81. **Miss S.Testud [13]** (FRA)
82. (W) Miss J.M.Pullin (GBR)
83. Miss D.Chladkova (CZE)
84. Miss B.Rittner (GER)
85. Miss M.Drake (CAN)
86. Miss E.Koulikovskaya (RUS)
87. Miss T.Tanasugarn (THA)
88. Miss K.Hrdlickova (CZE)
89. Miss M.Diaz Oliva (ARG)
90. Miss A.Smashnova (ISR)
91. (Q) Miss E.R.De Lone (USA)
92. Miss M.Lucic (CRO)
93. (W) Miss J.Ward (GBR)
94. Miss M.Weingartner (GER)
95. Miss C.Torrens-Valero (ESP)
96. **Miss M.Seles [4]** (USA)
97. **Miss V.Williams [6]** (USA)
98. Miss M.Oremans (NED)
99. Miss J.Chi (USA)
100. Miss E.Tatarkova (UKR)
101. Miss K.Srebotnik (SLO)
102. Miss S.Pitkowski (FRA)
103. Miss A-G.Sidot (FRA)
104. (W) Miss L.Latimer (GBR)
105. Miss R.Dragomir (ROM)
106. Miss P.Suarez (ARG)
107. Miss I.Gorrochategui (ARG)
108. Miss S.Smith (GBR)
109. Miss M.A.Vento (VEN)
110. Miss E.Gagliardi (SUI)
111. (W) Miss B.Schwartz (AUT)
112. **Miss A.Kournikova [17]** (RUS)
113. **Miss A.J.Coetzer [12]** (RSA)
114. Miss N.J.Pratt (AUS)
115. Miss C.Papadaki (GRE)
116. Miss M.Saeki (JPN)
117. Miss J.Kruger (RSA)
118. (Q) Miss K.Clijsters (BEL)
119. Miss L.Osterloh (USA)
120. (W) Miss K.M.Cross (GBR)
121. Miss K-A.Guse (AUS)
122. Miss J.Lee (TPE)
123. Miss C.Morariu (USA)
124. Miss L.Courtois (BEL)
125. Miss J.Watanabe (USA)
126. Miss M.de Swardt (RSA)
127. Miss L.Cervanova (SVK)
128. **Miss S.Graf [2]** (GER)

Second Round

- Miss J.Dokic 6/2 6/0
- Miss K.Studenikova 6/1 6/3
- Miss A.Kremer 6/3 4/6 7/5
- Miss B.Rippner 6/4 6/1
- Miss M.Shaughnessy 6/3 3/6 6/3
- Mrs E.Wagner 6/0 6/2
- Miss R.Grande 6/2 1/6 6/3
- **Miss M.Pierce [9]** 6/3 6/2
- **Mrs J.Halard-Decugis [11]** 6/1 6/0
- Miss S.Farina 6/2 6/1
- Miss A.Stevenson 6/1 3/6 6/3
- Miss O.Barabanschikova 6/2 6/3
- Miss T.Snyder 6/2 7/5
- Miss C.Martinez 6/2 6/1
- Miss L.M.Raymond 6/3 3/6 8/6
- **Miss A.Sanchez Vicario [7]** 4/6 6/3 6/4
- **Miss L.A.Davenport [3]** 6/0 6/3
- Miss K.Habsudova 6/3 6/2
- Miss L.Golarsa 6/2 6/2
- Miss A.Cocheteux 6/0 6/3
- Miss N.Arendt 6/3 7/6(4)
- Mrs L.Neiland 0/6 7/5 6/2
- Mrs A.Dechaume-Balleret 6/4 4/6 6/4
- **Miss B.Schett [14]** 7/5 6/2
- **Miss N.Zvereva [16]** 5/7 6/1 6/3
- Miss T.Panova 6/3 6/3
- Miss N.Dechy 5/7 6/3 6/3
- Miss S.Appelmans 6/3 6/7(5) 6/3
- Miss M.A.Sanchez Lorenzo 6/3 7/6(4)
- Miss N.Petrova 3/6 6/3 6/4
- Miss S.Plischke 7/6(5) 7/5
- **Miss J.Novotna [5]** 6/2 6/1
- **Miss N.Tauziat [8]** 6/3 6/2
- Miss A.Hopmans 6/4 6/2
- Miss S.Noorlander 6/3 6/3
- Miss J.Capriati 5/7 6/3 9/7
- Miss A.Sugiyama 6/1 6/2
- Miss E.Likhovtseva 6/2 6/0
- Miss K.Boogert 6/4 7/5
- **Mrs D.Van Roost [15]** 3/6 6/4 6/4
- **Miss S.Testud [13]** 6/1 6/3
- Miss B.Rittner 6/4 6/2
- Miss M.Drake 6/3 6/0
- Miss T.Tanasugarn 6/1 6/4
- Miss M.Diaz Oliva 7/6(3) 7/5
- Miss M.Lucic 3/6 7/6(4) 7/5
- Miss M.Weingartner 4/6 7/5 6/3
- **Miss M.Seles [4]** 6/3 6/1
- **Miss V.Williams [6]** 6/1 7/5
- Miss E.Tatarkova 7/5 6/0
- Miss S.Pitkowski 7/6(5) 5/7 6/1
- Miss L.Latimer 6/4 6/2
- Miss R.Dragomir 6/4 6/1
- Miss I.Gorrochategui 6/2 1/6 6/2
- Miss M.A.Vento 7/5 6/3
- **Miss A.Kournikova [17]** 7/6(2) 4/6 6/2
- **Miss A.J.Coetzer [12]** 6/2 7/5
- Miss M.Saeki 6/3 6/2
- Miss K.Clijsters 6/2 6/3
- Miss K.M.Cross 6/1 6/4
- Miss J.Lee 3/6 6/4 6/1
- Miss C.Morariu 7/6(8) 3/6 6/2
- Miss M.de Swardt 6/1 6/4
- **Miss S.Graf [2]** 6/1 6/4

Third Round

- Miss J.Dokic 6/0 4/6 8/6
- Miss A.Kremer 6/2 6/3
- Mrs E.Wagner 7/6(3) 6/3
- **Miss M.Pierce [9]** 6/1 6/3
- **Mrs J.Halard-Decugis [11]** 6/2 3/6 8/6
- Miss A.Stevenson 6/2 6/7(3) 6/3
- Miss C.Martinez 6/4 6/1
- Miss L.M.Raymond 7/6(4) 6/1
- **Miss L.A.Davenport [3]** 6/2 6/2
- Miss L.Golarsa 6/4 6/2
- Mrs L.Neiland 2/6 7/5 6/4
- **Miss B.Schett [14]** 6/7(6) 6/3 6/1
- Miss T.Panova 6/4 7/5
- Miss N.Dechy 6/3 7/6(6)
- Miss M.A.Sanchez Lorenzo 7/5 6/1
- **Miss J.Novotna [5]** 6/3 6/1
- **Miss N.Tauziat [8]** 6/3 6/4
- Miss S.Noorlander 6/1 6/3
- Miss E.Likhovtseva 7/6(6) 6/1
- **Mrs D.Van Roost [15]** 6/3 6/3
- **Miss S.Testud [13]** 7/6(2) 6/1
- Miss T.Tanasugarn 6/4 6/3
- Miss M.Lucic 6/2 6/1
- **Miss M.Seles [4]** 6/0 6/0
- **Miss V.Williams [6]** 6/3 6/4
- Miss S.Pitkowski 7/5 5/7 6/3
- Miss I.Gorrochategui 6/2 6/2
- **Miss A.Kournikova [17]** 7/5 6/4
- **Miss A.J.Coetzer [12]** 6/4 6/1
- Miss K.Clijsters 6/2 6/0
- Miss C.Morariu 6/2 6/4
- **Miss S.Graf [2]** 4/6 6/3 6/2

Fourth Round

- Miss J.Dokic 6/7(7) 6/3 6/4
- **Miss M.Pierce [9]** 6/3 6/0
- Miss A.Stevenson 6/3 6/3
- Miss L.M.Raymond 6/3 6/1
- **Miss L.A.Davenport [3]** 6/3 6/2
- **Miss B.Schett [14]** 6/2 6/3
- Miss N.Dechy 6/0 6/3
- **Miss J.Novotna [5]** 6/4 6/3
- **Miss N.Tauziat [8]** 6/1 6/1
- **Mrs D.Van Roost [15]** 6/4 7/6(4)
- Miss T.Tanasugarn 6/2 1/6 6/3
- Miss M.Lucic 7/6(4) 7/6(4)
- **Miss V.Williams [6]** 6/1 6/1
- **Miss A.Kournikova [17]** 7/5 3/1 Ret'd
- Miss K.Clijsters 6/2 6/4
- **Miss S.Graf [2]** 6/1 6/3

Quarter-Finals

- Miss J.Dokic 6/4 6/3
- Miss A.Stevenson 2/6 7/6(8) 6/1
- **Miss L.A.Davenport [3]** 7/6(7) 6/1
- **Miss J.Novotna [5]** 6/3 7/5
- **Miss N.Tauziat [8]** 6/3 3/6 6/3
- Miss M.Lucic 7/5 6/3
- **Miss V.Williams [6]** 3/6 6/3 6/2
- **Miss S.Graf [2]** 6/2 6/2

Semi-Finals

- Miss A.Stevenson 6/3 1/6 6/3
- **Miss L.A.Davenport [3]** 6/3 6/4
- Miss M.Lucic 4/6 6/4 7/5
- **Miss S.Graf [2]** 6/2 3/6 6/4

Final

- **Miss L.A.Davenport [3]** 6/1 6/1
- **Miss S.Graf [2]** 6/7(3) 6/4 6/3

Heavy type denotes seeded players. The figure in brackets against names denotes the order in which they have been seeded. (W)=Wild card. (Q)=Qualifier. (L)=Lucky loser.

Maiden Names of Competitors and Abbreviations will be found on page 54

Event IV— The Ladies' Doubles Championship 1999
Holders: Miss M. Hingis and Miss J. Novotna

The Winners will become the holders, for the year only, of the CHALLENGE CUP presented by H.R.H. PRINCESS MARINA, DUCHESS OF KENT, the late President of The All England Lawn Tennis and Croquet Club. The Winners will receive silver replicas of the Challenge Cup. A Silver Salver will be presented to each of the Runners-up and a Bronze Medal to each defeated Semi-finalist. Details of Prize Money will be found on page 25. The matches will be the best of three sets.

First Round	Second Round	Third Round	Quarter-Finals	Semi-Finals	Final

1. **Miss J.Novotna** (CZE) **& Miss N.Zvereva** (BLR) ....[1]
2. Mrs A.Dechaume-Balleret (FRA) & Miss S.Testud (FRA) ....
  — Miss J.Novotna & Miss N.Zvereva [1] — 7/5 6/7(2) 6/4
3. Miss A.J.Coetzer (RSA) & Miss I.Gorrochategui (ARG)
4. Miss O.Lugina (UKR) & Miss M.Muric (CRO) ....
  — Miss A.J.Coetzer & Miss I.Gorrochategui — 6/3 6/0

Miss J.Novotna & Miss N.Zvereva [1] ....w/o

(Q) 5. Miss J.Abe (GER) & Miss N.Petrova (RUS)
6. Miss E.Kim (KOR) & Miss Y.Yoshida (JPN)
  — Miss J.Abe & Miss N.Petrova — 6/2 6/3
7. Miss L.Courtois (BEL) & Miss A.Molik (AUS)
8. **Miss B.Schett** (AUT) **& Miss P.Schnyder** (SUI) ....[15]
  — Miss L.Courtois & Miss A.Molik — 6/7(5) 7/5 6/1

Miss L.Courtois & Miss A.Molik — 6/3 3/6 7/5

Miss J.Novotna & Miss N.Zvereva [1] — 6/4 6/0

9. **Miss C.Cristea** (ROM) **& Miss R.Dragomir** (ROM) .....[17]
10. Miss E.Martincova (CZE) & Miss C.Torrens-Valero (ESP)
  — Miss E.Martincova & Miss C.Torrens-Valero — 6/3 6/4
11. Miss K.Hrdlickova (CZE) & Miss T.Krizan (SLO)
12. Miss S.Farina (ITA) & Miss L.Wild (USA)
  — Miss S.Farina & Miss L.Wild — 4/3

Miss S.Farina & Miss L.Wild — 6/4 6/3

(W)13. Miss S.De Beer (RSA) & Miss S.Smith (GBR)
14. Mrs K.Kunce (AUS) & Miss K.Po (USA)
  — Mrs K.Kunce & Miss K.Po — 6/1 6/4
15. Miss E.Bes (ESP) & Miss K.Freye (GER)
16. **Mrs L.Neiland** (LAT) **& Miss A.Sanchez Vicario** (ESP) ...[8]
  — Mrs L.Neiland & Miss A.Sanchez Vicario [8] — 6/2 6/1

Mrs L.Neiland & Miss A.Sanchez Vicario [8] — 6/2 6/3

Miss S.Farina & Miss L.Wild — 6/1 7/6(2)

17. **Miss E.Likhovtseva** (RUS) **& Miss A.Sugiyama** (JPN) .....[5]
18. Miss S.Appelmans (BEL) & Miss M.Oremans (NED)
  — Miss E.Likhovtseva & Miss A.Sugiyama [5] — 6/3 6/4
19. Miss E.Melicharova (CZE) & Miss H.Vildova (CZE)
(Q)20. Miss J.Dokic (AUS) & Miss T.Pisnik (SLO)
  — Miss J.Dokic & Miss T.Pisnik — 7/5 6/2

Miss J.Dokic & Miss T.Pisnik — 3/6 6/2 12/10

21. Miss O.Barabanschikova (BLR) & Miss B.Rittner (GER)
(L)22. Miss S.Reeves (USA) & Miss M.Washington (USA)
  — Miss O.Barabanschikova & Miss B.Rittner — 6/3 6/3
(L)23. Miss A.Jidkova (RUS) & Miss L.Schaerer (PAR)
24. **Miss M.J.Fernandez** (USA) **& Miss M.Seles** (USA) .....[12]
  — Miss M.J.Fernandez & Miss M.Seles [12] — 6/1 6/2

Miss M.J.Fernandez & Miss M.Seles [12] — 6/1 6/0

Miss M.J.Fernandez & Miss M.Seles [12] — 6/2 6/1

25. **Miss V.Ruano Pascual** (ESP) **& Miss P.Suarez** (ARG) ...[14]
26. Miss V.Menga (BRA) & Mrs E.Wagner (GER)
  — Miss V.Ruano Pascual & Miss P.Suarez [14] — 6/4 6/7(5) 6/3
27. Miss E.Gagliardi (SUI) & Miss K.Marosi (HUN)
28. Miss A.Cocheteux (FRA) & Miss E.Loit (FRA)
  — Miss A.Cocheteux & Miss E.Loit — 7/5 6/4

Miss V.Ruano Pascual & Miss P.Suarez [14] — 7/6(3) 3/6 6/1

29. Miss W.Probst (GER) & Miss C.Singer (GER)
30. Miss L.Montalvo (ARG) & Miss S-T.Wang (TPE)
  — Miss W.Probst & Miss C.Singer — 6/1 6/0
(W)31. Miss J.M.Pullin (GBR) & Miss L.A.Woodroffe (GBR)
32. **Miss M.de Swardt** (RSA) **& Miss E.Tatarkova** (UKR) .....[9]
  — **Miss M.de Swardt & Miss E.Tatarkova [9]** — 6/2 2/6 6/2

Miss M.de Swardt & Miss E.Tatarkova [9] — 6/1 7/6(3)

Miss M.de Swardt & Miss E.Tatarkova [9] — 6/4 6/3

Miss M.de Swardt & Miss E.Tatarkova [9] — 6/7(3) 6/1 6/4

Miss J.Novotna & Miss N.Zvereva [1] — 6/1 7/5

33. **Miss L.A.Davenport** (USA) **& Miss C.Morariu** (USA) .....[7]
34. Miss M. F.Landa (ARG) & Miss M.Weingartner (GER)
  — Miss L.A.Davenport & Miss C.Morariu [7] — 6/0 6/0
(W)35. Miss H.Crook (GBR) & Miss V.E.Davies (GBR)
36. Miss C.Papadaki (GRE) & Miss M.Shaughnessy (USA)
  — Miss C.Papadaki & Miss M.Shaughnessy — 6/4 6/1

Miss L.A.Davenport & Miss C.Morariu [7] — 6/2 6/2

37. Miss B.Stewart (AUS) & Miss P.Stoyanova (BUL)
38. Miss A.Frazier (USA) & Miss K.Schlukebir (USA)
  — Miss A.Frazier & Miss K.Schlukebir — 7/5 6/2
39. Miss K.M.Adams (USA) & Miss C.Rubin (USA)
40. **Miss E.S.H.Callens** (BEL) **& Mrs J.Halard-Decugis** (FRA) [13]
  — **Miss E.S.H.Callens & Mrs J.Halard-Decugis [13]** — 6/3 6/2

Miss A.Frazier & Miss K.Schlukebir — 1/6 6/4 6/3

Miss L.A.Davenport & Miss C.Morariu [7] — 6/2 7/5

41. **Miss C.Black** (ZIM) **& Miss I.Selyutina** (KAZ) ....[16]
42. Miss A.Ellwood (AUS) & Miss L.McShea (AUS)
  — Miss C.Black & Miss I.Selyutina [16] — 6/3 5/7 6/3
43. Miss F.Labat (ARG) & Mrs D.Van Roost (BEL)
44. Miss E.R.De Lone (USA) & Miss N.J.Pratt (AUS)
  — Miss F.Labat & Mrs D.Van Roost — 6/1 6/2

Miss F.Labat & Mrs D.Van Roost — 6/4 2/6 6/4

45. Miss A.Carlsson (SWE) & Miss S.Jeyaseelan (CAN)
46. Miss N.Arendt (USA) & Miss M.M.Bollegraf (NED)
  — Miss N.Arendt & Miss M.M.Bollegraf — 3/6 6/3 6/4
(W)47. Miss K.M.Cross (GBR) & Miss J.Ward (GBR)
48. **Miss A.Fusai** (FRA) **& Miss N.Tauziat** (FRA) ....[3]
  — **Miss A.Fusai & Miss N.Tauziat [3]** — 7/5 3/6 6/0

Miss N.Arendt & Miss M.M.Bollegraf — 6/3 6/2

Miss N.Arendt & Miss M.M.Bollegraf — 6/1 3/6 6/1

Miss L.A.Davenport & Miss C.Morariu [7] — 6/4 7/6(1)

49. **Miss L.M.Raymond** (USA) **& Miss R.P.Stubbs** (AUS) .....[6]
50. Miss C.G.Barclay (AUS) & Miss K-A.Guse (AUS)
  — Miss L.M.Raymond & Miss R.P.Stubbs [6] — 7/6(5) 4/6 6/3
51. Miss C.Dhenin (FRA) & Miss L.Pleming (AUS)
52. Miss M.Drake (CAN) & Miss J.Steck (RSA)
  — Miss C.Dhenin & Miss L.Pleming — 1/6 7/5 12/10

Miss L.M.Raymond & Miss R.P.Stubbs [6] — 6/3 7/5

53. Miss L.Horn (RSA) & Miss K.Srebotnik (SLO)
54. Miss R.McQuillan (AUS) & Miss N.Miyagi (JPN)
  — Miss L.Horn & Miss K.Srebotnik — 4/6 7/6(3) 6/2
55. Miss L.Nemeckova (CZE) & Miss A.Ortuno (ESP)
56. **Miss C.Martinez** (ESP) **& Miss P.Tarabini** (ARG) ....[11]
  — **Miss C.Martinez & Miss P.Tarabini [11]** — 6/0 6/0

Miss L.Horn & Miss K.Srebotnik — 3/6 6/4 7/5

Miss L.Horn & Miss K.Srebotnik — 6/4 6/2

57. **Miss I.Spirlea** (ROM) **& Miss C.M.Vis** (NED) ....[10]
58. Miss L.Golarsa (ITA) & Miss J.Husarova (SVK)
  — Miss I.Spirlea & Miss C.M.Vis [10] — 6/4 6/2
59. Miss K.Habsudova (SVK) & Miss T.Tanasugarn (THA)
60. Miss N.De Villiers (RSA) & Miss R.Hiraki (JPN)
  — Miss N.De Villiers & Miss R.Hiraki — 5/7 6/1 6/3

Miss I.Spirlea & Miss C.M.Vis [10] — 6/2 6/2

61. Miss R.Grande (ITA) & Miss M.Saeki (JPN)
62. Miss A.Olsza (POL) & Miss L.Osterloh (USA)
  — Miss A.Olsza & Miss L.Osterloh — 6/4 6/3
63. Miss K.Boogert (NED) & Miss A-G.Sidot (FRA)
64. **Miss D.A.Graham** (USA) **& Miss L.M.McNeil** (USA) ..[18]
  — Miss K.Boogert & Miss A-G.Sidot — 6/4 6/3

Miss K.Boogert & Miss A-G.Sidot — 6/4 6/3

Miss K.Boogert & Miss A-G.Sidot — 7/6(2) 6/3

Miss L.Horn & Miss K.Srebotnik — 6/4 1/6 17/15

Miss L.A.Davenport & Miss C.Morariu [7] — 7/6(0) 6/3

Miss M.de Swardt & Miss E.Tatarkova [9] — 6/4 2/6 7/5

Miss M.de Swardt & Miss E.Tatarkova [9]

Heavy type denotes seeded players. The figure in brackets against names denotes the order in which they have been seeded. (W)=Wild card. (Q)=Qualifier. (L)=Lucky loser. Maiden Names of Competitors and Abbreviations will be found on page 54

Event V— The Mixed Doubles Championship 1999
Holders: M. Mirnyi and Miss S. Williams

The Winners will become the holders, for the year only, of the CHALLENGE CUP presented by the family of the late Mr. S. H. SMITH. The Winners will receive silver replicas of the Challenge Cup.
A Silver Salver will be presented to each of the Runners-up and a Bronze Medal to each defeated Semi-finalist. Details of Prize Money will be found on page 25. The matches will be the best of three sets.

First Round	Second Round	Third Round	Quarter-Finals	Semi-Finals	Final

1. **L.Paes** (IND) **& Miss L.M.Raymond** (USA) ....[1]
2. D.Roditi (MEX) & Miss S.Jeyaseelan (CAN) ....
— L.Paes & Miss L.M.Raymond [1] 6/2 6/1

3. C.Haggard (RSA) & Miss E.S.H.Callens (BEL) ....
4. P.Vizner (CZE) & Miss S.Testud (FRA) ....
— P.Vizner & Miss S.Testud .... 6/2 6/7(3) 6/4

L.Paes & Miss L.M.Raymond [1] 6/3 6/4

5. P.Albano (ARG) & Miss M.M.Bollegraf (NED) ....
6. B.MacPhie (USA) & Miss D.A.Graham (USA) ....
— P.Albano & Miss M.M.Bollegraf 2/6 6/4 7/5

7. W.Arthurs (AUS) & Miss O.Barabanschikova (BLR) ....
8. **A.Florent** (AUS) **& Miss E.Tatarkova** (UKR) ....[12]
— A.Florent & Miss E.Tatarkova [12] 7/5 6/3

P.Albano & Miss M.M.Bollegraf .... 7/5 7/6(6)

L.Paes & Miss L.M.Raymond [1] .... 7/6(4) 6/2

9. **W.Black** (ZIM) **& Miss C.Black** (ZIM) ....[10]
10. D.Bowen (USA) & Miss L.Montalvo (ARG) ....
— W.Black & Miss C.Black [10] 6/2 6/1

11. N.Djordjevic (YUG) & Miss O.Lugina (UKR) ....
12. S.Humphries (USA) & Miss C.Cristea (ROM) ....
— S.Humphries & Miss C.Cristea 6/2 6/1

W.Black & Miss C.Black [10] .... 6/2 4/6 4/2 Ret'd

13. B.Bryan (USA) & Miss L.McShea (AUS) ....
14. N.Broad (GBR) & Miss A.J.Coetzer (RSA) ....
— B.Bryan & Miss L.McShea .... 7/6(7) 6/7(5) 6/4

15. M.Barnard (RSA) & Miss K.M.Adams (USA) ....
16. **C.Suk** (CZE) **& Miss C.M.Vis** (NED) ....[5]
— C.Suk & Miss C.M.Vis [5] 6/2 6/4

B.Bryan & Miss L.McShea 6/4 6/3

B.Bryan & Miss L.McShea 4/6 6/3 6/3

17. **M.Knowles** (BAH) **& Miss E.Likhovtseva** (RUS) ....[4]
18. M.Tebbutt (AUS) & Miss C.G.Barclay (AUS) ....
— M.Knowles & Miss E.Likhovtseva [4] 6/4 6/3

19. M.Bhupathi (IND) & Miss A.Ellwood (AUS) ....
20. B.Ellwood (AUS) & Miss A.Carlsson (SWE) ....
— M.Bhupathi & Miss A.Ellwood 2/6 6/4 10/8

M.Knowles & Miss E.Likhovtseva [4] .... w/o

21. K.Ullyett (RSA) & Miss L.Golarsa (ITA) ....
22. D.Flach (USA) & Miss R.Hiraki (JPN) ....
— K.Ullyett & Miss L.Golarsa .... 6/1 7/6(6)

23. P.Galbraith (USA) & Miss K.Boogert (NED) ....
24. **D.Rikl** (CZE) **& Miss K.Habsudova** (SVK) ....[13]
— P.Galbraith & Miss K.Boogert .... 6/7(3) 7/6(6) 6/3

P.Galbraith & Miss K.Boogert 3/6 7/5 6/3

M.Knowles & Miss E.Likhovtseva [4] .... 6/3 7/6(2)

25. **M.Mirnyi** (BLR) **& Miss M.Pierce** (FRA) ....[15]
26. P.Nyborg (SWE) & Miss S.Appelmans (BEL) ....
— M.Mirnyi & Miss M.Pierce [15] 6/3 6/4

27. M.Damm (CZE) & Miss B.Rittner (GER) ....
28. R.Koenig (RSA) & Miss N.J.Pratt (AUS) ....
— M.Damm & Miss B.Rittner 7/5 6/4

M.Damm & Miss B.Rittner 7/5 4/6 6/4

29. M.Merklein (USA) & Miss E.R.De Lone (USA) ....
30. T.Vanhoudt (BEL) & Mrs D.Van Roost (BEL) ....
— M.Merklein & Miss E.R.De Lone 6/3 6/4

31. A.Kitinov (MKD) & Miss N.Miyagi (JPN) ....
32. **D.Adams** (RSA) **& Miss M.de Swardt** (RSA) ....[7]
— D.Adams & Miss M.de Swardt [7] .... 6/2 6/7(2) 6/2

M.Merklein & Miss E.R.De Lone 3/6 6/3 6/4

M.Damm & Miss B.Rittner 6/1 7/5

33. **R.Leach** (USA) **& Mrs L.Neiland** (LAT) ....[6]
34. G.Grant (USA) & Miss L.Horn (RSA) ....
— R.Leach & Mrs L.Neiland [6] 6/1 6/4

35. D.Dilucia (USA) & Miss M.Shaughnessy (USA) ....
36. M.Rodriguez (ARG) & Miss F.Labat (ARG) ....
— M.Rodriguez & Miss F.Labat 6/2 6/4

R.Leach & Mrs L.Neiland [6] 3/6 6/3 6/2

37. B.Coupe (USA) & Miss L.Osterloh (USA) ....
38. D.Johnson (USA) & Miss A.Molik (AUS) ....
— D.Johnson & Miss A.Molik 7/5 6/3

39. B.Haygarth (RSA) & Miss J.Steck (RSA) ....
40. **S.Stolle** (AUS) **& Mrs K.Kunce** (AUS) ....[11]
— B.Haygarth & Miss J.Steck .... 7/5 7/6(0)

D.Johnson & Miss A.Molik .... 7/6(4) 6/4

R.Leach & Mrs L.Neiland [6] 6/4 3/6 6/2

41. **P.Norval** (RSA) **& Miss K.Srebotnik** (SLO) ....[16]
42. M.Hill (AUS) & Miss C.Morariu (USA) ....
— P.Norval & Miss K.Srebotnik [16] .... 3/0 Ret'd

(W)43. B.Cowan (GBR) & Miss J.M.Pullin (GBR) ....
44. G.Stafford (RSA) & Miss N.De Villiers (RSA) ....
— G.Stafford & Miss N.De Villiers 6/3 3/6 6/3

P.Norval & Miss K.Srebotnik [16] 6/3 3/6 6/3

(W)45. M.MacLagan (GBR) & Miss K.M.Cross (GBR) ....
46. J-L.De Jager (RSA) & Miss M.Oremans (NED) ....
— J-L.De Jager & Miss M.Oremans 6/2 4/6 7/5

47. M.Bryan (USA) & Miss K.Schlukebir (USA) ....
48. **J.Bjorkman** (SWE) **& Miss A.Kournikova** (RUS) ....[3]
— J.Bjorkman & Miss A.Kournikova [3] 6/4 6/1

J.Bjorkman & Miss A.Kournikova [3] 6/2 6/3

J.Bjorkman & Miss A.Kournikova [3] .... 7/6(0) 6/1

49. **J.Gimelstob** (USA) **& Miss V.Williams** (USA) ....[8]
50. L.Bale (RSA) & Miss I.Selyutina (KAZ) ....
— J.Gimelstob & Miss V.Williams [8] 6/1 6/2

51. D.Del Rio (ARG) & Miss M. F.Landa (ARG) ....
52. N.Zimonjic (YUG) & Miss T.Krizan (SLO) ....
— N.Zimonjic & Miss T.Krizan .... 5/2 Ret'd

J.Gimelstob & Miss V.Williams [8] .... w/o

(W)53. C.Wilkinson (GBR) & Miss S.Smith (GBR) ....
54. A.Kratzmann (AUS) & Miss K-A.Guse (AUS) ....
— A.Kratzmann & Miss K-A.Guse .... 6/7(1) 6/3 6/4

55. T.Kempers (NED) & Miss C.Papadaki (GRE) ....
56. **P.Tramacchi** (AUS) **& Miss A.Sugiyama** (JPN) ....[14]
— P.Tramacchi & Miss A.Sugiyama [14] 6/1 7/5

A.Kratzmann & Miss K-A.Guse 2/6 7/5 7/5

J.Gimelstob & Miss V.Williams [8] 6/3 6/3

(W)57. **J.P.McEnroe** (USA) **& Miss S.Graf** (GER) ....[9]
58. J.Coetzee (RSA) & Miss E.Melicharova (CZE) ....
— J.P.McEnroe & Miss S.Graf [9] 6/2 6/4

59. E.Ran (ISR) & Miss V.Menga (BRA) ....
60. J.Waite (USA) & Miss K.Po (USA) ....
— E.Ran & Miss V.Menga 7/5 2/6 6/4

J.P.McEnroe & Miss S.Graf [9] 6/3 6/4

(W)61. D.E.Sapsford (GBR) & Miss L.A.Woodroffe (GBR) ....
62. D.Macpherson (AUS) & Miss R.McQuillan (AUS) ....
— D.Macpherson & Miss R.McQuillan .... 6/7(1) 6/3 6/3

63. T.J.Middleton (USA) & Miss L.M.McNeil (USA) ....
64. **T.A.Woodbridge** (AUS) **& Miss L.A.Davenport** (USA) ...[2]
— T.A.Woodbridge & Miss L.A.Davenport [2] 6/4 6/2

T.A.Woodbridge & Miss L.A.Davenport [2] 6/1 6/4

J.P.McEnroe & Miss S.Graf [9] .... W/O

J.P.McEnroe & Miss S.Graf [9] 6/4 6/3

J.Bjorkman & Miss A.Kournikova [3] .... 7/6(6) 4/6 6/3

L.Paes & Miss L.M.Raymond [1] .... 6/4 7/6(2)

M.Knowles & Miss E.Likhovtseva [4] 6/3 7/5

J.Bjorkman & Miss A.Kournikova [3] .... w/o

Heavy type denotes seeded players. The figure in brackets against names denotes the order in which they have been seeded. (W)=Wild card. (Q)=Qualifier. (L)=Lucky loser.
Maiden Names of Competitors and Abbreviations will be found on page 54

Event VI— The 35 And Over Gentlemen's Invitation Doubles 1999
Holders: G. Mayer and T. Wilkinson

The Winners will become the holders, for the year only, of a Cup presented by The All England Lawn Tennis and Croquet Club. The Winners will receive miniature Silver Salvers. A Silver Medal will be presented to each of the Runners-up. Details of Prize Money will be found on page 25.

GROUP A					WINS	LOSSES	SEMI-FINAL	FINAL
M.J. Bates (GBR) and R. Krishnan (IND)	v	M.R. Edmondson and P. Fleming 6/7(5) 6/7(8)	M. Pernfors and S. Zivojinovic 6/4 3/6 6/1	J.B. Fitzgerald and W. Masur 6/4 6/7(5) 4/6	1	2		
M.R. Edmondson (AUS) and P. Fleming (USA)	v	**M.J. Bates and R. Krishnan** 7/6(5) 7/6(8)	J.B. Fitzgerald and W. Masur 3/6 6/4 5/7	M. Pernfors and S. Zivojinovic 6/2 6/2	2	1	J.B. Fitzgerald and W. Masur	
J.B. Fitzgerald (AUS) and W. Masur (AUS)	v	M. Pernfors and S. Zivojinovic 6/2 6/3	M.R. Edmondson and P. Fleming 6/3 4/6 7/5	**M.J. Bates and R. Krishnan** 4/6 7/6(5) 6/4	3	0		
M. Pernfors (SWE) and S. Zivojinovic (YUG)	v	J.B. Fitzgerald and W. Masur 2/6 3/6	**M.J. Bates and R. Krishnan** 4/6 6/3 1/6	M.R. Edmondson and P. Fleming 2/6 2/6	0	3		

GROUP B					WINS	LOSSES	SEMI-FINAL	FINAL
G.W. Donnelly (USA) and D. Visser (RSA)	v	C. Dowdeswell and C.J. Mottram 6/7(5) 3/6	P.B. McNamara and P.F. McNamee 3/6 6/7(5)	H. Guenthardt and B. Taroczy 6/1 6/4	1	2		
C. Dowdeswell (GBR) and C.J. Mottram (GBR)	v	**G.W. Donnelly and D. Visser** 7/6(5) 6/3	H. Guenthardt and B. Taroczy 7/5 6/3	P.B. McNamara and P.F. McNamee 3/6 6/7(3)	2	1	P.B. McNamara and P.F. McNamee	P.B. McNamara and P.F. McNamee 6/7(1) 7/6(6) 6/3
H. Guenthardt (SUI) and B. Taroczy (HUN)	v	P.B. McNamara and P.F. McNamee 5/7 7/6(5) 3/6	C. Dowdeswell and C.J. Mottram 5/7 4/6	**G.W. Donnelly and D. Visser** 1/6 4/6	0	3		
P.B. McNamara (AUS) and P.F. McNamee (AUS)	v	H. Guenthardt and B. Taroczy 7/5 6/7(5) 6/3	**G.W. Donnelly and D. Visser** 6/3 7/6(5)	C. Dowdeswell and C.J. Mottram 6/3 7/6(3)	3	0		

GROUP C					WINS	LOSSES	SEMI-FINAL	FINAL
G. Mayer (USA) and T. Wilkison (USA)	v	P. Slozil and T. Smid 6/4 6/7(5) 7/5	P. Dupre and C.J. Van Rensburg 6/4 7/5	A. Jarryd and J. Nystrom 4/6 4/6	2	1		
P. Dupre (USA) and C.J. Van Rensburg (RSA)	v	A. Jarryd and J. Nystrom 3/6 3/6	**G. Mayer and T. Wilkison** 4/6 5/7	P. Slozil and T. Smid 4/6 6/7(5)	0	3	A. Jarryd and J. Nystrom	
A. Jarryd (SWE) and J. Nystrom (SWE)	v	P. Dupre and C.J. Van Rensburg 6/3 6/3	P. Slozil and T. Smid 6/1 6/3	**G. Mayer and T. Wilkison** 6/4 6/4	3	0		
P. Slozil (CZE) and T. Smid (CZE)	v	**G. Mayer and T. Wilkison** 4/6 7/6(5) 5/7	A. Jarryd and J. Nystrom 1/6 3/6	P. Dupre and C.J. Van Rensburg 6/4 7/6(5)	1	2		

GROUP D					WINS	LOSSES	SEMI-FINAL	FINAL
K. Curren (USA) and J. Kriek (USA)	v	M. Bahrami and H. Leconte 7/5 6/7(5) 10/8	J. Grabb and J. Pugh 4/6 4/6	K. Flach and R. Seguso 6/3 3/6 9/8(3)	2	1		
M. Bahrami (IRI) and H. Leconte (FRA)	v	**K. Curren and J. Kriek** 5/7 7/6(5) 8/10	K. Flach and R. Seguso 4/6 0/6	J. Grabb and J. Pugh 2/6 4/6	0	3	K. Flach and R. Seguso	
K. Flach (USA) and R. Seguso (USA)	v	J. Grabb and J. Pugh 7/6(4) 6/3	M. Bahrami and H. Leconte 6/4 6/0	**K. Curren and J. Kriek** 3/6 6/3 8/9(3)	2	1		
J. Grabb (USA) and J. Pugh (USA)	v	K. Flach and R. Seguso 6/7(4) 3/6	**K. Curren and J. Kriek** 6/4 6/4	M. Bahrami and H. Leconte 6/2 6/4	2	1		

This event will be played on a 'round robin' basis. 16 invited pairs have been divided into 4 groups and each pair in each group will play one another. The pairs winning most matches will be the winners of their respective groups and will play semi-final and final rounds as indicated above.
If matches should be equal in any group, the head to head result between the two pairs with the same number of wins, will determine the winning pair of the group.

Heavy type denotes seeded players. The matches will be the best of three sets. The tie-break will operate at six games all in the first two sets.

Event VII. The 45 And Over Gentlemen's Invitation Doubles 1999
Holders: M.C. Riessen and S.E. Stewart

The Winners will become the holders, for the year only, of a Cup presented by The All England Lawn Tennis and Croquet Club. The Winners will receive miniature Silver Salvers. A Silver Medal will be presented to each of the Runners-up. Details of Prize Money will be found on page 25.

First Round

1. **M.C.Riessen (USA) & S.E.Stewart (USA)** ....[1]
2. I.Nastase (ROM) & T.S.Okker (NED) .... → I.Nastase & T.S.Okker 7/6(8) 6/7(6) 6/1
3. J.G.Alexander (AUS) & R.Drysdale (GBR) ....
4. A.A.Mayer (USA) & R.Tanner (USA) .... → J.G.Alexander & R.Drysdale 6/4 7/5
5. **O.K.Davidson (AUS) & E.C.Drysdale (RSA)** ....[3]
6. R.L.Case (AUS) & G.Masters (AUS) .... → R.L.Case & G.Masters 6/3 6/1
7. R.J.Frawley (AUS) & A.Metreveli (RUS) ....
8. M.Cox (GBR) & M.Santana (ESP) .... → R.J.Frawley & A.Metreveli 6/2 6/4
9. J.D.Newcombe (AUS) & A.D.Roche (AUS) ....
10. F.D.McMillan (RSA) & A.Stone (AUS) .... → J.D.Newcombe & A.D.Roche 6/4 6/3
11. K.R.Rosewall (AUS) & F.S.Stolle (AUS) ....
12. **J.Fillol (CHI) & R.L.Stockton (USA)** ....[4] → J.Fillol & R.L.Stockton [4] 6/2 6/3
13. R.C.Lutz (USA) & S.R.Smith (USA) ....
14. J.W.Feaver (GBR) & R.Taylor (GBR) .... → R.C.Lutz & S.R.Smith 6/4 6/2
15. A.Amritraj (IND) & V.Amritraj (IND) ....
16. **B.E.Gottfried (USA) & T.R.Gullikson (USA)** .....[2] → B.E.Gottfried & T.R.Gullikson [2] 6/1 3/6 11/9

Second Round
- I.Nastase & T.S.Okker
- J.G.Alexander & R.Drysdale
- R.L.Case & G.Masters
- R.J.Frawley & A.Metreveli
- J.D.Newcombe & A.D.Roche
- J.Fillol & R.L.Stockton [4] 6/2 6/3
- R.C.Lutz & S.R.Smith 6/4 6/2
- B.E.Gottfried & T.R.Gullikson [2]

Semi-Finals
- I.Nastase & T.S.Okker 7/6(5) 7/5
- R.L.Case & G.Masters 6/2 6/2
- J.Fillol & R.L.Stockton [4] 6/3 6/4
- B.E.Gottfried & T.R.Gullikson [2] 6/3 6/4

Final
- R.L.Case & G.Masters 6/4 6/7(5) 6/3
- B.E.Gottfried & T.R.Gullikson [2] 6/2 4/6 6/4

68

Heavy type denotes seeded players. The figure in brackets against names denotes the order in which they have been seeded. The matches will be the best of three sets. The tie-break will operate at six games all in the first two sets.

EVENT VIII. – The 35 And Over Ladies' Invitation Doubles 1999
Holders: Miss P.H. Shriver and Miss P.D. Smylie

The Winners will become the holders, for the year only, of a Cup presented by The All England Lawn Tennis and Croquet Club. The Winners will receive miniature Cups.
A Silver Medal will be presented to each of the Runners-up. Details of Prize Money will be found on page 25.

GROUP A

				WINS	LOSSES	FINAL
Miss G. Fernandez (USA) and Miss Y. Vermaak (RSA) v	Mrs G. Magers and Miss B.F. Stove 3/6 6/3 5/7	Miss R. Casals and Miss A. Hobbs 6/1 1/6 5/7	Miss H. Mandlikova and Miss S.V. Wade 6/2 3/0 Ret'd	1	2	
Mrs G. Magers (USA) and Miss B.F. Stove (NED) v	**Miss G. Fernandez and Miss Y. Vermaak** 6/3 3/6 7/5	Miss H. Mandlikova and Miss S.V. Wade 6/1 6/1	Miss R. Casals and Miss A. Hobbs 6/4 7/5	3	0	Mrs G. Magers and Miss B.F. Stove
Miss R. Casals (USA) and Miss A. Hobbs (GBR) v	Miss H. Mandlikova and Miss S.V. Wade 7/5 6/4	**Miss G. Fernandez and Miss Y. Vermaak** 1/6 6/1 7/5	Mrs G. Magers and Miss B.F. Stove 4/6 5/7	2	1	
Miss H. Mandlikova (AUS) and Miss S.V. Wade (GBR) v	Miss R. Casals and Miss A. Hobbs 5/7 4/6	Mrs G. Magers and Miss B.F. Stove 1/6 1/6	**Miss G. Fernandez and Miss Y. Vermaak** 2/6 0/3 Ret'd	0	3	

GROUP B

				WINS	LOSSES	FINAL
Mrs P.D. Smylie (AUS) and Miss W.M. Turnbull (AUS) v	Miss B. Nagelsen and Mrs R. Nideffer 6/4 6/4	Miss J.M. Durie and Miss J.C. Russell 7/5 6/3	Miss M. Jausovec and Miss C. Kohde-Kilsch 6/2 6/3	3	0	
Miss B. Nagelsen (USA) and Mrs R. Nideffer (RSA) v	**Mrs P.D. Smylie and Miss W.M. Turnbull** 4/6 4/6	Miss M. Jausovec and Miss C. Kohde-Kilsch 6/3 4/6 6/4	Miss J.M. Durie and Miss J.C. Russell 2/6 6/7(5)	1	2	Mrs P.D. Smylie and Miss W.M. Turnbull
Miss J.M. Durie (GBR) and Miss J.C. Russell (USA) v	Miss M. Jausovec and Miss C. Kohde-Kilsch 7/6(3) 2/6 7/9	**Mrs P.D. Smylie and Miss W.M. Turnbull** 5/7 3/6	Miss B. Nagelsen and Mrs R. Nideffer 6/2 7/6(5)	1	2	
Miss M. Jausovec (SLO) and Miss C. Kohde-Kilsch (GER) v	Miss J.M. Durie and Miss J.C. Russell 6/7(3) 6/2 9/7	Miss B. Nagelsen and Mrs R. Nideffer 3/6 6/4 4/6	**Mrs P.D. Smylie and Miss W.M. Turnbull** 2/6 3/6	1	2	

ALPHABETICAL LIST – 35 & OVER EVENTS
GENTLEMEN

Bahrami M. *(Iran)*
Bates M.J. *(Great Britain)*
Curren K. *(USA)*
Donnelly G.W. *(USA)*
Dowdeswell C. *(Great Britain)*
Dupre P. *(USA)*
Edmondson M.R. *(Australia)*
Fitzgerald J.B. *(Australia)*

Flach K. *(USA)*
Fleming P. *(USA)*
Grabb J. *(USA)*
Guenthardt H. *(Switzerland)*
Jarryd A. *(Sweden)*
Kriek J. *(USA)*
Krishnan R. *(India)*
Leconte H. *(France)*

Masur W. *(Australia)*
Mayer G. *(USA)*
McNamara P.B. *(Australia)*
McNamee P.F. *(Australia)*
Mottram C.J. *(Great Britain)*
Nystrom J. *(Sweden)*
Pernfors M. *(Sweden)*
Pugh J. *(USA)*

Seguso R. *(USA)*
Slozil P. *(Czech Republic)*
Smid T. *(Czech Republic)*
Taroczy B. *(Hungary)*
Van Rensburg C.J. *(South Africa)*
Visser D. *(South Africa)*
Wilkison T. *(USA)*
Zivojinovic S. *(Yugoslavia)*

LADIES

Casals Miss R. *(USA)*
Durie Miss J.M. *(Great Britain)*
Fernandez Miss G. *(USA)*
Hobbs Miss A. *(Great Britain)*

Jausovec Miss M. *(Slovenia)*
Kohde-Kilsch Miss C. *(Germany)*
Magers Mrs G. *(USA)*
Mandlikova Miss H. *(Australia)*

Nagelsen Miss B. *(USA)*
Nideffer Mrs R. *(South Africa)*
Russell Miss J.C. *(USA)*
Smylie Mrs P.D. *(Australia)*

Stove Miss B.F. *(Netherlands)*
Turnbull Miss W.M. *(Australia)*
Vermaak Miss Y. *(South Africa)*
Wade Miss S.V. *(Great Britain)*

ALPHABETICAL LIST – 45 & OVER EVENT
GENTLEMEN

Alexander J.G. *(Australia)*
Amritraj A. *(India)*
Amritraj V. *(India)*
Case R.L. *(Australia)*
Cox M. *(Great Britain)*
Davidson O.K. *(Australia)*
Drysdale E.C. *(South Africa)*
Drysdale R. *(Great Britain)*

Feaver J.W. *(Great Britain)*
Fillol J. *(Chile)*
Frawley R.J. *(Australia)*
Gottfried B.E. *(USA)*
Gullikson T.R. *(USA)*
Hewitt R.A.J. *(South Africa)*
Lutz R.C. *(USA)*
Masters G. *(Australia)*

Mayer A.A. *(USA)*
McMillan F.D. *(South Africa)*
Metreveli A. *(Russia)*
Nastase I. *(Romania)*
Newcombe J.D. *(Australia)*
Okker T.S. *(Netherlands)*
Riessen M.C. *(USA)*
Roche A.D. *(Australia)*

Rosewall K.R. *(Australia)*
Santana M. *(Spain)*
Smith S.R. *(USA)*
Stewart S.E. *(USA)*
Stockton R.L. *(USA)*
Stolle F.S. *(Australia)*
Tanner R. *(USA)*
Taylor R. *(Great Britain)*

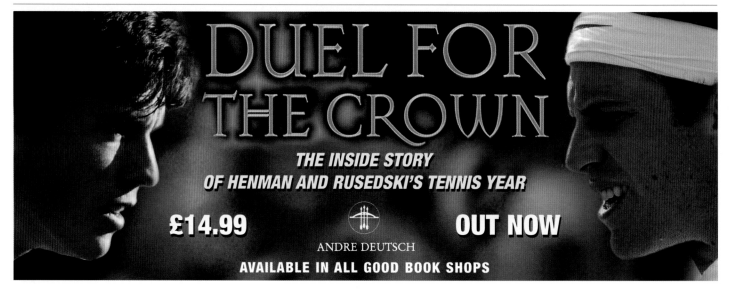

Event IX— The Boys' Singles Championship 1999

Holder: R. Federer

The Winner will become the holder, for the year only, of a Cup presented by The All England Lawn Tennis and Croquet Club.
The Winner will receive a miniature Cup and the Runner-up will receive a memento. The matches will be best of three sets.

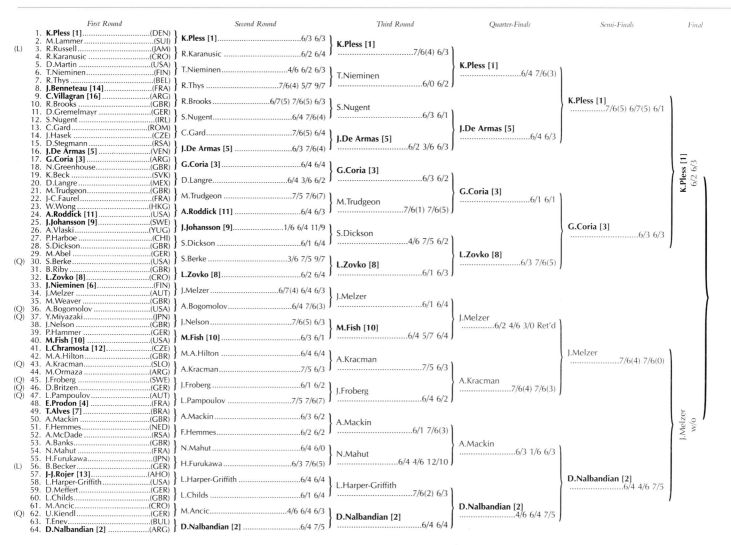

First Round	Second Round	Third Round	Quarter-Finals	Semi-Finals	Final
1. **K.Pless [1]** ....(DEN)	**K.Pless [1]** 6/3 6/3	**K.Pless [1]**			
2. M.Lammer ....(SUI)		........................7/6(4) 6/3			
(L) 3. R.Russell ....(JAM)	R.Karanusic 6/2 6/4		**K.Pless [1]**		
4. R.Karanusic ....(CRO)			...........6/4 7/6(3)		
5. D.Martin ....(USA)	T.Nieminen 4/6 6/2 6/3	T.Nieminen			
6. T.Nieminen ....(FIN)		..................6/0 6/2			
7. R.Thys ....(BEL)	R.Thys ....7/6(4) 5/7 9/7			**K.Pless [1]**	
8. J.Benneteau [14] ....(FRA)				.........7/6(5) 6/7(5) 6/1	
9. **C.Villagran [16]** ....(ARG)	R.Brooks ....6/7(5) 7/6(5) 6/3	S.Nugent			
10. R.Brooks ....(GBR)		..................6/3 6/1			
11. D.Gremelmayr ....(GER)	S.Nugent ....6/4 7/6(4)		**J.De Armas [5]**		
12. S.Nugent ....(IRL)			...........6/4 6/3		
13. C.Gard ....(ROM)	C.Gard ....7/6(5) 6/4	**J.De Armas [5]**			
14. J.Hasek ....(CZE)		..................6/2 3/6 6/3			
15. D.Stegmann ....(RSA)	**J.De Armas [5]** ....6/3 7/6(4)				**K.Pless [1]**
16. **J.De Armas [5]** ....(VEN)					6/2 6/3
17. **G.Coria [3]** ....(ARG)	**G.Coria [3]** 6/4 6/4	**G.Coria [3]**			
18. N.Greenhouse ....(GBR)		..................6/3 6/2			
19. K.Beck ....(SVK)	D.Langre 6/4 3/6 6/2		**G.Coria [3]**		
20. D.Langre ....(MEX)			...........6/1 6/1		
21. M.Trudgeon ....(GBR)	M.Trudgeon ....7/5 7/6(7)	M.Trudgeon			
22. J-C.Faurel ....(FRA)		..............7/6(1) 7/6(5)			
23. W.Wong ....(HKG)	**A.Roddick [11]** 6/4 6/3			**G.Coria [3]**	
24. **A.Roddick [11]** ....(USA)				.........6/3 6/3	
25. **J.Johansson [9]** ....(SWE)	J.Johansson [9] 1/6 6/4 11/9	S.Dickson			
26. A.Vlaski ....(YUG)		..............4/6 7/5 6/2			
27. P.Harboe ....(CHI)	S.Dickson 6/1 6/4		**L.Zovko [8]**		
28. S.Dickson ....(GBR)			...........6/3 7/6(5)		
29. M.Abel ....(GER)	S.Berke 3/6 7/5 9/7	**L.Zovko [8]**			
(Q) 30. S.Berke ....(USA)		..................6/1 6/3			
31. B.Riby ....(GBR)	**L.Zovko [8]** 6/2 6/4				
32. **L.Zovko [8]** ....(CRO)					
33. **J.Nieminen [6]** ....(FIN)	J.Melzer ....6/7(4) 6/4 6/3	J.Melzer			
34. J.Melzer ....(AUT)		..................6/1 6/4			
35. M.Weaver ....(GBR)	A.Bogomolov ....6/4 7/6(3)		J.Melzer		
(Q) 36. A.Bogomolov ....(USA)			......6/2 4/6 3/0 Ret'd		
(Q) 37. Y.Miyazaki ....(JPN)	J.Nelson ....7/6(5) 6/3	**M.Fish [10]**			
38. J.Nelson ....(GBR)		..................6/4 5/7 6/4			
39. P.Hammer ....(GER)	**M.Fish [10]** 6/3 6/1			J.Melzer	
40. **M.Fish [10]** ....(USA)				.........7/6(4) 7/6(0)	
41. **L.Chramosta [12]** ....(CZE)	M.A.Hilton 6/4 6/4	A.Kracman			
42. M.A.Hilton ....(GBR)		..................7/5 6/3			
(Q) 43. A.Kracman ....(SLO)	A.Kracman 7/5 6/3		A.Kracman		
44. M.Ormaza ....(ARG)			...........7/6(4) 7/6(3)		
(Q) 45. J.Froberg ....(SWE)	J.Froberg 6/1 6/2	J.Froberg			
(Q) 46. D.Britzen ....(GER)		..................6/4 6/2			
(Q) 47. L.Pampoulov ....(AUT)	L.Pampoulov ....7/5 7/6(7)			J.Melzer	
48. **E.Prodon [4]** ....(FRA)				w/o	
49. **T.Alves [7]** ....(BRA)	A.Mackin 6/3 6/2	A.Mackin			
50. A.Mackin ....(GBR)		..................6/1 7/6(3)			
51. F.Hemmes ....(NED)	F.Hemmes 6/2 6/2		A.Mackin		
52. A.McDade ....(RSA)			...........6/3 1/6 6/3		
53. A.Banks ....(GBR)	N.Mahut 6/4 6/0	N.Mahut			
54. N.Mahut ....(FRA)		..............6/4 4/6 12/10			
55. H.Furukawa ....(JPN)	H.Furukawa ....6/3 7/6(5)				
(L) 56. B.Becker ....(GER)					
57. **J-J.Rojer [13]** ....(AHO)	L.Harper-Griffith 6/4 6/4	L.Harper-Griffith			
58. L.Harper-Griffith ....(USA)		..................7/6(2) 6/3			
59. D.Meffert ....(GER)	L.Childs 6/1 6/4		**D.Nalbandian [2]**		
60. L.Childs ....(GBR)			...........4/6 6/4 7/5		
61. M.Ancic ....(CRO)	M.Ancic 4/6 6/4 6/3	**D.Nalbandian [2]**			
(Q) 62. U.Kiendl ....(GER)		..................6/4 6/4			
63. T.Enev ....(BUL)	**D.Nalbandian [2]** 6/4 7/5				
64. **D.Nalbandian [2]** ....(ARG)					

Heavy type denotes seeded players. The figure in brackets against names denotes the order in which they have been seeded. The Committee reserves the right to alter the seeding order in the event of withdrawls. (W) = Wild card. (Q) = Qualifier. (L) = Lucky loser. For particulars of Abbreviations, see page 54.

Event X— The Boys' Doubles Championship 1999

Holders: R. Federer and O. Rochus

The Winners will become the holders, for the year only, of a Cup presented by The All England Lawn Tennis and Croquet Club.
The Winners will receive miniature Cups and the Runners-up will receive mementoes. The matches will be best of three sets.

First Round	Second Round	Quarter-Finals	Semi-Finals	Final
1. **G.Coria (ARG) & D.Nalbandian (ARG)** ....[1]	**G.Coria & D.Nalbandian [1]** ....7/5 7/6(4)	G.Coria & D.Nalbandian [1]		
2. J.Gray (GBR) & T.Higgins (GBR)				
3. A.Mackin (GBR) & M.Trudgeon (GBR)	A.Mackin & M.Trudgeon 6/2 6/1		G.Coria & D.Nalbandian [1]	
4. T.Alves (BRA) & T.Nieminen (FIN)			...........6/3 6/4	
5. L.Harper-Griffith (USA) & A.Roddick (USA)	L.Harper-Griffith & A.Roddick ....7/6(2) 6/3	L.Childs & S.Dickson [5]		
6. C.Gard (ROM) & R.Karanusic (CRO)				
7. R.Brooks (GBR) & N.Greenhouse (GBR)	**L.Childs & S.Dickson [5]** 6/4 6/3			
8. **L.Childs (GBR) & S.Dickson (GBR)** ....[5]				
9. **J.Benneteau (FRA) & N.Mahut (FRA)** ....[4]	**J.Benneteau & N.Mahut [4]** 6/0 4/6 10/8	J.Benneteau & N.Mahut [4]		
10. M.Ormaza (ARG) & C.Villagran (ARG)				
11. A.Banks (GBR) & B.Riby (GBR)	A.Banks & B.Riby ....7/6(4) 6/4		M.A.Hilton & J.Nelson	
12. A.Vlaski (YUG) & B.Weir-Smith (RSA)			...........6/1 6/3	
13. M.A.Hilton (GBR) & J.Nelson (GBR)	M.A.Hilton & J.Nelson ....7/6(8) 6/3	M.A.Hilton & J.Nelson		
14. R.Russell (JAM) & W.Wong (HKG)				
15. T.Davis (USA) & A.Francis (USA)	**J.Johansson & L.Zovko [6]** ....7/6(4) 6/4			M.A.Hilton & J.Nelson
16. **J.Johansson (SWE) & L.Zovko (CRO)** ....[6]				..................7/6(5) 3/6 6/1
17. **L.Chramosta (CZE) & J.Hasek (CZE)** ....[7]	**L.Chramosta & J.Hasek [7]** ....6/7(4) 6/4 6/2	T.Enev & J.Nieminen		
18. F.Hemmes (NED) & L.Pampoulov (AUT)				
19. M.Lammer (SUI) & R.Thys (BEL)	T.Enev & J.Nieminen 6/3 6/1		T.Enev & J.Nieminen	
20. T.Enev (BUL) & J.Nieminen (FIN)			...........6/4 6/2	
21. A.Anderson (RSA) & D.Stegmann (RSA)	A.Anderson & D.Stegmann 6/4 6/4	J.Melzer & K.Pless [3]		
22. R.Green (USA) & M.Weaver (GBR)				
23. S.Berke (USA) & D.Britzen (GER)	**J.Melzer & K.Pless [3]** 6/3 6/4			T.Enev & J.Nieminen
24. **J.Melzer (AUT) & K.Pless (DEN)** ....[3]				..................7/6(4) 7/6(4)
25. **D.Martin (USA) & J-J.Rojer (AHO)** ....[8]	**D.Martin & J-J.Rojer [8]** ....7/6(4) 6/2	D.Martin & J-J.Rojer [8]		
26. K.Beck (SVK) & S.Nugent (IRL)				
27. M.Ancic (CRO) & A.Kracman (SLO)	H.Furukawa & Y.Miyazaki 4/6 6/3 6/4		J.De Armas & D.Langre [2]	
28. H.Furukawa (JPN) & Y.Miyazaki (JPN)			...........6/1 7/5	
29. J-C.Faurel (FRA) & E.Prodon (FRA)	A.Bogomolov & J-P.Fruttero 3/6 6/1 6/1	J.De Armas & D.Langre [2]		
30. A.Bogomolov (USA) & J-P.Fruttero (USA)				
31. P.Harboe (CHI) & A.McDade (RSA)	**J.De Armas & D.Langre [2]** 6/4 6/3			
32. **J.De Armas (VEN) & D.Langre (MEX)** ....[2]				

Heavy type denotes seeded players. The figure in brackets against names denotes the order in which they have been seeded. The Committee reserves the right to alter the seeding order in the event of withdrawls. For particulars of Abbreviations, see page 54.

Event XI— The Girls' Singles Championship 1999

Holder: Miss K. Srebotnik

The Winner will become the holder, for the year only, of a Cup presented by The All England Lawn Tennis and Croquet Club.
The Winner will receive a miniature Cup and the Runner-up will receive a memento. The matches will be best of three sets.

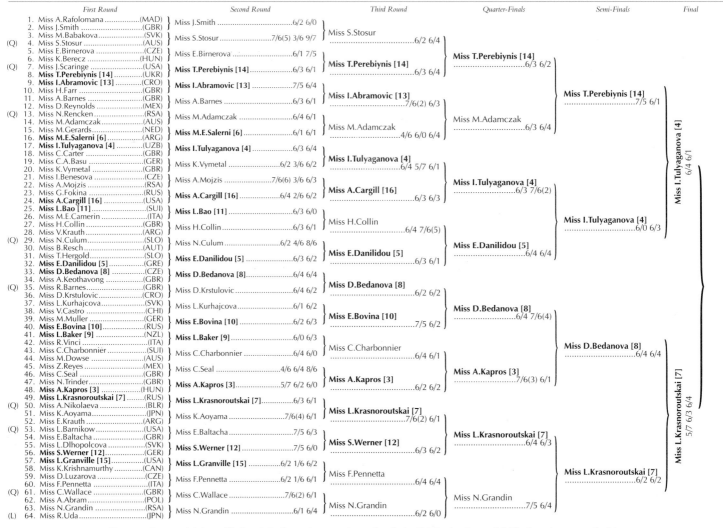

First Round	Second Round	Third Round	Quarter-Finals	Semi-Finals	Final
1. Miss A.Rafolomana ....(MAD)	Miss J.Smith 6/2 6/0				
2. Miss J.Smith ....(GBR)		Miss S.Stosur			
3. Miss M.Babakova................(SVK)	Miss S.Stosur ....7/6(5) 3/6 9/7	.................6/2 6/4			
(Q) 4. Miss S.Stosur ....(AUS)			Miss T.Perebiynis [14]		
5. Miss E.Birnerova................(CZE)	Miss E.Birnerova 6/1 7/5		.................6/3 6/2		
6. Miss K.Berecz ....(HUN)		Miss T.Perebiynis [14]			
(Q) 7. Miss J.Scaringe ....(USA)	Miss T.Perebiynis [14] 6/3 6/1	...............6/3 6/4			
8. Miss T.Perebiynis [14] ....(UKR)				Miss T.Perebiynis [14]	
9. Miss I.Abramovic [13] ....(CRO)	Miss I.Abramovic [13] 7/5 6/4			.................7/5 6/1	
10. Miss H.Farr ....(GBR)		Miss I.Abramovic [13]			
11. Miss A.Barnes ....(GBR)	Miss A.Barnes 6/3 6/1	............7/6(2) 6/3			
12. Miss D.Reynolds ....(MEX)			Miss M.Adamczak		
(Q) 13. Miss N.Rencken ....(RSA)	Miss M.Adamczak 6/4 6/1		...............6/3 6/4		
14. Miss M.Adamczak ....(AUS)		Miss M.Adamczak			
15. Miss M.Gerards ....(NED)	Miss M.E.Salerni [6] 6/1 6/1	...........4/6 6/0 6/4			
16. Miss M.E.Salerni [6] ....(ARG)					Miss I.Tulyaganova [4]
17. Miss I.Tulyaganova [4] ....(UZB)	Miss I.Tulyaganova [4] 6/3 6/4				6/4 6/1
18. Miss C.Carter ....(GBR)		Miss I.Tulyaganova [4]			
19. Miss C.A.Basu ....(GER)	Miss K.Vymetal 6/2 3/6 6/2	...........6/4 5/7 6/1			
20. Miss K.Vymetal ....(GBR)			Miss I.Tulyaganova [4]		
21. Miss I.Benesova ....(CZE)	Miss A.Mojzis ....7/6(6) 3/6 6/3		.............6/3 7/6(2)		
22. Miss A.Mojzis ....(RSA)		Miss A.Cargill [16]			
23. Miss G.Fokina ....(RUS)	Miss A.Cargill [16] 6/4 2/6 6/2	...............6/3 6/3			
24. Miss A.Cargill [16] ....(USA)				Miss I.Tulyaganova [4]	
25. Miss L.Bao [11] ....(SUI)	Miss L.Bao 6/3 6/0			.................6/0 6/3	
26. Miss M.E.Camerin ....(ITA)		Miss H.Collin			
27. Miss H.Collin ....(GBR)	Miss H.Collin 6/3 6/1	............6/4 7/6(5)			
28. Miss V.Krauth ....(ARG)			Miss E.Danilidou [5]		
(Q) 29. Miss N.Culum ....(SLO)	Miss N.Culum 6/2 4/6 8/6		...............6/4 6/4		
30. Miss B.Resch ....(AUT)		Miss E.Danilidou [5]			
31. Miss T.Hergold ....(SLO)	Miss E.Danilidou [5] 6/3 6/2	...............6/3 6/1			
32. Miss E.Danilidou [5] ....(GRE)					
33. Miss D.Bedanova [8] ....(CZE)	Miss D.Bedanova [8] 6/4 6/4				
34. Miss A.Keothavong ....(GBR)		Miss D.Bedanova [8]			
(Q) 35. Miss R.Barnes ....(GBR)	Miss D.Krstulovic 6/4 6/2	...............6/2 6/2			
36. Miss D.Krstulovic ....(CRO)			Miss D.Bedanova [8]		
37. Miss L.Kurhajcova ....(SVK)	Miss L.Kurhajcova 6/1 6/2		.............6/4 7/6(4)		
38. Miss V.Castro ....(CHI)		Miss E.Bovina [10]			
39. Miss M.Muller ....(GER)	Miss E.Bovina [10] 6/2 6/3	...............7/5 6/2			
40. Miss E.Bovina [10] ....(RUS)				Miss D.Bedanova [8]	
41. Miss L.Baker [9] ....(NZL)	Miss L.Baker [9] 6/0 6/3			.................6/4 6/4	
42. Miss R.Vinci ....(ITA)		Miss C.Charbonnier			
43. Miss C.Charbonnier ....(SUI)	Miss C.Charbonnier 6/4 6/0	...............6/4 6/1			
44. Miss M.Dowse ....(AUS)			Miss A.Kapros [3]		
45. Miss Z.Reyes ....(MEX)	Miss C.Seal 4/6 6/4 8/6		.............7/6(3) 6/1		
46. Miss C.Seal ....(GBR)		Miss A.Kapros [3]			
47. Miss N.Trinder ....(GBR)	Miss A.Kapros [3] 5/7 6/2 6/0	...............6/2 6/2			
48. Miss A.Kapros [3] ....(HUN)					Miss L.Krasnoroutskai [7]
49. Miss L.Krasnoroutskai [7] ....(RUS)	Miss L.Krasnoroutskai [7] 6/3 6/1				5/7 6/3 6/4
(Q) 50. Miss A.Nikolaeva ....(BLR)		Miss L.Krasnoroutskai [7]			
51. Miss K.Aoyama ....(JPN)	Miss K.Aoyama ....7/6(4) 6/1	............7/6(2) 6/1			
52. Miss E.Krauth ....(ARG)			Miss L.Krasnoroutskai [7]		
(Q) 53. Miss L.Barnikow ....(USA)	Miss E.Baltacha 7/5 6/3		.................6/4 6/3		
54. Miss E.Baltacha ....(GBR)		Miss S.Werner [12]			
55. Miss L.Dlhopolcova ....(SVK)	Miss S.Werner [12] 7/5 6/0	...............6/3 6/2			
56. Miss S.Werner [12] ....(GER)				Miss L.Krasnoroutskai [7]	
57. Miss L.Granville [15] ....(USA)	Miss L.Granville [15] 6/2 1/6 6/2			.................6/2 6/2	
58. Miss K.Krishnamurthy ....(CAN)		Miss F.Pennetta			
59. Miss D.Luzarova ....(CZE)	Miss F.Pennetta 6/2 1/6 6/1	...............6/4 6/4			
60. Miss F.Pennetta ....(ITA)			Miss N.Grandin		
(Q) 61. Miss C.Wallace ....(GBR)	Miss C.Wallace ....7/6(2) 6/1		...............7/5 6/4		
62. Miss A.Abram ....(POL)		Miss N.Grandin			
63. Miss N.Grandin ....(RSA)	Miss N.Grandin 6/1 6/4	...............6/2 6/0			
(L) 64. Miss R.Uda ....(JPN)					

Heavy type denotes seeded players. The figure in brackets against names denotes the order in which they have been seeded. The Committee reserves the right to alter the seeding order in the event of withdrawls. (W) = Wild card. (Q) = Qualifier. (L) = Lucky loser. For particulars of Abbreviations, see page 54.

Event XII— The Girls' Doubles Championship 1999

Holders: Miss E. Dyrberg and Miss J. Kostanic

The Winners will become the holders, for the year only, of a Cup presented by The All England Lawn Tennis and Croquet Club.
The Winners will receive miniature Cups and the Runners-up will receive mementoes. The matches will be best of three sets.

First Round	Second Round	Quarter-Finals	Semi-Finals	Final
1. Miss F.Pennetta (ITA) & Miss R.Vinci (ITA) ....[1]	Miss F.Pennetta & Miss R.Vinci [1]	Miss F.Pennetta & Miss R.Vinci [1]		
2. bye		.................2/6 6/2 6/4		
3. Miss M.Adamczak (AUS) & Miss M.Dowse (AUS)	Miss M.Adamczak & Miss M.Dowse 6/3 6/1			
4. Miss E.Baltacha (GBR) & Miss C.Seal (GBR)		Miss G.Fokina & Miss L.Krasnoroutskai		
5. Miss R.Barnes (GBR) & Miss A.Keothavong (GBR)	Miss G.Fokina & Miss L.Krasnoroutskai 6/0 6/2			
6. Miss G.Fokina (RUS) & Miss L.Krasnoroutskai (RUS) ...		.................6/4 6/3		
7. Miss A.Hawkins (GBR) & Miss E.Webley-Smith (GBR) ...	Miss N.Culum & Miss S.Stone [8] 6/4 6/1			
8. Miss N.Culum (SLO) & Miss S.Stone (SLO) ....[8]			Miss L.Baker & Miss K.Berecz	
9. Miss E.Krauth (ARG) & Miss V.Krauth (ARG) ....[3]	Miss E.Krauth & Miss V.Krauth [3] 4/6 6/3 6/2	Miss L.Baker & Miss K.Berecz		
10. Miss I.Benesova (CZE) & Miss E.Birnerova (CZE)			.................7/6(3) 6/0	
11. Miss L.Baker (NZL) & Miss K.Berecz (HUN)	Miss L.Baker & Miss K.Berecz 6/0 6/2			
12. Miss H.Farr (GBR) & Miss S.Gregg (GBR)		.................7/6(3) 6/0		
13. Miss K.Krishnamurthy (CAN) & Miss D.Reynolds (MEX)	Miss L.Bao & Miss C.Charbonnier 6/1 6/3	Miss T.Perebiynis & Miss I.Tulyaganova [7]		
14. Miss L.Bao (SUI) & Miss C.Charbonnier (SUI)				
15. Miss J.Smith (GBR) & Miss K.Vymetal (GBR)	Miss T.Perebiynis & Miss I.Tulyaganova [7] 4/6 6/1 8/6	.................6/1 4/6 6/2		
16. Miss T.Perebiynis (UKR) & Miss I.Tulyaganova (UZB) [7]			Miss A.Cargill & Miss L.Granville [6]	
17. Miss A.Cargill (USA) & Miss L.Granville (USA) ....[6]	Miss A.Cargill & Miss L.Granville [6] 7/5 6/4	Miss A.Cargill & Miss L.Granville [6]		
18. Miss L.Dlhopolcova (SVK) & Miss L.Kurhajcova (SVK)			.................7/6(5) 6/2	
19. Miss M.Babakova (SVK) & Miss V.Castro (CHI)	Miss M.Babakova & Miss V.Castro 6/3 6/4			Miss A.Cargill & Miss L.Granville [6]
20. Miss L.Barnikow (USA) & Miss J.Scaringe (USA)		.................6/2 6/3		.................6/2 6/1
21. Miss E.Bovina (RUS) & Miss M.Gerards (NED)	Miss E.Bovina & Miss M.Gerards 6/2 6/4	Miss E.Bovina & Miss M.Gerards		
22. Miss C.Wallace (GBR) & Miss L.Wood (GBR)				
23. Miss A.Abram (POL) & Miss B.Resch (AUT)	Miss A.Kapros & Miss A.Mojzis [4] ....w/o			
24. Miss A.Kapros (HUN) & Miss A.Mojzis (RSA) ....[4]			Miss N.Grandin & Miss N.Rencken [5]	
25. Miss N.Grandin (RSA) & Miss N.Rencken (RSA) ......[5]	Miss N.Grandin & Miss N.Rencken [5] 6/4 6/2	Miss N.Grandin & Miss N.Rencken [5]		
26. Miss D.Luzarova (CZE) & Miss S.Stosur (AUS)			.................6/2 6/1	
27. Miss A.Rafolomana (MAD) & Miss Z.Reyes (MEX)	Miss A.Barnes & Miss N.Trinder ....6/7(1) 6/4 6/3			
28. Miss A.Barnes (GBR) & Miss N.Trinder (GBR)		.................6/2 6/1		
29. Miss K.Aoyama (JPN) & Miss R.Uda (JPN)	Miss K.Aoyama & Miss R.Uda 6/3 3/6 6/3	Miss D.Bedanova & Miss M.E.Salerni [2]		
30. Miss I.Abramovic (CRO) & Miss D.Krstulovic (CRO)				
31. Miss H.Collin (GBR) & Miss T.Hergold (SLO)	Miss D.Bedanova & Miss M.E.Salerni [2] ...7/6(8) 6/7(1) 6/3	.................6/3 6/1		
32. Miss D.Bedanova (CZE) & Miss M.E.Salerni (ARG) .[2]				

Heavy type denotes seeded players. The figure in brackets against names denotes the order in which they have been seeded. The Committee reserves the right to alter the seeding order in the event of withdrawls. For particulars of Abbreviations, see page 54.

Quiz Answers

1. Chris Wilkinson
2. Dally Randriantefy
3. Steffi Graf (1988) and Conchita Martinez (1994)
4. Henry Billington
5. Susan Mascarin in 1984
6. Jo Durie, 1984
7. New Zealander
8. Martin Lee and James Trotman
9. Majorca
10. 1980

Arthur Roberts, without question the most successful coach this country has produced, stood outside his beloved courts at the Palace Hotel, Torquay, and puffing his ancient pipe told me: "If she gets a job behind the counter at Woolworth's she will finish as sales manager. Whatever she does in life she will get to the top." He was talking about Sue Barker.

She was then a blonde bubbly 13-year-old who may have had childish dreams of playing at Wimbledon, but her immediate ambition was to be considered good enough by "Mr Roberts", a man whom she both feared and adored, to hang her racket in the locker once used by Angela Mortimer.

By the 1970s Sue Barker was the pin-up of British tennis, with a forehand as good as Steffi Graf's. She was a member of the winning British Wightman Cup team in 1974, 1975 and 1978. In 1976 she won the French and German Opens, and in 1977 reached the final of the Virginia Slims World Championship at Madison Square Garden. Her highest ranking was World No.4.

Now as a BBC television presenter she seems to glide

Sue begins her Wimbledon at nine in the morning taking her three Rottweilers, Coco, Pebbles and Barney ("I feel pretty safe with them") along the lanes or around her own land. Then as calmly as if she were making out her shopping list she spends twenty minutes or so in the garden swing-seat browsing over the day's order of play.

On air Barker has the gift of making everything look easy, but if there were a crisis on camera she would not panic, as she proved when her resilience was put to an horrific test in 1980 and she survived a nightmare which could have left her blind or scarred. It happened while she was on holiday with her mother and aunt in Spain, and she tells the story as calmly as if she were reading a bedtime book about Pooh Bear losing his honey pot.

"Everyone was having drinks so I offered to do the washing up. The tea towels were in the laundry room, inside was a dog. I love dogs and when he growled I told him not to be silly and bent down to make a fuss of him. He lunged at my face and had two goes at it. Blood was everywhere, but mainly from my eye. They rushed me to a

To the Top—

through the pressures of live broadcasting with all the natural ease of a dolphin at play in a calm sea.

Unlike most of us at Wimbledon who feel when we hear a great roar from some distant court that we are in the wrong place, Sue Barker never goes to any court. Instead, from the moment the first ball is struck at noon until the last point in the evening gloom, she sits in the sophisticated Wimbledon Broadcasting Centre facing a bank of television screens so that she does not miss any dramatic moment that might be the big story of the day, and also keeps in touch for any interviews she may have to do. When that is all over, often with less than an hour to spare, and without the luxury of an autocue, she presents her "Today at Wimbledon" round-up. On a good day she arrives home around midnight.

Home with her husband Lance Tankard is a 16th century farmhouse hidden in the heartland of the Surrey countryside. It's their fifth move in ten years, and this time they plan to stay put. They have 25 acres of land, a tennis court, as yet unused, and an ancient barn in which there is a snooker table, a massive television set and a selection of sofas for sprawling. "We call it our play-pen."

small local hospital; there were flies everywhere and I watched them sew on a man's ear. Mum was in such a state that the doctors had to see her first. (laugh)

"They gave me twenty-five stitches but the wound was so close to my eye they could not give me an anaesthetic. It was agony. I was blind for twenty-four hours, but one of the worst parts was when they told me that I could not leave Spain for ten days while the dog was tested for rabies." (no laugh).

With the relentless pressure of computer ranking points at stake Sue Barker was back in action as soon as the doctors gave her the go-ahead, but by the time the 1985 Australian Open came around she had slumped from 16 to 63 on the world list.

A series of leg injuries were now affecting her game, for like so many professionals she had pushed her body too hard and too far.

In her heart she probably knew she was chasing tennis rainbows; what she didn't know was that her early defeat would bring her a pot of gold. "When I was badly beaten I announced my retirement and everyone wanted to talk to me, and I did loads of interviews; they must have lasted a couple of hours. When I got back to the hotel there was a message to 'phone Channel 7. My first reaction was "Oh no! Not another" but I knew that I'd better do the polite thing and return the call. When I did, there was this guy, his name was Gordon Bennett (I thought it was a joke at first), offering me a job as a tennis commentator on Australian TV. I had only been out of work for two and a half hours!"

Three years later Sky Television, making big inroads into sports coverage, picked her up. Good looking, quick-witted and camera-comfortable she was soon headhunted by the BBC. For Barker it was "a dream come true". Soon there was a place on Grandstand, the BBC's sporting flagship with the irrepressible Des Lynam at the helm, and there followed the quizmaster's chair in "Question of Sport"—a great success.

She has covered the Olympic Games—Winter and Summer—World Figure Skating Championships, with an abundance of ghastly names to master, and is just as much at home with the All Blacks rugby team as she is in the

Twice

LAURIE PIGNON

elegant surrounds of Longchamps. Such is her gregarious nature that very soon her "subjects" become her friends.

At Wimbledon Miss Barker admits that she is both lucky and privileged to be a member of the BBC team which is streets ahead of all its international rivals. Fronted by the imperturbable Lynam it includes David Mercer (the regular tennis correspondent), John Barrett—the new Dan Maskell—Mark Cox, Bill Threlfall and the ubiquitous Barry Davies. The back-up squad includes such players as Chris Bailey, Pat Cash, Jo Durie, Pam Shriver, Virginia Wade and Ann Jones.

Working for overseas channels there is an array of former stars including Chris Evert, Martina Navratilova, Billie Jean King, Wendy Turnbull, John McEnroe, Fred Stolle, Cliff Drysdale and Boris Becker.

Sue Barker has no time to socialise with any of them over lunch… she has a take-away in her studio.

Pity Arthur Roberts is no longer around to light his pipe and switch on his television, for his golden girl has reached the top twice.

Double the Pleasure

BARRY WOOD

THERE IS AN ENIGMA IN THE TENNIS WORLD. IN MOST CLUBS AROUND THE COUNTRY, THE GAME OF CHOICE IS doubles. It's more sociable, with couples being able to play together—which of course does have its hazards, as a few ill-chosen comments could result in no dinner that evening!

The game of doubles can also be immensely entertaining to watch, because of the pace of play and lightning quick reflexes. But most doubles matches are played at the end of the day, and at indoor tournaments that can mean still being on court past midnight and playing in front of just a coach and a few friends or family members.

The reason for doubles being relegated to the role of a supporting cast is that singles matches will always take priority because that is where the money and attention is. If a player is involved in singles and doubles, common in the women's game, then doubles must wait until the singles has been played first.

Which means many people have often missed some terrific tennis from an elite handful of teams who have gone down in the history books for their astonishing achievements.

The most successful team of modern times was the combination of Martina Navratilova and Pam Shriver, who claimed an impressive 79 titles together, including 20 Grand Slams. Only one other team in history has matched their Grand Slam record, with Louise Brough and Margaret Osborne duPont winning 12 US Opens, five Wimbledons and 3 French Opens between 1942 and 1957.

Competition was less fierce in those distant days, of course, although that was tempered by the more difficult life-style they had to endure. Back in the 40's and 50's, and indeed until quite recently, tennis players were not treated as celebrities with people falling over themselves to fall at their feet. And they didn't jet around the world all the time. Travel was extremely challenging and time-consuming.

Although Martina and Pam could enjoy the trappings of stardom and travelled in luxury, the competition was tough. All the more remarkable, then, that they managed to dominate the doubles game for so long during their 10-year partnership.

Their first title came in Chicago in February 1981, where they defeated Barbara Potter and Sharon Walsh, and their last came at the US Hardcourt Championships in April 1992 against Patty Fendick and Andrea Strnadova, now Mrs Jason Stoltenberg. In between, they established several records that will surely never be broken.

Between April 1983 and July 1985, they remained undefeated for 109 matches, a winning streak that was eventually ended in the Wimbledon final by Kathy Jordan and Elizabeth Smylie. They won a calendar year Grand Slam in 1984, and in a run stretching from Wimbledon 1983 to the French Open 1985, they won eight consecutive Grand Slams which also included another two non-calendar year Grand Slams.

In total they won seven Australian Opens, five Wimbledons, and four titles at both the French and US Opens. Their accomplishments brought them more than $2 million in combined prize money, and also earned them the title of Doubles Team of the Year for a remarkable eight consecutive years.

There's an interesting story about Pam and Martina, by the way. They were playing each other in singles in Washington one year, and Navratilova was dominating as usual. In fact, Shriver was being humiliated, so she went over and changed the scoreboard to show that she, instead of Navratilova, was winning. Then she sat down on the court and went 'on strike'. "Play on", ordered the umpire. "I don't want to," Shriver wailed, before eventually continuing along the road to an inevitable defeat. A much better reaction than throwing her racket in anger and frustration.

Martina Navratilova and Pam Shriver lift the Ladies' Doubles Trophy in 1984

As that partnership dissolved, another highly successful team evolved, with Gigi Fernandez and Natasha Zvereva combining to earn a total of 14 Grand Slam titles composed of five French Opens, four wins at Wimbledon and three at the US Open, and two Australian victories. They also put together an impressive Grand Slam run, remaining undefeated for six events running from the 1992 French Open through to and including Wimbledon 1993.

To find any other team that even came close to matching these modern day heroines, we have to go back to Thelma Coyne (Long) and Nancye Wynne (Bolton), who won 10 Australian Open titles between 1936 and 1952.

Last year, Martina Hingis established an individual record by winning a doubles Grand Slam, with Mirjana Lucic at the Australian Open (and they still had to qualify in Tokyo the following week!), and with Jana Novotna at the French Open, Wimbledon and the US Open. She was only the fourth player ever to win a women's doubles Grand Slam, along with Maria Bueno in 1960, and Shriver and Navratilova in 1984.

In 1996, Hingis had already become the youngest player ever to win an 'adult' title at Wimbledon when she partnered Helena Sukova to the title, breaking by three days the record set in 1887 when Lottie Dod won the singles. By winning the 1998 Australian Open doubles title, by the way, Lucic became the first player to win her debut tournaments in both singles and doubles.

Last year, also, Zvereva, with partner Lindsay Davenport, also established a place in the history books but probably wished they had not, as they contested all four Grand Slam finals but failed to win any of them.

Battle of the Generations

BIOGRAPHIES OF THIS YEAR'S LEADING LADIES

DAVID MERCER *BBC TV*

'T*he beauty of the Women's Tour is that it has both elements, youth and experience.' So said three times Wimbledon champion Chris Evert last year, and how right she was. The battle of the generations is one of the factors that has led to a dramatic revival in the fortunes of the women's game, with record attendances at tournaments, greatly increased television ratings and unprecedented media interest.*

Last year's Ladies' Championship was a triumph for experience as Jana Novotna at last achieved the Grand Slam title that her talent had long deserved. This year the teenagers, led by a resurgent Martina Hingis, will be out for revenge.

Jana Novotna

CZECH REPUBLIC

30; 5'9"; 139lb; RH; Champion 1998, F 93, 97, SF 95, QF 90, 94, 96

Providing she has recovered from the ankle injury she suffered at the French Open, Jana can expect a rapturous reception when she begins the defence of her title on the second day of this year's Championships. There have been few more popular winners than the Czech, who seemed destined to be the perpetual bridesmaid at the All England Lawn Tennis Club until she overcame Nathalie Tauziat in last year's final. It was an emotional moment for all of us who have followed the long career of one of the most naturally gifted and complete players in the women's game. Her all-court style of play should have brought her the game's greatest prize in 1993, but just when she seemed certain to defeat Steffi Graf in the final, nerves set in and Jana's subsequent sobbing on the shoulder of the Duchess of Kent entered sporting folklore. In 1997 she again looked set for victory against Martina Hingis, only to be denied by a combination of a stomach muscle problem and the superb ability of the "Swiss Miss" to adjust her tactics to the demands of any situation. Last year though Jana finally claimed her first Grand Slam title. As she said afterwards: "It was a big thing for me and I can see from the comments from so many people the match was a big thing for them as well. I'm glad I not only did it for myself, but also for everyone rooting and cheering for me." There will be plenty of people rooting for her again this year, and with her reputation as a "choker" laid to rest there is no reason why Jana should not make a successful defence of her title.

79

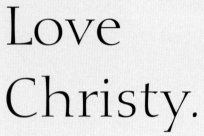

Love Christy.

Be onto a winner for Wimbledon 1999.

Christy's collection of Championship towels*

feature the stylish check design and

tournament logo.

Available in traditional green and purple and

the new aquamarine and geranium

colourways, you'll be sporting a new look

in your bathroom, in the gym and of course

on the tennis court.

*Available for a limited period only.

Christy bathroom towels. Every body deserves a little luxury

The Christy tournament collection is available from the Wimbledon shop.

Lindsay Davenport

USA

23; 6'2"; 175lb; RH 2HB; QF 1994, 98

In August of last year Lindsay Davenport was asked about her chances of becoming the world's number one ranked player. She replied prophetically, "If I am going to do it, I'll have to win the US Open." A month later she had claimed her first Grand Slam title and on 12th October 1998 Lindsay became the eighth player to reach the top spot. "I've dreamed of being the best, ever since I was a little kid," was the reaction then of the likeable Californian who was brought up in a sporting household. Her father, Wink, played volleyball for the United States in the 1968 Olympic Games, and her mother, Ann, and sisters Shannon and Leiann have also been volleyball players. "I can remember, when I was about 4 or 5, my Dad telling me I had to do a sport after school, so I wouldn't just come home and watch TV and be really lazy. Sport is very prevalent in the household. We are always watching it on TV at the weekends, and the whole family is athletic and always on the go, and that's the way I was brought up." So, did Lindsay make a deliberate decision to play tennis rather than follow the rest of the family into volleyball? "Not really. I was only about 6 when my Mum put me in tennis lessons after school to kind of get me out of the house. It just kind of took off from there. I kept playing and playing, and I'm very happy that I did, but I was too young to really make a decision that tennis was my sport when I started". Over the last couple of years Lindsay has made tremendous efforts to slim down and improve her mobility. Even so, she may need a drier than normal British summer, with the courts firmer and the balls bouncing higher, if she is to improve on her previous best of a place in the quarter-finals at the All England Lawn Tennis Club.

Steffi Graf

GERMANY

30; 5'9"; 132lb; RH;

Champion 1988, 89, 91, 92, 93, 95, 96, F 87, SF 90

"It is a thrill to be where I am right now and I hope I don't have to answer any more questions about why am I still trying what I am doing. I think it speaks for itself." That is how Steffi Graf summed up her feelings after beating Monica Seles 1-6 6-4 6-4 in last November's Chase Championships in New York, in what was one of the best matches of the year. The result meant Graf had won twelve straight matches since returning to tennis from her latest injury lay-off, and beaten the first, second, third, sixth and eighth ranked players. "It has been amazing. It is not possible to describe what I am going through but it is paying off the hard work and the difficult times. I am sitting here and I can't believe it. It is excitement and disbelief. Disbelief at seeing myself where I am right now and the excitement of pulling through these matches when it's difficult to see that I am going to make it." When she was in her early twenties Steffi was adamant that she would retire well before her thirtieth birthday. Now though she has discovered that her competitive instincts are as strong as ever and that she still loves performing on the game's greatest stages. In her eyes there is no greater stage than Wimbledon's Centre Court and she would love to crown her glittering career with an eighth Ladies' Championship. Can she do it? If the body is fit and the mind does not become too anxious there is no reason why not, especially after her remarkable triumph at the French Open.

Martina Hingis

SWITZERLAND

18; 5'7"; 130lb; RH 2HB;

Champion 1997, SF 98

When Martina Hingis retained her Australian Open title at the start of 1998, and then followed that up with tournament victories in Indian Wells, Hamburg and Rome, her grip on the world number one ranking seemed impregnable. Complacency though can be an insidious enemy and a touch of it crept in. The "Swiss Miss" put on a little bit of weight and lost a little bit of her sharpness around the court. Very understandably the then seventeen-year-old discovered that there are other things in life than tennis, including romance. To use the word the players use, Martina was no longer "focused". There were defeats in the semi-finals at the French Open and Wimbledon, a loss in the final of the US Open. By the time mid-October came around Martina had gone five months without a tournament victory and was no longer number one. She had a choice to make and she decided to re-dedicate herself to tennis. She took herself off to Florida to work on her fitness and reaped an immediate reward when she overcame Lindsay Davenport in the final of the season-ending Chase Championships in New York. As she said then:- "It was about time for me to show people again that I can win a big tournament." She did so again in Melbourne at the start of this year, claiming a third successive double of singles and doubles titles at the Australian Open. One week later victory in Tokyo saw her move back to the top of the world rankings. Now it will be fascinating to see if she can maintain her motivation throughout 1999. If she does she will deservedly be the favourite to win every tournament she enters, including Wimbledon.

contem
porary
art

contemporary art, part 1 london wednesday 23 june 1999 at 7pm

enquiries: elena geuna, cheyenne westphal, benjamin brown tel: +44 171 293 5401 fax: +44 171 293 5921
catalogues: tel: +44 171 293 6444 fax: +44 171 293 5909, quoting ref: WI 99 above: georg baselitz,
orangenesser II, estimate: £180,000–220,000 34-35 new bond street, london, W1A 2AA www.sothebys.com

SOTHEBY'S

Anna Kournikova

RUSSIA

18; 5'8"; 123lb; RH 2HB; SF 1997

Anna Kournikova may not yet be the world's best female tennis player but she is certainly the most photographed. Her long golden hair and glamorous looks have added another dimension to the women's game, and quite rightly she sees no need to apologise for that. As she told Sports Illustrated magazine last year:- "People ask me, 'Why do you have to look good on the court? Why not just play?' But to me, whenever I'm on the court it's like theatre and I have to express myself. Why should I have to look ugly just because I'm an athlete?" Why indeed, and although it is Anna's looks that have so far attracted most attention, we should not for one moment ignore what she has achieved on the court. In 1995 she was the World Junior Champion and two years later made a remarkable senior debut here at Wimbledon, reaching the semi-finals. A thumb injury kept her away from last year's Championships, but during the course of the year she moved into the world's top ten for the first time and, in Florida in March 1998, recorded successive victories over four players ranked in the top ten, Monica Seles, Conchita Martinez, Lindsay Davenport and Arantxa Sanchez-Vicario. At the end of the year though she suddenly developed an acute case of "double faultitis". In her last three matches of 1998 she double faulted fifty six times. The problem was still afflicting her at this year's Australian Open, but provided she finds a way of overcoming it there is no reason why Anna's tennis as well as her looks should not be attracting the headlines during this year's Championships.

Conchita Martinez

SPAIN

27; 5'7"; 132lb; RH;

Champion 1994, SF 93, 95

In the twenty six years that I have been coming to Wimbledon, few results have surprised me more than that of the 1994 Ladies' Singles final. After all the queen of Wimbledon, Martina Navratilova, was bidding for a tenth title against a Spanish clay-courter who had been a member of the "grass is fit only for cows" club. On the day though Conchita Martinez played superbly and thoroughly deserved her 6-4 3-6 6-3 victory, becoming the first and so far only Spanish woman to win at the All England Lawn Tennis Club. Now the surprise is that that remains Conchita's only Grand Slam title. She did reach the final of the Australian Open at the start of last year, but on her favourite clay courts she has never advanced beyond the semi-finals of the French Open. Why is this? Perhaps her entry in the Player Guide of the women's WTA Tour gives the game away. Conchita is listed as enjoying riding horses and motorcycles; playing golf, soccer, beach volleyball; shopping, nice restaurants and red wine. Here is a well-rounded woman for whom tennis is not the be-all and end-all of life. Indeed the same guide says that Conchita wants to have her own wine cellar. A nice thought, isn't it, to be able to open a bottle of Rioja and reflect on the day you became Wimbledon Champion. Especially when, as I suspect will be the case, it was a once in a lifetime experience.

Amelie Mauresmo

FRANCE

19; 5'9"; 142lb; RH

You are entitled to ask what a nineteen-year-old, who in her only previous appearance at The Championships lost in the second round, is doing in this list of title contenders? There are three reasons why. First, Amelie states that grass courts are her favourite surface. Secondly, she has won here at Wimbledon before. She was the junior champion in 1996, a year in which she also won the junior title at the French Open and was named by the International Tennis Federation as World Junior Champion. Thirdly, and most importantly, is her remarkable run to the final of the Australian Open in January including a magnificent win over Lindsay Davenport in the semi-finals. Suddenly junior promise was being turned into senior achievement and the whole of the tennis world was sitting up and taking notice. "I have worked for this for all my young career," said Amelie after losing to Martina Hingis in the final, "so it's a special moment. To get on the Centre Court to play a Grand Slam final is very big. Emotionally it is very intense out there." The first sign that Amelie was ready to make a major breakthrough came at last year's German Open where, having saved a match point during qualifying, she became the first qualifier to reach the final of a Tier One tournament on the WTA Tour, before falling to Conchita Martinez. Since linking up with new coach Christophe Fournerie at the end of last year, Amelie has worked hard on improving her fitness and strength. Long hours in the gym have broadened her shoulders and enabled her to hit powerfully from all parts of the court. Whether she is ready yet to mount a sustained challenge for a Wimbledon title is a good question especially as she injured an ankle at the French Open, but after what she achieved in Melbourne few will be surprised to see her still around in the second week.

Advantage Wimbledon!

Mary Pierce

FRANCE

24; 5'10"; 150lb; RH 2HB; QF 1996

Such is the strength of women's tennis in France that three of my sixteen picks as contenders for the Ladies' Championship come from the other side of the Channel. Mind you Mary Pierce's original roots were in Montreal where she was born to an American father and French mother. Like Amelie Mauresmo, she reached her first Grand Slam final while still a teenager, sweeping all opponents, including Steffi Graf, aside on her way to the 1994 French Open final. In it she found Arantxa Sanchez-Vicario's defensive skills a little too much to overcome. Seven months later though she conceded just five games to the Spaniard in the final of the Australian Open. With a first Grand Slam crown safely secured, Mary seemed destined to be challenging for all the game's major titles. Things have not gone quite to plan. True she did reach the Australian Open final again in 1997, but her great potential still seems a little unfulfilled. There have perhaps been too many niggling injuries and too many changes of coach. Mary still though possesses some of the most powerful ground strokes in the women's game, and a more than useful serve. So why hasn't she done better at Wimbledon, where her record is one quarter-final appearance in four attempts? Well perhaps it is because Mary is not the most flexible of players. Give her time and give her an even bouncing ball and she is a formidable opponent. Those though are often missing factors on grass courts, especially slightly damp ones.

Arantxa Sanchez Vicario

SPAIN

27; 5'6"; 124lb; RH 2HB;

Finalist 1995, 96, SF 97, QF 89, 91, 98

When Arantxa Sanchez-Vicario failed to win a singles title throughout the whole of 1997, there were those who were ready to suggest that her time as one of the game's leading ladies was over. They said the "Barcelona bumble-bee" was losing her sting. She might have been only twenty six but those legs had covered thousands of miles scrambling across baselines all over the world, and the indomitable spirit seemed a little weaker. Well, Arantxa silenced those doubters at the start of 1998, winning her twenty fifth career title in Sydney, beating the Williams sisters Serena and Venus in the semis and final. Any lingering thoughts of a Spanish decline were emphatically dispelled when wins over Lindsay Davenport and Monica Seles brought Arantxa a third French Open title and a fourth Grand Slam singles crown. That collection does not include a Wimbledon singles title although she did contest memorable finals with Steffi Graf in 1995 and 1996, and last year was not far away from beating Martina Hingis in the quarter-finals. So the pedigree is there, the legs and the heart are still strong, and Arantxa has a habit of making her critics eat humble pie. So it is with some trepidation that I suggest that her best chances of winning Wimbledon have probably gone. I just feel that the new crop of teenage stars have games better suited to the demands of grass courts. I also wonder whether humble pie will taste a little better when it's covered in tomato sauce!

Patty Schnyder

SWITZERLAND

20; 5'6"; 129lb; LH 2HB

If I asked you which two Swiss players each won five titles on the WTA Tour in 1998, I am sure you would all be able to name Martina Hingis, but I wonder how many of you would know the second name, that of Patty Schnyder. Well, the woman who has almost inevitably been nicknamed "Swiss Miss Two" claimed her victories in Hobart, Hanover, Madrid, Maria Lankowitz and Palermo. Perhaps not the most glamorous stops on the women's circuit but they still represented a considerable advance for the left-hander from Basle, who began 1998 at twenty sixth in the rankings and finished at number eleven. She might have been in the top ten if she had not let a one set to love lead slip away against Zimbabwe's Cara Black in the second round of last year's Championships, but at least she had made it beyond the first round for the first time in three attempts. Patty is most at home on slow clay courts, but showed in Hanover that she can play on faster ones. After all you do not beat the likes of Jana Novotna and Nathalie Tauziat on an indoor carpet unless you can cope with a speedy surface. One disappointment for Patty was that she finished 1998 just outside the top ten. You see she had agreed with both her father and her agent that if she ended the year inside it they would quit smoking. Presumably they are still puffing away.

BECOME
WHAT
YOU ARE.

LACOSTE

LACOSTE

www.lacoste.fr

Monica Seles

USA

25; 5'10"; 155lb; LH 2HB 2HF;

Finalist 1992, QF 90, 98

The main hope for Monica Seles in 1999 must surely be that she stays free of the traumas that have dogged her ever since that awful day in April 1993, when she was stabbed in the back while playing in Hamburg. That kept her out of the game for over two years, and after returning she had to watch her father, Karolj, fight a long and brave battle with cancer. A fight he finally lost in May of last year. It was perhaps his memory that inspired Monica to reach the final of the French Open just weeks later. Now though her wish for 1999 is understandable. "If I keep really working hard and hopefully have no… not distractions, but things that have happened in the last five years… if I can have that for the next couple of years that will definitely help. I have a greater peace of mind this year and I'm really committed to what I can control." At her best, at the start of the 1990's, Monica was controlling the women's game, winning three Grand Slam Championships in both 1991 and 1992. The one title to elude her was Wimbledon. She did reach the final in 1992 but, affected by all the tabloid publicity concerning the loudness of her grunting, decided to keep silent against Steffi Graf. Her performance that day was not only quiet but also anonymous as she won just three games. Given what she has had to endure since, Monica will never allow herself to be influenced in such a way again. If she reaches the later stages of this year's Championships we will see and hear the full Monica.

Nathalie Tauziat

FRANCE

31; 5'5"; 120lb; RH;

Finalist 1998, QF 92, 97

1967 may not have been a vintage year for French wine, but it did produce a French tennis player who has matured as richly as any bottle of Chateau Petrus, Nathalie Tauziat. Last year she reached the top ten of the world rankings for the first time and, in her forty third Grand Slam tournament, reached her first final here at Wimbledon with wins over the likes of Iva Majoli, Lindsay Davenport and the British heroine of last year's Championships, Sam Smith. Not content to rest on her laurels, Nathalie has this year become the eighteenth woman in professional tennis history to record her five hundredth singles victory. The other seventeen? In chronological order they are Margaret Court, Virginia Wade, Evonne Goolagong, Billie Jean King, Chris Evert, Martina Navratilova, Rosie Casals, Wendy Turnbull, Hana Mandlikova, Pam Shriver, Steffi Graf, Helena Sukova, Zina Garrison, Gabriela Sabatini, Arantxa Sanchez-Vicario, Jana Novotna and Conchita Martinez. Pretty impressive company to keep. So perhaps it should not have been a surprise to see Nathalie tasting such success on the lawns of the All England Lawn Tennis Club, especially when two of her four career titles have come on grass. She won in Eastbourne in 1995 and at Edgbaston in Birmingham two years later. In an age of baseliners with double handed backhands, Nathalie has always played to a different beat. Although she has never possessed one particularly big shot, she has been prepared to take the ball early, move forward and seek to put away the volley. Not a bad brew for success on fast courts. There was perhaps another reason for her great run here in 1998. She was being inspired by the exploits of her cousin, Didier Deschamps, who was captaining France to victory in football's World Cup. It certainly was a champagne time for Nathalie's family.

Dominique Van Roost

BELGIUM

26; 5'7"; 122lb; RH

Sadly I have never had the chance to visit Belgium, so when I think of that country my thoughts turn either to chocolates or the bureaucracy based in Brussels. Certainly I do not associate it with tennis players. After all, until last year, Belgium had never produced a player, man or woman, who had ever been ranked in the world's top ten. That all changed last autumn when successive victories over Martina Hingis and Venus Williams at a tournament in Filderstadt in Germany, saw Dominique Van Roost reach a career high of ninth in the world. An achievement which resulted in her being voted her country's athlete of the year. Yet when you first see Dominique you do not automatically think of an athlete. She is so slender that you think a gust of wind may blow her over at any moment. Appearances can be very deceptive. Dominique may lack the sheer power of some of her rivals, but she does possess the ability to use any pace created by her opponents and return it with interest. There is strength of character too, with a steely stubbornness that has been honed by her husband and coach Bart. Dominique has been a Grand Slam quarter-finalist, at the 1997 Australian Open, and last year she produced her best performance at Wimbledon, reaching the fourth round before losing in three sets to Arantxa Sanchez-Vicario. She could be ready to go even further in 1999.

the ultimate golfing shopping experience…

GOLF EXHIBITION

The National Golf Show

golf*live*'99

Try out and buy the latest in equipment & apparel ●

Meet top pros and golf celebrities ●

Get advice from the top instructors ●

- ● **Pitching & Putting Greens**
- ● **Driving Bays**
- ● **Electronic 3D Simulators & Analysers**
- ● **Fashion Shows**
- ● **Holidays & Resorts Feature Area**
- ● **Junior Coaching Feature Area**
- ● **Virtual Zone**
- ● **Free prize draws and Competitions**
  to win equipment, apparel, tickets to tournaments and a fabulous golf vacation
- ● **Free admission to under 16's**
- ● **Interactive Fun for all the family!**
- ● **Live coverage of the Dutch Open**
- ● **Refreshments available all day**

Official Charity

NSPCC ●
Cruelty to children must stop. FULL STOP.

Reg. Charity No. 216401

…don't miss the golfing extravaganza of the year!

ticket hotline **0870 739 9777**

Tickets available in advance £8.00 ● On the day £12.00 ● Under 16's No charge

National Rate - approx. 10p per minute (Under 16's must be accompanied by an adult & Identity may be required) *www.golflive.co.uk*

London ● Wembley Exhibition Centre ● 23rd–25th July 1999
10.00am - 7.00pm Friday & Saturday ● 10.00am - 6.00pm Sunday

Serena Williams

USA

17; 5'10"; 145lb; RH 2HB

"My main goal this year is to get an 'A' in zoology." So said the youngest of the five Williams sisters, Serena, last year. I confess I do not know if she succeeded, but she did collect a Wimbledon title at the tender age of sixteen, claiming the Mixed Doubles with Max Mirnyi from Belarus. They also won the Mixed at the US Open to complete a remarkable Grand Slam of Mixed titles for the Williams family, for sister Venus had won the Australian and French Opens in partnership with fellow American Justin Gimelstob. I am constantly changing my mind about whether Serena or Venus is the more naturally talented. It took Serena just sixteen matches on the WTA Tour to record five wins over players ranked in the world's top ten. That smashed the record previously held by Monica Seles who had taken thirty three matches. In her first ever clay court tournament she beat both Conchita Martinez and Nathalie Tauziat. Last year, on her debut at Wimbledon, she advanced to the third round before succumbing to injury. All this is strong evidence to suggest that Serena is the more naturally gifted, but when it comes to playing against her sister there only seems to be one outcome, a win for Venus. That is hardly likely to provoke a smile from Serena, but when the two sisters play together in doubles it is always a case of smiles all round. Indeed the greatest problem for them then is not to collapse into an uncontrollable fit of giggles. If you are at Wimbledon on a grey and damp day seek out the sisters for they are sure to put some sunshine back into your life.

Venus Williams

USA

19; 6'1"; 169lb; RH 2HB; QF 1998

Venus Williams was making tennis headlines even before she made a dramatic debut on the Women's Circuit. That was in 1994 when she won her first professional match and led Arantxa Sanchez-Vicario 6-3 3-0 in her second. There were stories of how this hugely talented athlete had been brought up in one of the roughest areas of Southern California; of how, after shots had been fired near to where Venus and her sister Serena had been practising on public courts, her parents had arranged for a local gang to protect them from similar disturbances; of how her father had insisted that she should not play in junior tournaments; and of how he stated that his two daughters were destined to reach the top. Many regarded such claims with a great deal of scepticism until, in her debut at the US Open in 1997, Venus stormed her way through to the final. In post-match press conferences Venus will frequently say that she will become the world number one and that her biggest rival is likely to be her sister Serena. Inevitably such comments have ruffled several feathers in the locker room, but Venus is not concerned. "I wouldn't consider myself cocky and arrogant. I'm confident and I tell the truth." Mind you there has definitely been an improvement in relations between the Williams sisters and their fellow players and a mellowing of Venus' comments. "I am not the only player out there who is doing great things. I am doing the best I can do and definitely other players are competing and competing well." Yes, Venus is maturing as a person and if her game continues to mature as well then she is surely destined to become a Wimbledon champion one day.

Natasha Zvereva

BELARUS

28; 5'8"; 138lb; RH 2HB;
SF 1998, QF 90, 92, 93

Back in 1988 I saw a seventeen-year-old from Minsk beat Martina Navratilova in the fourth round of the French Open and subsequently make her way into the final. It seemed the tennis world lay at the feet of Natasha Zvereva. But then she came up against Steffi Graf and suffered the humiliation of failing to win a single game in the final. Since then it has seemed that the singles career of the "Minx from Minsk", as Natasha is affectionately known, has been permanently blighted. Her skills have shone like a beacon in doubles, in which Natasha has claimed eighteen Grand Slam titles plus another two in Mixed Doubles, but on her own she seemed destined never to fulfil her capabilities. That all changed though at the 1998 Championships. In the third round she again faced Steffi Graf who had won all seventeen of their previous matches. This time Natasha never dropped her serve and recorded a famous 6-4 7-5 victory. Two rounds later Monica Seles was also beaten and Natasha was through to her first Grand Slam singles semi-final since the 1988 French. She had chances to go even further, but eventually lost to Nathalie Tauziat in three sets. How good it was though to see Natasha in the later stages of a Grand Slam singles after such a long absence. She has the ability to do just as well again this year but then the only thing that is really predictable about her is her unpredictability. Still, no matter how she is playing you can also be sure that with Natasha on court the tennis will never be dull.

Canon

IXUS

**IXUS
Z70**

-THE IXUS Z70.
CARRY THE RIGHT
ATTITUDE.

**IXUS
L-1**

EYE-OPENING DESIGNER

PHOTOGRAPHY.

CARVED IN STAINLESS

STEEL. ADVANCED

PHOTO SYSTEM AND

A 3X ZOOM LENS

SEIZE THE MOMENT.

**IXUS
M-1**

Canon Europa N.V., P.O. Box 2262, 1180 EG Amstelveen, The Netherlands. http://www.canon-europa.com

THE WORLD CHAMPIONS

Pete Sampras

At the age of 27 Pete Sampras was elected World Champion by the International Tennis Federation for the sixth year in succession; a record which outstrips all of his illustrious predecessors. Although he won Wimbledon for the fifth time in six years he did not dominate the game as he did in the past, and his only other tournament wins were in Philadelphia, Atlanta and Vienna. Greg Rusedski beat him in the Paris Indoor final. His win/lose record for the year was 61-17.

Lindsay Davenport

This 23-year-old Californian is the first American in twelve years to hold the World title and achieved it in great style despite failing to justify her No.2 seeding at Wimbledon. She reached a total of ten finals, five of which were against her great rival Martina Hingis. She defeated the Swiss player in Tokyo, Manhattan Beach and the US Open, but lost to her in Indian Wells and in the WTA Championship in New York. Her win/lose record for the year was 69-15.

MALE I.T.F. WORLD CHAMPIONS

1978	B. BORG	SWEDEN
1979	B. BORG	SWEDEN
1980	B. BORG	SWEDEN
1981	J.P. MCENROE	U.S.A.
1982	J.S. CONNORS	U.S.A.
1983	J.P. MCENROE	U.S.A.
1984	J.P. MCENROE	U.S.A.
1985	I. LENDL	CZECHOSLOVAKIA
1986	I. LENDL	CZECHOSLOVAKIA
1987	I. LENDL	CZECHOSLOVAKIA
1988	M. WILANDER	SWEDEN
1989	B. BECKER	W. GERMANY
1990	I. LENDL	CZECHOSLOVAKIA
1991	S. EDBERG	SWEDEN
1992	J. COURIER	U.S.A.
1993	P. SAMPRAS	U.S.A.
1994	P. SAMPRAS	U.S.A.
1995	P. SAMPRAS	U.S.A.
1996	P. SAMPRAS	U.S.A.
1997	P. SAMPRAS	U.S.A.
1998	P. SAMPRAS	U.S.A.

FEMALE I.T.F. WORLD CHAMPIONS

1978	MISS C.M. EVERT	U.S.A.
1979	MISS M. NAVRATILOVA	U.S.A.
1980	MRS J.M. LLOYD (MISS EVERT)	U.S.A.
1981	MRS J.M. LLOYD (MISS EVERT)	U.S.A.
1982	MISS M. NAVRATILOVA	U.S.A.
1983	MISS M. NAVRATILOVA	U.S.A.
1984	MISS M. NAVRATILOVA	U.S.A.
1985	MISS M. NAVRATILOVA	U.S.A.
1986	MISS M. NAVRATILOVA	U.S.A.
1987	MISS S. GRAF	W. GERMANY
1988	MISS S. GRAF	W. GERMANY
1989	MISS S. GRAF	W. GERMANY
1990	MISS S. GRAF	W. GERMANY
1991	MISS M. SELES	YUGOSLAVIA
1992	MISS M. SELES	YUGOSLAVIA
1993	MISS S. GRAF	W. GERMANY
1994	MISS A. SANCHEZ VICARIO	SPAIN
1995	MISS S. GRAF	GERMANY
1996	MISS S. GRAF	GERMANY
1997	MISS M. HINGIS	SWITZERLAND
1998	MISS L. DAVENPORT	U.S.A

TICKET HOLDERS

If you leave before the end of play, you are urged to return your showcourt tickets to the red ticket boxes when leaving the grounds

Tickets will be priced at £5.00 for any ticket before 5 p.m. and £3.00 after 5 p.m.
The proceeds are divided between the National Playing Fields Association, SPARKS (the Sportsmans Charity),
the Dan Maskell Fund – to help the disabled and disadvantaged to play tennis,
St. John Ambulance, for whom 1999 represents their 900th anniversary and the WRVS, in recognition of 50 years at The Championships.
Collecting boxes are situated at all exits to the stands and Grounds. Tickets must be placed only in the collecting boxes.

THE AMOUNT COLLECTED AT THE 1998 CHAMPIONSHIPS WAS £45,995 (NET OF VAT)—A RECORD

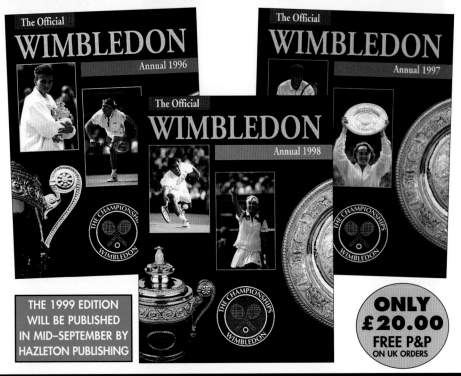

The Long-Term Plan

I N THE SPRING OF 1993, THE CLUB ANNOUNCED ITS 20 YEAR MASTER PLAN TO TAKE THE CHAMPIONSHIPS INTO THE 21st Century. The overriding goal of this plan is to maintain The Championships' international leadership by improving the quality of the event for players, spectators, the media, officials and neighbours. In August 1994, work began on the building of a new No.1 Court in the Aorangi Park area. This first phase of the All England Club's Long Term Plan also included a tunnel linking Somerset Road and Church Road, two additional grass courts and a new Broadcast Centre. These facilities were in use for the 1997 Championships. Stage 2 of the Long Term Plan, which commenced in 1997, is currently in progress and includes a new Facilities Building, which is scheduled for completion prior to the 2000 Championships. This will provide improved amenities for players, the media, officials, members of the Club and LTA Council members, and will release areas to improve the facilities of Debenture Holders and other spectator groups. At the same time, the terracing and public access to the west side of the Centre Court are being extended and will be completed a year ahead of schedule, in time for this summer's Championships. This will provide 728 additional seats on the Centre Court, which will now seat 13,813 people.

93

WTA TOUR-
Skill, Elegance and Athleticism

If you took a poll asking for the top names in women's professional sports, not only would the stars of the WTA TOUR dominate the list, but they would also be recognized by their first names alone: Martina, Steffi, Monica, Venus, Serena, Lindsay, Anna and others. Of course these and over 1,000 other professional players from nearly 80 countries are sustaining a long-standing tradition.

Ever since Suzanne Lenglen first captivated both the social and sporting worlds in the 1920's with her daring play and dominant personality, tennis has always been accepted as perhaps the sport in which women are best able to present and exploit those essential qualities of skill, elegance and athleticism.

The list of outstanding champions over the last 30 years speaks for itself. Names such as Billie Jean King, Chris Evert, Martina Navratilova, Margaret Court, Evonne Goolagong and Virginia Wade helped to build recognition of women's professional tennis around the world with a geographical diversity of talent that has been essential for the growth of tennis in terms of popularity, sponsorship and television coverage. For instance, last year each winner of the Grand Slam tournaments was from a different country.

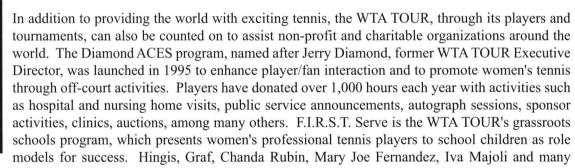

Throughout the 1970's and then into the 1980's, the WTA TOUR featured several well-known names including King, Court, Wade, Goolagong, Evert, Navratilova and a teenage newcomer, Tracy Austin. The 1990's saw the emergence of yet another legendary rivalry between Graf and Seles. Arantxa Sanchez-Vicario also challenged for the top spot until Hingis, the precocious teenager, took the lead. Now Davenport and the exciting Williams sisters have established themselves as legitimate contenders.

The last year and a half has proven to be the dawn of a new era. The more established players, known affectionately as the Tour veterans, have been forced to raise their games to keep up with a talented and entertaining mix of young competitors led by Martina Hingis, Venus and Serena Williams, Anna Kournikova, Patty Schnyder and Amelie Mauresmo, just to name a few. These budding rivalries, along with more competitive tournaments and improved fitness and equipment, have drawn more interest to women's professional tennis than ever before, and new attendance and television ratings records are continually being set.

In addition to providing the world with exciting tennis, the WTA TOUR, through its players and tournaments, can also be counted on to assist non-profit and charitable organizations around the world. The Diamond ACES program, named after Jerry Diamond, former WTA TOUR Executive Director, was launched in 1995 to enhance player/fan interaction and to promote women's tennis through off-court activities. Players have donated over 1,000 hours each year with activities such as hospital and nursing home visits, public service announcements, autograph sessions, sponsor activities, clinics, auctions, among many others. F.I.R.S.T. Serve is the WTA TOUR's grassroots schools program, which presents women's professional tennis players to school children as role models for success. Hingis, Graf, Chanda Rubin, Mary Joe Fernandez, Iva Majoli and many others are also actively involved with individual charities.

We can never forget those who made all of today's success possible. One thinks particularly of Billie Jean King, Rosie Casals and Gladys Heldman, who in the early 1970's courageously broke away from the establishment and helped form what is now known as the WTA TOUR, the premier women's sporting circuit in the world. They led the charge for more equitable distribution of prize money, and while the US Open has long since offered equal prize money, Wimbledon, Roland Garros and the Australian Open are getting closer all the time.

In 1999, the WTA TOUR is comprised of 59 events, including the four Grand Slams and the KB Fed Cup, in 26 countries over an 11-month schedule, concluding with the Chase Championships in mid-November at Madison Square Garden in New York. The players compete for a record-breaking total of over $45 million in prize money before more than 3.7 million fans in person and via television in over 11.1 billion homes worldwide.

1999 WTA TOUR

www.wtatour.com

THINK OF MUTUALLY BENEFICIAL PARTNERSHIPS IN THIS SPORT AND YOU MIGHT COME UP WITH FLEMING AND McEnroe, Hewitt and McMillan perhaps, or Navratilova and Shriver, but closer to home how about this one: Greg Rusedski and British tennis.

Surely few relationships can have had such a positive effect on both sides, and while there will always be those who will look at it as a marriage of convenience it is hard to argue against the dividends it has paid.

For the domestic game the benefits of his presence on the British scene have been in some ways less obvious and in others more tangible.

For example, the sheaf of press cuttings about tennis now consumes more paper probably in a week than it used to do in a month.

In the desperate fight to attract and keep youngsters from other sports he has become one half of a role model duo, even going so far as winning the BBC Sports Personality of the Year in 1997. (Disappointingly, this has not seemed to rub off on the already established other British professionals).

There have been sell-outs at the national championships in Telford, and a renewed effort in the Davis Cup. It is hard to imagine that Battersea's Guardian Direct Cup would ever have been born without him.

Of course there has been another crucial player in all this—Tim Henman, although he will testify to the spurring effect the arrival of the 25-year-old left-hander onto the British scene had on him.

When Henman began emerging as a player of genuine class there was always the concern that he might suffer from the same problem that Jeremy Bates had, in that he might be left to roam the upper echelons of the circuit all on his own. It was not loneliness that was the problem for Bates, but the lack of anyone pushing him for the domestic top spot over the years—and its concomitant rewards—must have had an impact on his career.

With Rusedski around that has not been a difficulty for Henman, and after all those years of British tennis being a rarely stirred backwater in the national consciousness their rivalry has provided one of the great on-going stories in British sport.

On the other side the benefits have been considerable, both ranking-wise and materially, for Montreal-born Rusedski.

It will always be a matter of conjecture, but the chances of him developing so swiftly into a top ten player and US Open finalist would surely have been reduced had he not taken the quantum leap across the Atlantic.

In deciding to throw in his lot with the land of his mother's birth, and by then his residency, he had to prove

G.R.

himself as a player and person to a sceptical British scene, and, already a hugely motivated and dedicated professional, it sparked an even greater desire within.

With the rise of Henman, and the sight of him mopping up some lucrative commercial deals, there was even greater incentive to dig deep. By talent, bloody-minded determination and with the help of that trademark grin, there has been no shortage of fame, fortune and wide acceptance to come his way.

There has, of course, been some cynicism about his motives, and he is undoubtedly a richer man for flying under the Union Jack in what is a larger tennis market than Canada, yet it is peculiar that the hue of his passport comes under far greater scrutiny than Britain's many other imports in other sports.

It is rarely mentioned, for instance, that representing Britain offered no new avenues for Rusedski to pursue his trade. Unlike, say, a South African cricketer with a British connection he did not gain entrance to the international scene by making the decision, as Canada has never been a

G.B.

pariah state and has its own Davis Cup team.

He accepts the recurring question with admirable good grace, saying "What matters most to me is that people think of me as a good person, rather than whether they think of me as a pure Brit."

For the record, there are few who know him who doubt his enthusiasm for his adopted country, and his links have only been cemented by the announcement in February—in the kind of glossy magazine that is the stamp that your celebrity transcends mere sport—that he is to marry his long-standing girlfriend Lucy Connor.

Few will remember it anyway if he emerges triumphant from the Men's Singles on the final Sunday, a prospect that has become realistic in the last few years.

To do that he will have to banish the memory of this time twelve months ago, which provided probably the roughest stretch of his career.

Ten days before The Championships started, with his preparations going perfectly at the Stella Artois event at Queen's, he fell badly on his ankle. Repairing it was a race against time he could not win, and after an abortive attempt to play his first round match there was further aggravation with the subsequent acrimonious split from his coach Tony Pickard.

It was not the first time that Rusedski had fallen out with a coach as, for all the easy smile, he has never been one to linger on sentimentally with an adviser when he feels it is time for a change.

Californian Brian Teacher had discovered first hand the split nature of Rusedski's character shortly after he coached him to the US Open final in September 1997. In the year leading up to that, Teacher had helped transform his client's game, adding guile to the God-given sledgehammer serve, shoring up his suspect backhand and steadily improving his return of serve.

By the time he made the final at Flushing Meadow, Rusedski was transformed from one of the tour's many decent journeymen to a devastating all-court player, but for reasons best known to himself the player soon opted to change his mentor.

It was a vivid illustration of the Rusedski dichotomy. Away from the tennis court he is friendly and affable, the sort of bloke who if stopped to ask the way in the street would spend five minutes poring over your A to Z with you. He also enjoys some of the trappings of his fame; happy to mix with personalities from other worlds and bask in the limelight he has created for himself.

Yet the last thing he would do is see it interfere with the business of becoming the best player he can be. Near a tennis court he is a contrastingly uncharitable competitor with a rare drive to succeed—and he needs to make no apology for that.

It is for certain that no player will like to see his name near that of Rusedski in this year's draw, for there is nowhere, other possibly than a fast indoor court, where his game is more dangerous.

His serve—timed last year at a world record, altitude-assisted 149 m.p.h. in California—works its left-handed magic perfectly on the grass, which is also well-suited to the sliced backhand, the standard product from that flank.

Above all, though, you sense it is the intensity of the Wimbledon occasion, the knife-edge quality of the brief points and the knowledge that this is his biggest fortnight of the year, that counts most in his favour.

From falling in love with a ball girl at Thames Ditton, to winning the junior doubles here, to moving to London, to asserting his citizenship, there is the feeling that the winning of Wimbledon—as for Henman—is a life's ambition. You wonder if Greg Rusedski can ever properly rest until his mission is complete.

MIKE DICKSON *Daily Mail*

Eye on the Box

IAN EDWARDS *Television Marketing Director*

THE CHAMPIONSHIPS RECEIVED A TOTAL OF 5,552 HOURS OF COVERAGE IN 175 TERRITORIES IN 1998. THIS REPRESENTS a decline of 183 hours (3%) compared with 1997, but an increase in the number of territories by one. The decrease in hours can be attributed mainly to the reduction of 14 hours by ESPN/Star Sports in Asia and the Far East and the competing attraction of soccer's World Cup. This World Cup effect was most noticeable in the less developed television markets.

Because of the methodology used when calculating ESPN/Star's coverage, only the 13 major Star TV territories are counted, though Star currently transmits to 64 territories. Elsewhere, the hours of coverage by broadcasters reaching more than one territory have been counted only once, so as not to overstate coverage.

Additional coverage received via news services, inflight distribution, the British and American armed forces' radio and television services and Trans World Sport are not counted, in keeping with the methodology of previous years.

Though Wimbledon can now be seen in as many as 520 million homes worldwide, this figure should be treated with caution because of the continuously growing overlap of international terrestrial, cable and satellite broadcasters' transmission footprints.

In the UK, Tim Henman's semi-final against Pete Sampras provided an audience of 8.8 million for the BBC. The Ladies' Final peaked at 8.6 million and the Men's Final at 7.1 million.

This year, Wimbledon is keeping pace with the fast changing developments in television, co-operating for the third year in succession with DFI in Germany. DFI offers a choice of four of Wimbledon's televised showcourts in digital format. In addition, viewers of digital terrrestial TV signals in the UK will be able to follow an interactive digital service offered by BBC Choice, to further enhance the Wimbledon experience.

	1990	1991	1992	1993	1994	1995	1996	1997	1998
Total countries	71	78	100	121	118	145	167	174	175
Total hours	2,133	2,378	4,121	4,820	4,767	6,004	6,287	5,737	5,552

	Hours	Mins
EUROPE		
Austria	5	23
Belgium	24	35
Bosnia	20	00
Bulgaria	3	30
Croatia	26	00
Cyprus	39	15
Czech Republic	6	55
Denmark	17	41
Finland	17	41
France	58	00
Germany	195	20
Greece	39	15
Hungary	32	00
Ireland	13	00
Italy	95	15
Malta	45	00
Moldova	66	36
Monaco	95	15
Netherlands	69	39
Norway	17	41
Poland	4	50
Portugal	5	41
Romania	28	35
Russia	96	25
San Marino	95	15
Slovak Republic	11	00
Slovenia	19	52
Spain	162	07
Sweden	17	41
Switzerland	87	25
Turkey	37	00
Ukraine	12	43
United Kingdom	163	02
CENTRAL AND SOUTH AMERICA		
Argentina	12	00
Barbados	24	44
Belize	96	00
Bermuda	22	00
Bolivia	96	00
Brazil	46	37
Chile	10	04
Colombia	13	00
Costa Rica	5	40
Cuba	96	00
Dominican Republic	96	00
Ecuador	15	35
El Salvador	96	00
French Guiana	96	00
Guatemala	96	00
Guyana	96	00
Honduras	87	00
Jamaica	20	40
Mexico	8	00
Nicaragua	96	00
Panama	96	00
Paraguay	12	00
Peru	17	40
Puerto Rico	96	00
Surinam	96	00
Trinidad & Tobago	31	16
Uruguay	12	00
Venezuela	12	00

	Hours	Mins
NORTH AMERICA		
Canada	79	45
United States	86	30
AFRICA		
Algeria	83	10
Angola	83	10
Benin	83	10
Botswana	83	10
Burkina Faso	83	10
Burundi	83	10
Cameroon	83	10
Central Africa	83	10
Central African Rep.	3	40
Chad	83	10
Commores	83	10
Congo	83	10
Djibouti	83	10
Equatorial Guinea	83	10
Eritrea	83	10
Ethiopia	83	10
Gabon	83	10
Gambia	83	10
Ghana	83	10
Guinea	83	10
Guinea-Bissau	83	10
Ivory Coast	83	10
Kenya	83	10
Lesotho	83	10
Liberia	83	10
Libya	78	00
Madagascar	83	10
Malawi	83	10
Mali	83	10
Mauritania	83	10
Mauritius	83	10
Morocco	8	49
Mozambique	83	10
Namibia	83	10
Niger	83	10
Nigeria	83	10
Reunion	83	10
Rwanda	83	10
Sao Tome	83	10
Senegal	83	10
Seychelles	83	10
Sierra Leone	83	10
Somalia	83	10
South Africa	158	10
Sudan	83	10
Swaziland	83	10
Tanzania	4	09
Togo	3	40
Tunisia	3	40
Uganda	83	10
Western Sahara	83	10
Zaire	83	10
Zambia	83	10
Zanzibar	83	10
Zimbabwe	5	10
MIDDLE EAST		
Bahrain	78	00
Egypt	78	00
Iran	78	00
Iraq	78	00

	Hours	Mins
Israel	9	17
Jordan	78	00
Kuwait	78	00
Lebanon	50	00
Oman	78	00
Qatar	78	00
Saudi Arabia	78	00
Syria	3	40
United Arab Emirates	78	00
Yemen	78	00
ASIA PACIFIC		
Afghanistan	166	36
Armenia	166	36
Australia	218	20
Azerbaijan	166	36
Bangladesh	18	20
Bhutan	166	36
Brunei	166	36
Cambodia	166	36
China	26	30
Fiji	19	45
Georgia	166	36
Guam	165	56
Hong Kong	16	05
India	19	00
Indonesia	6	00
Japan	136	35
Kazakhstan	166	36
Kyrgyzstan	166	36
Laos	166	36
Macau	166	36
Malaysia	166	36
Maldives	166	36
Micronesia	166	36
Mongolia	166	36
Myanmar	166	36
Nepal	166	36
New Caledonia	166	36
New Zealand	272	30
North Korea	165	56
Pakistan	5	00
Papua New Guinea	166	36
Philippines	165	56
Singapore	14	00
Solomon Islands	166	36
South Korea	165	56
Sri Lanka	29	17
Taiwan	1	00
Tajikistan	166	36
Thailand	166	36
Turkmenistan	166	36
Uzbekistan	166	36
Vanuatu	166	36
Vietnam	16	30

Sampras

BARRY FLATMAN
The Express

WITH THE MILLENNIUM NOW ONLY A MATTER OF MONTHS AWAY, THE ALL ENGLAND LAWN TENNIS CLUB IS A delicately balanced mix between the traditional and the technological. As far as Pete Sampras is concerned that is as close to perfect as it is possible to get.

The defending Gentlemen's champion has good reason to be particularly fond of the lawns of London SW19 and could quite easily take the attitude that nothing needs to change. After all, five of his eleven Grand Slam titles have been collected on Centre Court.

Yet there is more to Sampras' affection for Wimbledon than just memories of past glories and immense financial gain. Though he has been infatuated with the creeper-clad walls since growing to understand what a tennis racket was for, he is a realist as well as a sentimentalist and understands that anything or anybody wanting to remain the very best needs to move with the times.

There are those who mourned the demolition of the old No.1 Court as sacrilege nearly three years ago. Similarly many a tear will be shed when the bulldozers move in on the current Players' Centre next to the Centre Court after this year's competition. But not Sampras, even though it housed his private reactions to both triumph and disaster.

"The thing I like about Wimbledon is they seem to do things just right," said the American who will go down in The Championships' history as the man who dominated the 1990s. "Of course it was sad to see the old No.1 Court go because it was an arena which had its own unique atmosphere, and it will be the same walking out of the locker rooms for a last time this year."

"Still, however much they modernise and change things, it will always be Wimbledon and for me it will always be special. It's got to move with the times, everything has to and that's just a fact of life. But you are not going to lose that wonderful aura."

Sampras' enthusiasm is deep-rooted and dates back to his childhood spent in Palos Verdes, just part of that vast Californian conurbation called Los Angeles. By the time he reached his tenth birthday, tennis was already a major part

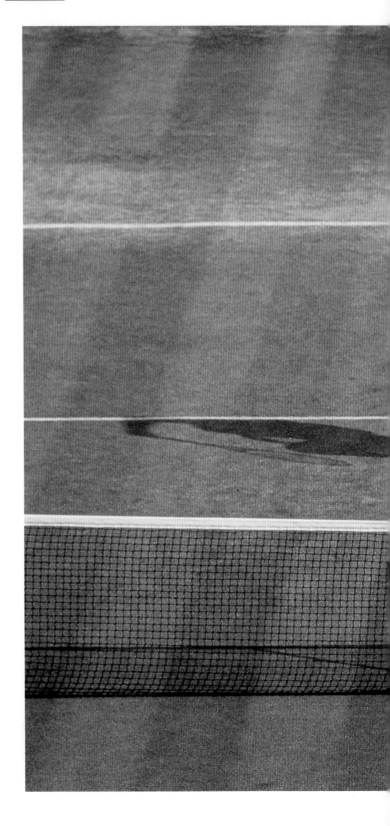

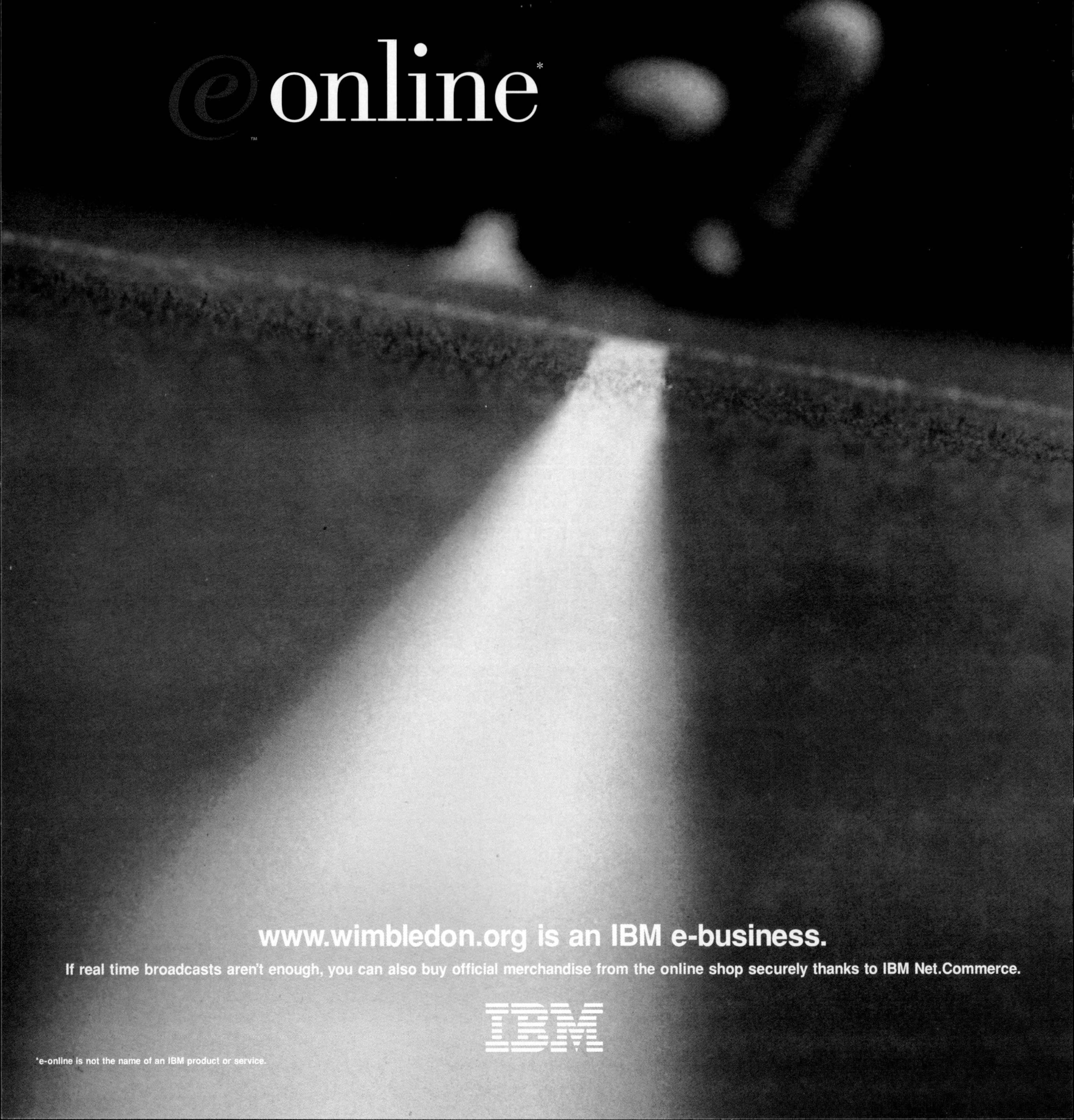

e online*
TM
www.wimbledon.org is an IBM e-business.
If real time broadcasts aren't enough, you can also buy official merchandise from the online shop securely thanks to IBM Net.Commerce.
IBM
*e-online is not the name of an IBM product or service.

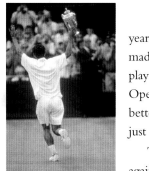

of his life. He began practising regularly at the Jack Kramer Tennis Club at Manhattan Beach but it was another court, more than 5,500 miles away that featured prominently in both his dreams and early morning waking moments.

"The whole family used to get up just after 5 a.m. to watch Wimbledon on the television," he recalled. "For me it was just as exciting as waking up on Christmas morning to open my presents. My first memories of Wimbledon were those finals between Bjorn Borg and John McEnroe of 1980 and '81. I must have been only nine or ten years old at the time so was too young to be really in awe of what I was watching.

"But it all had a very lasting effect. I remember Dick Enberg and Bud Collins doing the commentary and thinking Centre Court was such a massive arena. It always seemed such a special place, so kind of different from anything I knew at the time in California, and when I finally went there to play for the first time as a 17-year-old in 1989 I was shocked by how the whole place is really so compact."

Before too long Sampras became acquainted with Wimbledon in a previous era. A Californian coach called Des Little owned an old fashioned movie-projector and footage of legends such as Rod Laver, Lew Hoad and Ken Rosewall playing on the famous grass. It opened the youngster's eyes to the greatness of the Australians, role-models which he still holds in the highest esteem to this day. And it heightened the levels of reverence with which he held Centre Court.

He recalled: "It was jumpy old film and obviously in black and white but I could make out the brilliance of the Aussies which is something I have always tried to emulate. And of course it was Wimbledon so that made it even more special for me."

Eventually dreams became reality and at the age of 17 he came to walk through the gates of the All England Club, and it was a feeling he will never forget. "It was very, very special," he said. "Suddenly here I was walking around the place I had seen so many times on the TV and movie screen."

"I can remember going to practise on the weekend before the tournament started and going up to sit in the Centre Court while it was quiet with nobody else around. I know it's something so many other players have done but to me it seemed so unique. I thought about all the great players who had performed out there and all the wonderful finals. I can't say I felt a sense of destiny but I can remember being with my brother and just saying to him that the whole place was just totally awesome."

Unfortunately Sampras' initial playing experiences left him with more than a sense of anti-climax. First round defeats against first Todd Woodbridge in 1989 and then a year later at the hands of Christo van Rensburg made him wonder whether he was equipped to play on grass. Despite arriving as reigning US Open champion in 1991 things did not get much better as Derrick Rostagno sent him home after just two rounds.

Twelve months later he reached the semi-final against Goran Ivanisevic only to suffer another defeat. And the man who has won five of the last six Wimbledon Gentlemen's singles titles admitted: "For three years I was almost convinced grass was never going to be my surface."

"I had built it up as such a big thing and then almost came to the conclusion I couldn't play on the stuff. Admittedly it was all on the outside courts and to this day I'm happier when I'm on the big ones. But it wasn't until the year I reached the semi-final that I convinced myself I had a future at Wimbledon."

And what a future it has turned out to be. Since losing that four-setter to Ivanisevic and the chance of figuring in an all-American final against Andre Agassi, and until the beginning of this year's tournament, Sampras' Wimbledon record read: Played 40, Won 39. Even the 1996 quarter-final defeat by Richard Krajicek did not affect his pride as he said: "Without doubt I feel more comfortable on the Centre Court than I do on any other tennis arena in the world."

"There is just something natural about it to me. On the first Monday I will walk under the quotation from Rudyard Kipling's *If* and take a glance at the words. I have a look at the trophy which will be standing there and then I'll walk out on court knowing when to turn and take a bow to the Royal Box. It's all so different from everywhere else but it's also become so familiar. There are no speeches on court after the final, no thanking the sponsor and the ball kids. And you actually get a chance to do a lap of honour with the trophy which doesn't happen anywhere else. Long after I retire it's those memories that will live with me as the most special."

And he will not forget either those celebration evenings at the Savoy-staged Champions' Dinner when the influence of All England Club chairman John Curry has seen Sampras develop a taste for a big cigar. "For a couple of years I frankly didn't want to go to the dinner and felt very uncomfortable sitting there in a dinner suit and having to make a speech," he said. "Now I kind of enjoy it. I relax, have a few drinks, smoke my cigar and take in everything that has happened."

It's a long way from that young kid waking up early in the morning to watch Wimbledon on television to a champion puffing away on the finest Havana. The story is quite simply Pete Sampras' love affair with Wimbledon and there are undoubtedly a few more chapters yet to be written.

Bjorn Borg—Wimbledon 1979

*Ann Jones on her way
to beating Billie-Jean King
in the Ladies' Singles Final
—4th July 1969*

Wimbledon
59 69
79 89

JOHN ROBERTS
The Independent

WHEN MARIA BUENO WON THE FIRST OF HER THREE WIMBLEDON SINGLES TITLES IN 1959, BRAZIL CELEBRATED with rather more than a samba. A stamp was issued in La Bueno's honour, and a statue was commissioned. The aircraft taking the heroine back to São Paulo was diverted because of a storm, and when she finally arrived, after midnight, all the lights in the city's buildings were switched on to greet her.

Two British players, Christine Truman and Angela Mortimer, were seeded to meet in the final, but their contest would have to wait until 1961. Bueno's elegant style mesmerised opponents and captivated spectators. The American Darlene Hard, who had been unable to withstand the power and athleticism of her compatriot Althea Gibson in the 1957 final, was upstaged by the balletic Bueno this time, the No.6 seed winning 6-4 6-3.

Latin American-born players dominated The Championships, with the tall, graceful Alex Olmedo fulfilling his No.1 seeding by winning the Men's singles title. Olmedo, the son of a groundsman in Arequipa, Peru, had won a scholarship to the University of Southern California in Los Angeles and had taken United States citizenship.

Although a strike prevented the daily order of play and results of matches being printed in the Wimbledon Programme, tennis followers were well aware of the exploits of Bueno and Olmedo and were also beginning to respond to the exceptional talent of an unseeded, 20-year-old Australian left-hander named Rod Laver, who was defeated by Olmedo in the final, 6-4 6-3 6-4.

A decade later, Laver was acclaimed as possibly the greatest player the game had known. The short (5ft 9in), slightly bandy, shy, red-haired Queenslander had developed into "The Rockhampton Rocket". When Laver came to Wimbledon in 1969, he was on the third leg of his second Grand Slam, primed for the unique distinction of repeating as a professional what he accomplished as an amateur in 1962.

Laver won the Wimbledon singles title four times in total, twice in succession either side of a five-year gap when he competed on the old professional tour prior to the advent of the open era in 1968. In spite of the hiatus, Laver's magnificent career was adorned with 11 Grand Slam singles championships. In the 1969 Wimbledon final, he defeated his compatriot John Newcombe, 6-4 5-7 6-4 6-4.

Pancho Gonzales, whose best years were spent playing in the professional tennis circuit, made an impact at the All England Lawn Tennis Club at the age of 41, winning his first round match against Charlie Pasarell, a fellow American, after a record 112 games. Their marathon lasted 5 hours and 12 minutes, Gonzales prevailing 22-24 1-6 16-14 6-3 11-9.

Ann Jones, from Birmingham, won the Ladies' singles title with a characteristic display of persistence against two of the sport's greatest players. Jones, seeded No.4, overcame the Australian Margaret Court, the top seed, in the semi-finals, 10-12 6-3 6-2, and defeated the American Billie Jean King, the No.2 seed, in the final, 3-6 6-3 6-2. Jones was the first left-handed player to win the Ladies' singles (Laver was the fourth "leftie" to win the Men's singles).

Martina Navratilova, the second left-handed Ladies' singles champion, not only made a successful defence of the title in 1979 but also partnered Billie Jean King in the doubles as King won a record 20th Wimbledon title (6 singles, 10 doubles, 4 mixed). Sadly, on the eve of the Ladies' doubles final, Elizabeth Ryan, the winner of 19 Wimbledon titles (12 doubles, 7 mixed) was taken ill at the All England Lawn Tennis Club and died, aged 87.

Navratilova, who defeated her great rival Chris Evert in three sets in the 1978 final to win the first of her record nine singles titles, beat the same player in the 1979 final, 6-4 6-4, the difference being that her opponent had married and become Mrs John Lloyd.

The phenomenal Bjorn Borg continued to defy logic by moving smoothly from success on the slow clay courts at the French Open in Paris to triumph on the fast Wimbledon lawns thanks to a combination of unwavering concentration, heavy top-spin, and awesome stamina. The Swede won his fourth consecutive Wimbledon singles title, defeating the big-serving Roscoe Tanner, from Lookout Mountain, Tennessee, 6-7 6-1 3-6 6-3 6-4, in a tense final that drained the spectators almost as much as the protagonists.

Borg's timing was matched by the new digital clocks fitted to the Centre Court and No.1 Court scoreboards, which also indicated the duration of each match. Tardiness was discouraged. Tie-break regulations were changed to operate at 6-all instead of 8-all, and umpires were issued with stopwatches to ensure players did not exceed the time limit between change of ends.

There was never a need to check if Steffi Graf was wasting time, and Boris Becker was no slouch, either. In 1989, having already established themselves as prodigious competitors, the young Germans made Wimbledon their own. Graf successfully defended the Ladies' singles title, defeating Navratilova for a second time, and Becker overcame Sweden's Stefan Edberg in the second of their three consecutive finals.

Chris Evert bid farewell to Wimbledon after losing to Graf in the semi-finals, 6-2 6-1. Evert, the singles champion in 1974, 1976 and 1981, had gained the affection of the crowds over an 18-year period, first impressions having prompted the nickname "The Ice Maiden". Evert won 96 of her 111 singles matches at the All England Lawn Tennis Club. Her last victory, seized after being two points from defeat against Italy's Laura Golarsa in the quarter-finals on No.1 Court, guaranteed a valedictory appearance on the Centre Court.

Rain interrupted play towards the end of the tournament, causing the Men's singles semi-finals to be played on different days and the Men's and Ladies' singles finals both to be played on the Sunday.

Graf and Navratilova had been seeded to meet in the final, as in the previous two years. Graf made it two wins to one with a 6-2 6-7 6-1 victory. Becker, who had fought through a difficult semi-final against Ivan Lendl on the Saturday, while Edberg was resting, played magnificently to win the final, 6-0 7-6 6-4, completing the German double. Smiling at Graf, Becker said, "It's only when I'm a grandfather and she's a grandmother that people will realise what we have achieved."

Compaq Grand Slam Cup 1998

BILL BABCOCK *Administrator—Grand Slam Cup*

VENUS WILLIAMS BEGAN A FRESH PAGE OF TENNIS HISTORY AT THE OLYMPIAHALLE IN MUNICH LAST OCTOBER WHEN SHE claimed the inaugural Women's Compaq Grand Slam Cup title and picked up $800,000—the richest prize money winner's purse in the women's game. The eighteen-year-old unseeded American defeated Patty Schnyder 6-2 3-6 6-2 in the final.

In the men's competition, Marcelo Rios, the 1998 Australian Open finalist allowed himself a broad smile when he defeated wild card entry Andre Agassi 6-4 2-6 7-6 5-7 6-3 in a three hour final that left the audience breathless.

The addition of women to the competition came eight years after the Grand Slam Cup was introduced to the tennis calendar, and the eight most successful women players in the four Grand Slams each year now receive invitations to play alongside the twelve most successful men.

Unseeded, Williams secured her berth in the Women's final with a resounding 6-3 6-2 win over No.3 seed and Roland Garros champion Arantxa Sanchez Vicario and a 6-4 6-0 victory over Wimbledon finalist Nathalie Tauziat in the semi-finals. Schnyder's path to the final however, was a little more fraught.

Surviving one match point in the second set against Wimbledon champion Jana Novotna, Schnyder eventually came through to win their quarter-final match 2-6 7-5 7-5. Her reward? The unenviable task of a semi-final meeting with compatriot and world No.1 Martina Hingis. In a match full of breathtaking counter-attacking strokes, stunning baseline winners and adventurous net play, the score between the cream of women's Swiss and world tennis reached one set-all. Hingis, nearly two years Schnyder's junior, then built up a 5-1 lead in the third, but Schnyder regained two service breaks and saved another match point and the score rebounded to 5-5. Then, to the disappointment of the crowd, Australian Open champion Hingis unfortunately was forced to retire suffering from acute cramps in both legs.

In the final, Williams' powerful service, cat-like quickness and ferocious ground strokes wore down the resilient 19-year-old Swiss and the American finally prevailed in 94 minutes.

In her post-match interview, Williams said "She really wanted this title... and I really wanted this title too. So it was just a matter of who played a little bit better in the end. I got an early break ... so I was happy."

Schnyder was reflective about her week "I know I can play against the top players. That's good to know," she smiled.

As the Oktoberfest fizzed in the background, Rios' journey to the Men's final had been simple enough.

Venus Williams

Straight set victories over Felix Mantilla and then Mark Philippoussis assured him of his Sunday berth.

Agassi, however, like Schnyder, trod a far less stable path on his way to the final. Blowing away Cedric Pioline 6-0 6-0 in 34 minutes in the opening round, the American lost the first set of his second match to the No.1 seed and Australian Open title holder Petr Korda before recovering to take the next two sets 6-0 6-1. Agassi went on to score a sensational five set victory in his semi-final clash with Karol Kucera—who had jetted in from a Davis Cup tie in Argentina just a few days earlier. Facing a 7-6 6-7 2-6 2-5 deficit, the former world No.1 made an incredible comeback—winning the next 11 games in a row—and secured his place across the net from Rios.

The final lived up to all expectations. On one particular point, Rios slipped and fell flat on his back after a volley, but was still able to execute a perfect overhead smash for a winner—from a mid-court sitting position. By the fifth set, the labours of Agassi's semi-final match began to show and at the same time Rios' early back spasms began to ease. In the end Rios finally wore down a drained Agassi and seized victory after two hours and 55 minutes of sparkling tennis.

Rios was delighted with his performance. "I played one of my best matches and I'm really proud I can win a match like that," he said.

Agassi, who just one year previously had been floundering at No.141 in the world, said "I think this week was the first week I really started feeling like I can be the best again. I started really hitting my shots. I enjoyed this week very much on that level."

Public interest in this 'Best of the Best' competition was so high that the official tournament website compaqgrand-slam.net registered a staggering 10 million hits across 76 countries during the week—three times more than last year and a record for the event.

As more and more people learn each year, the Compaq Grand Slam Cup is not only a generous event for the current stars but also represents a unique partnership with the Grand Slams and the ITF that helps create the next generation of players.

Since the inaugural 1990 event, the Compaq Grand Slam Cup has allowed the Grand Slams to donate more than $17,000,000 for the future of tennis to the Grand Slam Development Fund administered by the ITF. No other events in the sport offer such a remarkable international contribution.

In 1998 alone, the Fund provided prize money for 45 weeks of men's professional events (Satellite Circuits and Futures events), 17 weeks of women's $10,000 events and three weeks of women's $25,000 events.

In addition, the Fund enabled 151 players from 73 countries to join ITF Junior Teams, allowing them to participate in tournaments outside their own region under the guidance of an ITF coach. For the best of these juniors, the International Junior Team, consisting of 12 players all now ranked within the top 40 on the ITF Junior World Ranking, competed in eight weeks of high level events in Europe including Roland Garros and Wimbledon.

Marcelo Rios

Not just juniors, but men's and women's professional teams were also subsidised in 1998. Encouraging achievements included that of Cara Black of Zimbabwe, who improved her WTA Tour ranking to finish the year at 43. In addition to these professional team grants, individual Grand Slam Development Fund travel grants were awarded to players from 32 nations to enable them to play in an approved schedule of professional events.

Finally, the Grand Slams' commitment through the Compaq Grand Slam Cup to the Grand Slam Development Fund also meant that National Associations from Bangladesh to Zambia were able to construct or refurbish tennis facilities for players in their countries. All in all, an unprecedented ethical commitment to the future of the sport made possible by the Grand Slams and the Grand Slam Cup.

The 1999 race to Munich has now reached the halfway point. Keep an eye on the matches and the leader board during this year's Championships to see which Grand Slam players will earn one of the treasured invitations to compete in the sport's most lucrative and beneficial week-long event.

The All England Club's UK policy in the development of the Wimbledon brand is to appoint mainly British companies who are regarded as market leaders in their product field. This policy has created a consistently high quality image and enabled the Wimbledon brand to be marketed in areas not restricted solely to tennis.

First opened in June 1996 in the new No. 1 Court stadium, the Wimbledon shop has floor space of 1600 square metres, offering an extensive range of Wimbledon merchandise, from both UK and international licensees, for sale each year during The Championships. Wimbledon merchandise is also available in the UK, throughout the year, from the Wimbledon Shop in the Royal Arcade, Old Bond Street, the Wimbledon 'shop in shop' at Harrods and duty free outlets at Heathrow and Gatwick airports.

• *www.wimbledon.org*

Wimbledon Collection

The long-term marketing strategy of the All England Club is to further develop the Wimbledon Shop concept. Over the last twenty years, a carefully selected group of international companies have worked closely with the All England Club to develop and promote a prestigious selection of Wimbledon merchandise sold under licence in key world markets.

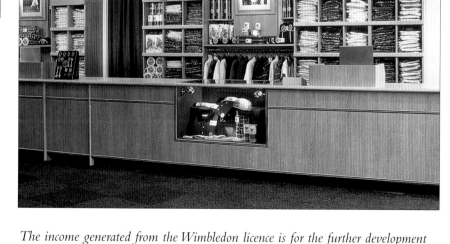

The income generated from the Wimbledon licence is for the further development of the game of tennis. Some thirty six companies, primarily in the UK, USA, Japan and Asia, are today actively marketing the Wimbledon brand.

Keep it in

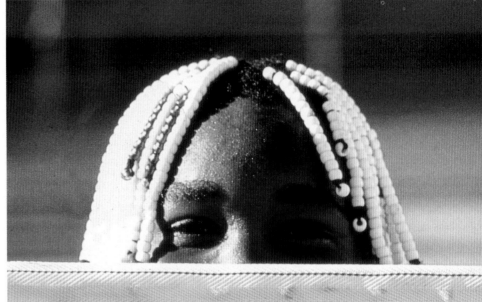

THE DEEPER YOU DIG INTO THE ANNALS OF TENNIS THE MORE YOU REALISE how much the game runs in families. The Williams sisters, Venus and Serena, are the latest illustration of the sibling factor as they illuminate the tournaments of the world; dreadlocked, ambitious, supportive of each other's prowess and an astonishing tribute to the belief of their father, Richard, who fashioned their rise to the top.

It all started on shabby public courts in the crime-ridden suburb of Compton in Los Angeles where practice sessions were often threatened by gang disputes. Now they are the most famous sisters in tennis with a lot more going for them than the hair braids and beads that have become their flailing hallmark.

Venus and Serena represent another instalment in the ongoing family affair called tennis, which, as far as Wimbledon is concerned began around the turn of the century with the Renshaw brothers, the Baddeley brothers and the Doherty brothers. William Renshaw, for the benefit of tennis anoraks everywhere, won the singles title a record seven times between 1881 and 1889; his twin brother Ernest once in 1888.

As a pair they captured the Wimbledon doubles seven times, but they were not the only talented twins around at the time. Wilfred Baddeley won the first of his three singles titles at the age of 19 in 1891 and was the youngest champion until 17-year-old Boris Becker in 1985. He also won the doubles four times—1891, 1894, 1895, 1896—partnering his twin brother, Herbert.

The brotherly saga was maintained by the Dohertys, Reggie and Laurie, whose achievements are commemorated by the memorial gates at the main Church Road entrance. Reggie, one of the great stylists of his era, took the Wimbledon singles title four times in a row between 1897 and 1900; Laurie five successive years from 1902 to 1906. A magnificent doubles team, they won the doubles eight times, 1897–1901, 1903–05. It's worth a thought as you pass through the gates dedicated to their memory.

Fast-forward to more recent times and it becomes more a question of who to leave out rather than unearthing family connections in tennis. According to my trusty Wimbledon Compendium, 1977 was the first time that three brothers competed in the Men's singles. The brothers? Yes, I'm sure you got it—David, John and Tony Lloyd, pride of Leigh-on-Sea, Essex and living proof that tennis can not only run through families but almost envelop them.

The Mottrams have a distinguished place among British tennis dynasties, too. Tony Mottram was a pillar of the post-war game in Britain, with 25 singles Davis Cup victories to his credit and a battling third round win over Jaroslav Drobny at Wimbledon in 1951 which quickened the pulse of the nation. His wife Joy Gannon played in the Wightman Cup. Their son Buster Mottram was British number one like his dad and a resolute Davis Cup competitor with 27 singles wins. Daughter Linda played at

the *Family*

REGINALD BRACE

a touch of razzamatazz to doubles with varying degrees of success.

The most successful brother-and-sister combinations at Wimbledon were Cyril Suk and Helena Sukova, who won the Wimbledon mixed in 1996 and 1997, and John and Tracy Austin who were successful in 1980. In 1962 two sons of an Australian High Court judge, Neale Fraser and Dr John Fraser, became the first brothers to reach the Wimbledon singles semi-finals in the same year. Neale, who had won the title in 1960, was beaten by Rod Laver while John went down to Martin Mulligan.

Fred Stolle, Wimbledon runner-up in three successive years between 1963–65, now looks down from the TV commentary box on the performances of his son Sandon. Ramanathan Krishnan, a Wimbledon semi-finalist in 1960–61, saw the family name enhanced with the stalwart performances of his son Ramesh. Patrick McEnroe, a much less volatile version of brother John, proved there was more than one tennis player in the clan.

Spain has the tennis equivalent of a royal family in Arantxa Sanchez Vicario and her brothers Emilio and Javier. Bulgaria's Manuela, Katerina and Magdalena Maleeva made Grand Slam history in 1993 when all three sisters were seeded in the Australian Open, French Open and Wimbledon. And let's not forget the Blacks of Zimbabwe. Brothers Byron and Wayne toppled Britain in the Davis Cup in 1997 and beat Australia last year while sister Cara is a rising talent in the women's game.

Nancy and Cliff Richey, Gordon and Jean Forbes, Barbara and Kathy Jordan… the list seems endless and in this case is certainly incomplete. Tim Henman comes from tennis stock and it is unlikely that the line will end with him. Could there be a Martina Hingis Mk.II at some future date? If she takes after her mother, Melanie, very probably. It is hard to escape the conclusion that tennis is sustained by the families who play the game.

Wimbledon in the Seventies and was picked for the British Federation Cup team in 1977.

The Truman family had a special niche in the affections of the British public during the Sixties. Christine, a popular figure then and now, was runner-up to Angela Mortimer in the final of 1961, played Wightman Cup doubles with her accomplished sister Nell and partnered her brother Humphrey in the mixed at Wimbledon. Today we have Christine's daughter, Amanda Janes, maintaining the tradition.

One tennis player in the family usually leads to another. The Amritraj brothers, Vijay, Anand and Ashok, were popular figures on the tennis scene of the 1970s. The Gullikson twins were so alike we devised a way of identifying them in the Press Box; Tim was the right-hander because he had an 'i' in his name; Tom the southpaw. Today we have the colourful Jensens, Luke and Murphy, bringing

The Championship Roll

GENTLEMEN'S SINGLES — CHAMPIONS & RUNNERS UP

1877	S. W. Gore / W. C. Marshall	1909	A. W. Gore / M. J. G. Ritchie	1929	H. Cochet / J. Borotra	1951	R. Savitt / K. McGregor	1967	J. D. Newcombe / W. P. Bungert

1877 S. W. Gore / W. C. Marshall
1878 P. F. Hadow / S. W. Gore
★ 1879 J. T. Hartley / V. St. L. Goold
1880 J. T. Hartley / H. F. Lawford
1881 W. Renshaw / J. T. Hartley
1882 W. Renshaw / E. Renshaw
1883 W. Renshaw / E. Renshaw
1884 W. Renshaw / H. F. Lawford
1885 W. Renshaw / H. F. Lawford
1886 W. Renshaw / H. F. Lawford
★ 1887 H. F. Lawford / E. Renshaw
1888 E. Renshaw / H. F. Lawford
1889 W. Renshaw / E. Renshaw
1890 W. J. Hamilton / W. Renshaw
★ 1891 W. Baddeley / J. Pim
1892 W. Baddeley / J. Pim
1893 J. Pim / W. Baddeley
1894 J. Pim / W. Baddeley
★ 1895 W. Baddeley / W. V. Eaves
1896 H. S. Mahony / W. Baddeley
1897 R. F. Doherty / H. S. Mahony
1898 R. F. Doherty / H. L. Doherty
1899 R. F. Doherty / A. W. Gore
1900 R. F. Doherty / S. H. Smith
1901 A. W. Gore / R. F. Doherty
1902 H. L. Doherty / A. W. Gore
1903 H. L. Doherty / F. L. Riseley
1904 H. L. Doherty / F. L. Riseley
1905 – H. L. Doherty / N. E. Brookes
1906 – H. L. Doherty / F. L. Riseley
★ 1907 – N. E. Brookes / A. W. Gore
★ 1908 – A. W. Gore / H. Roper Barrett

1909 A. W. Gore / M. J. G. Ritchie
1910 A. F. Wilding / A. W. Gore
1911 A. F. Wilding / H. Roper Barrett
1912 A. F. Wilding / A. W. Gore
1913 A. F. Wilding / M. E. McLoughlin
1914 N. E. Brookes / A. F. Wilding
1919 G. L. Patterson / N. E. Brookes
1920 W. T. Tilden / G. L. Patterson
1921 W. T. Tilden / B. I. C. Norton
★†1922 G. L. Patterson / R. Lycett
★ 1923 W. M. Johnston / F. T. Hunter
★ 1924 J. Borotra / R. Lacoste
1925 R. Lacoste / J. Borotra
1926 J. Borotra / H. Kinsey
1927 H. Cochet / J. Borotra
1928 R. Lacoste / H. Cochet

1929 H. Cochet / J. Borotra
1930 W. T. Tilden / W. Allison
★ 1931 S. B. Wood / F. X. Shields
1932 H. E. Vines / H. W. Austin
1933 J. H. Crawford / H. E. Vines
1934 F. J. Perry / J. H. Crawford
1935 F. J. Perry / G. von Cramm
1936 F. J. Perry / G. von Cramm
★ 1937 J. D. Budge / G. von Cramm
1938 J. D. Budge / H. W. Austin
★ 1939 R. L. Riggs / E. T. Cooke
★ 1946 Y. Petra / G. E. Brown
1947 J. Kramer / T. Brown
★ 1948 R. Falkenburg / J. E. Bromwich
1949 F. R. Schroeder / J. Drobny
★ 1950 B. Patty / F. A. Sedgman

1951 R. Savitt / K. McGregor
1952 F. A. Sedgman / J. Drobny
★ 1953 V. Seixas / K. Nielsen
1954 J. Drobny / K. R. Rosewall
1955 T. Trabert / K. Nielsen
★ 1956 L. A. Hoad / K. R. Rosewall
1957 L. A. Hoad / A. J. Cooper
★ 1958 A. J. Cooper / N. A. Fraser
★ 1959 A. Olmedo / R. Laver
★ 1960 N. A. Fraser / R. Laver
1961 R. Laver / C. R. McKinley
1962 R. Laver / M. F. Mulligan
★ 1963 C. R. McKinley / F. S. Stolle
1964 R. Emerson / F. S. Stolle
1965 R. Emerson / F. S. Stolle
1966 M. Santana / R. D. Ralston

1967 J. D. Newcombe / W. P. Bungert
1968 R. Laver / A. D. Roche
1969 R. Laver / J. D. Newcombe
1970 J. D. Newcombe / K. R. Rosewall
1971 J. D. Newcombe / S. R. Smith
★ 1972 S. R. Smith / I. Nastase
★ 1973 J. Kodes / A. Metreveli
1974 J. S. Connors / K. R. Rosewall
1975 A. R. Ashe / J. S. Connors
1976 B. Borg / I. Nastase
1977 B. Borg / J. S. Connors
1978 B. Borg / J. S. Connors
1979 B. Borg / R. Tanner
1980 B. Borg / J. P. McEnroe
1981 J. P. McEnroe / B. Borg
1982 J. S. Connors / J. P. McEnroe
1983 J. P. McEnroe / C. J. Lewis
1984 J. P. McEnroe / J. S. Connors
1985 B. Becker / K. Curren
1986 B. Becker / I. Lendl
1987 P. Cash / I. Lendl
1988 S. Edberg / B. Becker
1989 B. Becker / S. Edberg
1990 S. Edberg / B. Becker
1991 M. Stich / B. Becker
1992 A. Agassi / G. Ivanisevic
1993 P. Sampras / J. Courier
1994 P. Sampras / G. Ivanisevic
1995 P. Sampras / B. Becker
1996 R. Krajicek / M. Washington
1997 P. Sampras / C. Pioline
1998 P. Sampras / G. Ivanisevic

For the years 1913, 1914 and 1919-1923 inclusive the above records include the "World's Championships on Grass" granted to The Lawn Tennis Association by The International Lawn Tennis Federation.
This title was then abolished and commencing in 1924 they became The Official Lawn Tennis Championships recognised by The International Lawn Tennis Federation.
Prior to 1922 the holders in the Singles Events and Gentlemen's Doubles did not compete in the Championships but met the winners of these events in the Challenge Rounds.

† Challenge Round abolished: holders subsequently played through. ★ The holder did not defend the title.

The Championship Roll

1884   Miss M. Watson
Miss L. Watson

1885   Miss M. Watson
Miss B. Bingley

1886   Miss B. Bingley
Miss M. Watson

1887   Miss L. Dod
Miss B. Bingley

1888   Miss L. Dod
Mrs. G. W. Hillyard

★1889   Mrs. G. W. Hillyard
Miss L. Rice

★1890   Miss L. Rice
Miss M. Jacks

★1891   Miss L. Dod
Mrs. G. W. Hillyard

1892   Miss L. Dod
Mrs. G. W. Hillyard

1893   Miss L. Dod
Mrs. G. W. Hillyard

★1894   Mrs. G. W. Hillyard
Miss E. L. Austin

★1895   Miss C. Cooper
Miss H. Jackson

1896   Miss C. Cooper
Mrs. W. H. Pickering

1897   Mrs. G. W. Hillyard
Miss C. Cooper

★1898   Miss C. Cooper
Miss L Martin

1899   Mrs. G. W. Hillyard
Miss C. Cooper

1900   Mrs. G. W. Hillyard
Miss C. Cooper

1901   Mrs. A. Sterry
Mrs. G. W. Hillyard

1902   Miss M. E. Robb
Mrs. A. Sterry

★1903   Miss D. K. Douglass
Miss E. W. Thomson

1904   Miss D. K. Douglass
Mrs. A. Sterry

1905   Miss M. Sutton
Miss D. K. Douglass

1906   Miss D. K. Douglass
Miss M. Sutton

1907   Miss M. Sutton
Mrs. Lambert Chambers

★1908   Mrs. A. Sterry
Miss A. M. Morton

★1909   Miss D. P. Boothby
Miss A. M. Morton

1910   Mrs. Lambert Chambers
Miss D. P. Boothby

1911   Mrs. Lambert Chambers
Miss D. P. Boothby

★1912   Mrs. D. R. Larcombe
Mrs. A. Sterry

★1913   Mrs. Lambert Chambers
Mrs. R. J. McNair

1914   Mrs. Lambert Chambers
Mrs. D. R. Larcombe

1919   Mlle. S. Lenglen
Mrs. Lambert Chambers

1920   Mlle. S. Lenglen
Mrs. Lambert Chambers

1921   Mlle. S. Lenglen
Miss E. Ryan

†1922   Mlle. S. Lenglen
Mrs. F. Mallory

1923   Mlle. S. Lenglen
Miss K. McKane

1924   Miss K. McKane
Miss H. Wills

1925   Mlle. S. Lenglen
Miss J. Fry

1926   Mrs. L. A. Godfree
Sta. L. de Alvarez

1927   Miss H. Wills
Sta. L. de Alvarez

1928   Miss H. Wills
Sta. L. de Alvarez

1929   Miss H. Wills
Miss H. H. Jacobs

1930   Mrs. F. S. Moody
Miss E. Ryan

★1931   Fraulein C. Aussem
Fraulein H. Krahwinkel

★1932   Mrs. F. S. Moody
Miss H. H. Jacobs

1933   Mrs. F. S. Moody
Miss D. E. Round

★1934   Miss D. E. Round
Miss H. H. Jacobs

1935   Mrs. F. S. Moody
Miss H. H. Jacobs

★1936   Miss H. H. Jacobs
Frau. S. Sperling

1937   Miss D. E. Round
Miss J. Jedrzejowska

★1938   Mrs. F. S. Moody
Miss H. H. Jacobs

★1939   Miss A. Marble
Miss K. E. Stammers

★1946   Miss P. Betz
Miss L. Brough

★1947   Miss M. Osborne
Miss D. Hart

1948   Miss L. Brough
Miss D. Hart

1949   Miss L. Brough
Mrs. W. du Pont

1950   Miss L. Brough
Mrs. W. du Pont

1951   Miss D. Hart
Miss S. Fry

1952   Miss M. Connolly
Miss L. Brough

1953   Miss M. Connolly
Miss D. Hart

1954   Miss M. Connolly
Miss L. Brough

★1955   Miss L. Brough
Mrs. J. G. Fleitz

1956   Miss S. Fry
Miss A. Buxton

★1957   Miss A. Gibson
Miss D. R. Hard

1958   Miss A. Gibson
Miss A. Mortimer

★1959   Miss M. E. Bueno
Miss D. R. Hard

1960   Miss M. E. Bueno
Miss S. Reynolds

★1961   Miss A. Mortimer
Miss C. C. Truman

1962   Mrs. J. R. Susman
Mrs. V. Sukova

★1963   Miss M. Smith
Miss B. J. Moffitt

1964   Miss M. E. Bueno
Miss M. Smith

1965   Miss M. Smith
Miss M. E. Bueno

1966   Mrs. L. W. King
Miss M. E. Bueno

1967   Mrs. L. W. King
Mrs. P. F. Jones

1968   Mrs. L. W. King
Miss J. A. M. Tegart

1969   Mrs. P. F. Jones
Mrs. L. W. King

★1970   Mrs. B. M. Court
Mrs. L. W. King

1971   Miss E. F. Goolagong
Mrs. B. M. Court

1972   Mrs. L. W. King
Miss E. F. Goolagong

1973   Mrs. L. W. King
Miss C. M. Evert

1974   Miss C. M. Evert
Mrs. O. Morozova

1975   Mrs. L. W. King
Mrs. R. Cawley

★1976   Miss C. M. Evert
Mrs. R. Cawley

1977   Miss S. V. Wade
Miss B. F. Stove

1978   Miss M. Navratilova
Miss C. M. Evert

1979   Miss M. Navratilova
Mrs. J. M. Lloyd

1980   Mrs. R. Cawley
Mrs. J. M. Lloyd

1981   Mrs. J. M. Lloyd
Miss H. Mandlikova

1982   Miss M. Navratilova
Mrs. J. M. Lloyd

1983   Miss M. Navratilova
Miss A. Jaeger

1984   Miss M. Navratilova
Mrs. J. M. Lloyd

1985   Miss M. Navratilova
Mrs. J. M. Lloyd

1986   Miss M. Navratilova
Miss H. Mandlikova

1987   Miss M. Navratilova
Miss S. Graf

1988   Miss S. Graf
Miss M. Navratilova

1989   Miss S. Graf
Miss M. Navratilova

1990   Miss M. Navratilova
Miss Z. Garrison

1991   Miss S. Graf
Miss G. Sabatini

1992   Miss S. Graf
Miss M. Seles

1993   Miss S. Graf
Miss J. Novotna

1994   Miss C. Martinez
Miss M. Navratilova

1995   Miss S. Graf
Miss A. Sanchez Vicario

1996   Miss S. Graf
Miss A. Sanchez Vicario

1997   Miss M. Hingis
Miss J. Novotna

1998   Miss J. Novotna
Miss N. Tauziat

MAIDEN NAMES OF LADY CHAMPIONS

In the tables the following have been recorded in both married and single identities.

Mrs. R. Cawley .... Miss E. F. Goolagong	Mrs. G. W. Hillyard .... Miss B. Bingley	Mrs. F. S. Moody .... Miss H. Wills
Mrs. Lambert Chambers .... Miss D. K. Douglass	Mrs. P. F. Jones .... Miss A. S. Haydon	Mrs. O. Morozova .... Miss O. Morozova
Mrs. B. M. Court .... Miss M. Smith	Mrs. L. W. King .... Miss B. J. Moffitt	Mrs. L. E. G. Price .... Miss S. Reynolds
Mrs. B. C. Covell .... Miss P. L. Howkins	Mrs. M. R. King .... Miss P. E. Mudford	Mrs. G. E. Reid .... Miss K. Melville
Mrs. D. E. Dalton .... Miss J. A. M. Tegart	Mrs. D. R. Larcombe .... Miss E. W. Thomson	Mrs. P. D. Smylie .... Miss E. M. Sayers
Mrs. W. du Pont .... Miss M. Osborne	Mrs. J. M. Lloyd .... Miss C. M. Evert	Frau. S. Sperling .... Fraulein H. Krahwinkel
Mrs. L. A. Godfree .... Miss K. McKane		Mrs. A. Sterry .... Miss C. Cooper
Mrs. H. F. Gourlay Cawley .... Miss H. F. Gourlay		Mrs. J. R. Susman .... Miss K. Hantze

The Championship Roll

GENTLEMEN'S DOUBLES — CHAMPIONS & RUNNERS UP

1879 L. R. Erskine and H. F. Lawford
F. Durant and G. E. Tabor

1880 W. Renshaw and E. Renshaw
O. E. Woodhouse and C. J. Cole

1881 W. Renshaw and E. Renshaw
W. J. Down and H. Vaughan

1882 J. T. Hartley and R. T. Richardson
J. G. Horn and C. B. Russell

1883 C. W. Grinstead and C. E. Welldon
C. B. Russell and R. T. Milford

1884 W. Renshaw and E. Renshaw
E. W. Lewis and E. L Williams

1885 W. Renshaw and E. Renshaw
C. E. Farrer and A. J. Stanley

1886 W. Renshaw and E. Renshaw
C. E. Farrer and A. J. Stanley

1887 P. Bowes-Lyon and H. W. W. Wilberforce
J. H. Crispe and E. Barratt Smith

1888 W. Renshaw and E. Renshaw
P. Bowes-Lyon and H. W. W. Wilberforce

1889 W. Renshaw and E. Renshaw
E. W. Lewis and G. W. Hillyard

1890 J. Pim and F. O. Stoker
E. W. Lewis and G. W. Hillyard

1891 W. Baddeley and H. Baddeley
J. Pim and F. O. Stoker

1892 H. S. Barlow and E. W. Lewis
W. Baddeley and H. Baddeley

1893 J. Pim and F. O. Stoker
E. W. Lewis and H. S. Barlow

1894 W. Baddeley and H. Baddeley
H. S. Barlow and C. H. Martin

1895 W. Baddeley and H. Baddeley
E. W. Lewis and W. V. Eaves

1896 W. Baddeley and H. Baddeley
R. F. Doherty and H. A. Nisbet

1897 R. F. Doherty and H. L. Doherty
W. Baddeley and H. Baddeley

1898 R. F. Doherty and H. L . Doherty
H. A. Nisbet and C. Hobart

1899 R. F. Doherty and H. L. Doherty
H. A. Nisbet and C. Hobart

1900 R. F. Doherty and H. L. Doherty
H. Roper Barrett and H. A. Nisbet

1901 R. F. Doherty and H. L. Doherty
Dwight Davis and Holcombe Ward

1902 S. H. Smith and F. L. Riseley
R. F. Doherty and H. L. Doherty

1903 R. F. Doherty and H. L. Doherty
S. H. Smith and F. L. Riseley

1904 R. F. Doherty and H. L. Doherty
S. H. Smith and F. L. Riseley

1905 R. F. Doherty and H. L. Doherty
S. H. Smith and F. L. Riseley

1906 S. H. Smith and F. L. Riseley
R. F. Doherty and H. L. Doherty

1907 N. E. Brooks and A. F. Wilding
B. C. Wright and K. H. Behr

1908 A. F. Wilding and M. J. G. Ritchie
A. W. Gore and H. Roper Barrett

1909 A. W. Gore and H. Roper Barrett
S. N. Doust and H. A. Parker

1910 A. F. Wilding and M. J. G. Ritchie
A. W. Gore and H. Roper Barrett

1911 M. Decugis and A. H. Gobert
M. J. G. Ritchie and A. F. Wilding

1912 H. Roper Barrett and C. P. Dixon
M. Decugis and A. H. Gobert

1913 H. Roper Barrett and C. P. Dixon
F. W. Rahe and H. Kleinschroth

1914 N. E. Brookes and A. F. Wilding
H. Roper Barrett and C. P. Dixon

1919 R. V. Thomas and P. O'Hara-Wood
R. Lycett and R. W. Heath

1920 R. N. Williams and C. S. Garland
A. R. F. Kingscote and J. C. Parke

1921 R. Lycett and M. Woosnam
F. G. Lowe and A. H. Lowe

1922 R. Lycett and J. O. Anderson
G. L. Patterson and P. O'Hara-Wood

1923 R. Lycett and L. A. Godfree
Count de Gomar and E. Flaquer

1924 F. T. Hunter and V. Richards
R. N. Williams and W. M. Washburn

1925 J. Borotra and R. Lacoste
J. Hennessey and R. Casey

1926 H. Cochet and J. Brugnon
V. Richards and H. Kinsey

1927 F. T. Hunter and W. T. Tilden
J. Brugnon and H. Cochet

1928 H. Cochet and J. Brugnon
G. L. Patterson and J. B. Hawkes

1929 W. Allison and J. Van Ryn
J. C. Gregory and I. G. Collins

1930 W. Allison and J. Van Ryn
J. H. Doeg and G. M. Lott

1931 G. M Lott and J. Van Ryn
H. Cochet and J. Brugnon

1932 J. Borotra and J. Brugnon
G. P. Hughes and F. J. Perry

1933 J. Borotra and J. Brugnon
R. Nunoi and J. Satoh

1934 G. M. Lott and L. R. Stoefen
J. Borotra and J. Brugnon

1935 J. H. Crawford and A. K . Quist
W. Allison and J. Van Ryn

1936 G. P. Hughes and C. R. D. Tuckey
C. E. Hare and F. H. D. Wilde

1937 J. D. Budge and G. Mako
G. P. Hughes and C. R. D. Tuckey

1938 J. D. Budge and G. Mako
H. Henkel and G. von Metaxa

1939 R. L. Riggs and E. T. Cooke
C. E. Hare and F. H. D. Wilde

1946 T. Brown and J. Kramer
G. E. Brown and D. Pails

1947 R. Falkenburg and J. Kramer
A. J. Mottram and O. W. Sidwell

1948 J. E. Bromwich and F. A. Sedgman
T. Brown and G. Mulloy

1949 R. Gonzales and F. Parker
G. Mulloy and F. R. Schroeder

1950 J. E. Bromwich and A. K. Quist
G. E. Brown and O. W. Sidwell

1951 K. McGregor and F. A. Sedgman
J. Drobny and E. W. Sturgess

1952 K. McGregor and F. A. Sedgman
V. Seixas and E. W. Sturgess

1953 L. A. Hoad and K. R. Rosewall
R. N. Hartwig and M. G. Rose

1954 R. N. Hartwig and M. G. Rose
V. Seixas and T. Trabert

1955 R. N. Hartwig and L. A. Hoad
N. A. Fraser and K. R. Rosewall

1956 L. A. Hoad and K. R. Rosewall
N. Pietrangeli and O. Sirola

1957 G. Mulloy and B. Patty
N. A. Fraser and L. A. Hoad

1958 S. Davidson and U. Schmidt
A. J. Cooper and N. A. Fraser

1959 R. Emerson and N. A. Fraser
R. Laver and R. Mark

1960 R. H. Osuna and R. D. Ralston
M. G. Davies and R. K. Wilson

1961 R. Emerson and N. A. Fraser
R. A. J. Hewitt and F. S. Stolle

1962 R. A. J. Hewitt and F. S. Stolle
B. Jovanovic and N. Pilic

1963 R. H. Osuna and A. Palafox
J. C. Barclay and P. Darmon

1964 R. A. J. Hewitt and F. S. Stolle
R. Emerson and K. N. Fletcher

1965 J. D. Newcombe and A. D. Roche
K. N. Fletcher and R. A. J. Hewitt

1966 K. N. Fletcher and J. D. Newcombe
W. W. Bowrey and O. K. Davidson

1967 R. A. J. Hewitt and F. D. McMillan
R. Emerson and K. N. Fletcher

1968 J. D. Newcombe and A. D. Roche
K. R. Rosewall and F. S. Stolle

1969 J. D. Newcombe and A. D. Roche
T. S. Okker and M. C. Reissen

1970 J. D. Newcombe and A. D. Roche
K. R. Rosewall and F. S. Stolle

1971 R. S. Emerson and R. G. Laver
A. R. Ashe and R. D. Ralston

1972 R. A. J. Hewitt and F. D. McMillan
S. R. Smith and E. J. van Dillen

1973 J. S. Connors and I. Nastase
J. R. Cooper and N. A. Fraser

1974 J. D. Newcombe and A. D. Roche
R. C. Lutz and S. R. Smith

1975 V. Gerulaitis and A. Mayer
C. Dowdeswell and A. J. Stone

1976 B. E. Gottfried and R. Ramirez
R. L. Case and G. Masters

1977 R. L. Case and G. Masters
J. G. Alexander and P. C. Dent

1978 R. A. J. Hewitt and F. D. McMillan
P. Fleming and J. P. McEnroe

1979 P. Fleming and J. P . McEnroe
B. E. Gottfried and R. Ramirez

1980 P. McNamara and P. McNamee
R. C. Lutz and S. R. Smith

1981 P. Fleming and J. P. McEnroe
R. C. Lutz and S. R. Smith

1982 P. McNamara and P. McNamee
P. Fleming and J. P. McEnroe

1983 P. Fleming and J. P McEnroe
T. E. Gullikson and T. R. Gullikson

1984 P. Fleming and J. P. McEnroe
P. Cash and P. McNamee

1985 H. P. Guenthardt and B. Taroczy
P. Cash and J. B. Fitzgerald

1986 J. Nystrom and M. Wilander
G. Donnelly and P. Fleming

1987 K. Flach and R. Seguso
S. Casal and E. Sanchez

1988 K. Flach and R. Seguso
J. B. Fitzgerald and A. Jarryd

1989 J. B. Fitzgerald and A. Jarryd
R. Leach and J. Pugh

1990 R. Leach and J. Pugh
P. Aldrich and D. T. Visser

1991 J. B. Fitzgerald and A. Jarryd
J. Frana and L. Lavalle

1992 J. P. McEnroe and M. Stich
J. Grabb and R. A. Reneberg

1993 T. A. Woodbridge and M. Woodforde
G. Connell and P. Galbraith

1994 T. A. Woodbridge and M. Woodforde
G. Connell and P. Galbraith

1995 T. A. Woodbridge and M. Woodforde
R. Leach and S. Melville

1996 T. A. Woodbridge and M. Woodforde
B. Black and G. Connell

1997 T. A. Woodbridge and M. Woodforde
J. Eltingh and P. Haarhuis

1998 J. Eltingh and P. Haarhuis
T. A. Woodbridge and M. Woodforde

LADIES' DOUBLES — CHAMPIONS & RUNNERS UP

1913 Mrs. R. J. McNair and Miss D. P. Boothby
Mrs. A, Sterry and Mrs. Lambert Chambers

1914 Miss E. Ryan and Miss A. M. Morton
Mrs. D. R. Larcombe and Mrs. F. J. Hannam

1919 Mlle. S. Lenglen and Miss E. Ryan
Mrs. Lambert Chambers and Mrs. D. R. Larcombe

1920 Mlle. S. Lenglen and Miss E. Ryan
Mrs. Lambert Chambers and Mrs. D. R. Larcombe

1921 Mlle. S. Lenglen and Miss E. Ryan
Mrs. A. E. Beamish and Mrs. G. E. Peacock

1922 Mlle. S. Lenglen and Miss E. Ryan
Mrs. A. D. Stocks and Miss K. McKane

1923 Mlle. S. Lenglen and Miss E. Ryan
Miss J. Austin and Miss E. L. Colyer

1924 Mrs. H. Wightman and Miss H. Wills
Mrs. B. C. Covell and Miss K. McKane

1925 Mlle. S. Lenglen and Miss E. Ryan
Mrs. A. V. Bridge and Mrs. C. G. McIlquham

1926 Miss E. Ryan and Miss M. K. Browne
Mrs. L. A. Godfree and Miss E. L. Colyer

1927 Miss H. Wills and Miss E. Ryan
Miss E. L. Heine and Mrs. G. E. Peacock

1928 Mrs. Holcroft-Watson and Miss P. Saunders
Miss E. H. Harvey and Miss E. Bennett

1929 Mrs. Holcroft-Watson and Mrs. L. R. C. Michell
Mrs. B. C. Covell and Mrs. D. C. Shepherd-Barron

1930 Mrs. F. S. Moody and Miss E. Ryan
Miss E. Cross and Miss S. Palfrey

1931 Mrs. D. C. Shepherd-Barron and Miss P. E. Mudford
Mlle. D. Metaxa and Mlle. J. Sigart

1932 Mlle. D. Metaxa and Mlle. J. Sigart
Miss E. Ryan and Miss H. H. Jacobs

1933 Mme. R. Mathieu and Miss E. Ryan
Miss F. James and Miss A. M. Yorke

1934 Mme. R. Mathieu and Miss E. Ryan
Mrs. D. Andrus and Mme. S. Henrotin

1935 Miss F. James and Miss K. E. Stammers
Mme. R. Mathieu and Frau. S. Sperling

1936 Miss F. James and Miss K. E. Stammers
Mrs. S. P. Fabyan and Miss H. H. Jacobs

1937 Mme. R. Mathieu and Miss A. M. Yorke
Mrs. M. R. King and Mrs. J. B. Pittman

1938 Mrs. S. P. Fabyan and Miss A. Marble
Mme. R. Mathieu and Miss A. M. Yorke

1939 Mrs S. P. Fabyan and Miss A. Marble
Miss H. H. Jacobs and Miss A. M. Yorke

1946 Miss L. Brough and Miss M. Osborne
Miss P. Betz and Miss D. Hart

1947 Miss D. Hart and Mrs. P. C. Todd
Miss L. Brough and Miss M. Osborne

1948 Miss L. Brough and Mrs. W. du Pont
Miss D. Hart and Mrs. P. C. Todd

1949 Miss L. Brough and Mrs. W. du Pont
Miss G. Moran and Mrs. P. C. Todd

1950 Miss L. Brough and Mrs. W. du Pont
Miss S. Fry and Miss D. Hart

1951 Miss S. Fry and Miss D. Hart
Miss L. Brough and Mrs. W. du Pont

1952 Miss S. Fry and Miss D. Hart
Miss L. Brough and Miss M. Connolly

1953 Miss S. Fry and Miss D. Hart
Miss M. Connolly and Miss J. Sampson

1954 Miss L. Brough and Mrs. W. du Pont
Miss S. Fry and Miss D. Hart

1955 Miss A. Mortimer and Miss J. A. Shilcock
Miss S. J. Bloomer and Miss P. E. Ward

1956 Miss A. Buxton and Miss A. Gibson
Miss F. Muller and Miss D. G. Seeney

1957 Miss A. Gibson and Miss D. R. Hard
Mrs. K. Hawton and Mrs. T. D. Long

1958 Miss M. E. Bueno and Miss A. Gibson
Mrs. W. du Pont and Miss M. Varner

1959 Miss J. Arth and Miss D. R. Hard
Mrs. J. G. Fleitz and Miss C. C. Truman

1960 Miss M. E. Bueno and Miss D. R. Hard
Miss S. Reynolds and Miss R. Schuurman

1961 Miss K. Hantze and Miss B. J. Moffitt
Miss J. Lehane and Miss M. Smith

1962 Miss B. J. Moffitt and Mrs. J. R. Susman
Mrs. L. E. G. Price and Miss R. Schuurman

1963 Miss M. E. Bueno and Miss D. R. Hard
Miss R. A. Ebbern and Miss M. Smith

1964 Miss M. Smith and Miss L. R. Turner
Miss B. J. Moffitt and Mrs. J. R. Susman

1965 Miss M. E. Bueno and Miss B. J. Moffitt
Miss F. Durr and Miss J. Lieffrig

1966 Miss M. E. Bueno and Miss N. Richey
Miss M. Smith and Miss J. A. M. Tegart

1967 Miss R. Casals and Mrs. L. W. King
Miss M. E. Bueno and Miss N. Richey

1968 Miss R. Casals and Mrs. L. W. King
Miss F. Durr and Mrs. P. F. Jones

1969 Mrs. B. M. Court and Miss J. A. M. Tegart
Miss P. S. A. Hogan and Miss M. Michel

1970 Miss R. Casals and Mrs. L. W. King
Miss F. Durr and Miss S. V. Wade

1971 Miss R. Casals and Mrs. L. W. King
Mrs. B. M. Court and Miss E. F. Goolagong

1972 Mrs. L. W. King and Miss B. F. Stove
Mrs. D. E. Dalton and Miss F. Durr

1973 Miss R. Casals and Mrs. L. W. King
Miss F. Durr and Miss B. F. Stove

1974 Miss E. F. Goolagong and Miss M. Michel
Miss H. F. Gourlay and Miss K. M. Krantzcke

1975 Miss A. Kiyomura and Miss K. Sawamatsu
Miss F. Durr and Miss B. F. Stove

1976 Miss C. M. Evert and Miss M. Navratilova
Mrs. L. W. King and Miss B. F. Stove

1977 Mrs. H. F. Gourlay Cawley and Miss J. C. Russell
Miss M. Navratilova and Miss B. F . Stove

1978 Mrs. G. E. Reid and Miss. W. M. Turnbull
Miss M. Jausovec and Miss V. Ruzici

1979 Mrs. L. W. King and Miss M. Navratilova
Miss B. F. Stove and Miss W. M. Turnbull

1980 Miss K. Jordan and Miss A. E. Smith
Miss R. Casals and Miss W. M. Turnbull

1981 Miss M. Navratilova and Miss P. H. Shriver
Miss K. Jordan and Miss A. E. Smith

1982 Miss M. Navratilova and Miss P. H. Shriver
Miss K. Jordan and Miss A. E. Smith

1983 Miss M. Navratilova and Miss P. H. Shriver
Miss R. Casals and Miss W. M. Turnbull

1984 Miss M. Navratilova and Miss P. H. Shriver
Miss K. Jordan and Miss A. E. Smith

1985 Miss K. Jordan and Mrs. P. D. Smylie
Miss M. Navratilova and Miss P. H. Shriver

1986 Miss M. Navratilova and Miss P. H. Shriver
Miss H. Mandlikova and Miss W. M. Turnbull

1987 Miss C. Kohde-Kilsch and Miss H. Sukova
Miss B. Nagelsen and Mrs. P. D. Smylie

1988 Miss S. Graf and Miss G. Sabatini
Miss L. Savchenko and Miss N. Zvereva

1989 Miss J. Novotna and Miss H. Sukova
Miss L. Savchenko and Miss N. Zvereva

1990 Miss J. Novotna and Miss H. Sukova
Miss K. Jordan and Mrs. P. D. Smylie

1991 Miss L. Savchenko and Miss N. Zvereva
Miss G. Fernandez and Miss J. Novotna

1992 Miss G. Fernandez and Miss N. Zvereva
Miss J. Novotna and Mrs. L. Savchenko-Neiland

1993 Miss G. Fernandez and Miss N. Zvereva
Mrs. L. Neiland and Miss J. Novotna

1994 Miss G. Fernandez and Miss N. Zvereva
Miss J. Novotna and Miss A. Sanchez Vicario

1995 Miss J. Novotna and Miss A. Sanchez Vicario
Miss G. Fernandez and Miss N. Zvereva

1996 Miss M. Hingis and Miss H. Sukova
Miss M.J. McGrath and Mrs. L. Neiland

1997 Miss G. Fernandez and Miss N. Zvereva
Miss N.J. Arendt and Miss M.M. Bollegraf

1998 Miss M. Hingis and Miss J. Novotna
Miss L.A. Davenport and Miss N. Zvereva

The Championship Roll

MIXED DOUBLES—CHAMPIONS & RUNNERS UP

1913	Hope Crisp and Mrs. C. O. Tuckey
	J. C. Parke and Mrs. D. R. Larcombe
1914	J. C. Parke and Mrs. D.R. Larcombe
	A. F. Wilding and Mlle. M. Broquedis
1919	R. Lycett and Miss E. Ryan
	A. D. Prebble and Mrs. Lambert Chambers
1920	G. L. Patterson and Mlle. S. Lenglen
	R. Lycett and Miss E. Ryan
1921	R. Lycett and Miss E. Ryan
	M. Woosnam and Miss P. L. Howkins
1922	P. O'Hara-Wood and Mlle. S. Lenglen
	R. Lycett and Miss E. Ryan
1923	R. Lycett and Miss E. Ryan
	L. S. Deane and Mrs. D. C. Shepherd-Barron
1924	J. B. Gilbert and Miss K. McKane
	L. A. Godfree and Mrs. D. C. Shepherd-Barron
1925	J. Borotra and Mlle. S. Lenglen
	H. L. de Morpurgo and Miss E. Ryan
1926	L. A. Godfree and Mrs. L. A. Godfree
	H. Kinsey and Miss M. K. Browne
1927	F. T. Hunter and Miss E. Ryan
	L. A. Godfree and Mrs. L. A. Godfree
1928	P. D. B. Spence and Miss E. Ryan
	J. Crawford and Miss D. Akhurst
1929	F. T. Hunter and Miss H. Wills
	I. G. Collins and Miss J. Fry
1930	J. H. Crawford and Miss E. Ryan
	D. Prenn and Fraulein H. Krahwinkel
1931	G. M. Lott and Mrs L. A. Harper
	I. G. Collins and Miss J. C. Ridley
1932	E. Maier and Miss E. Ryan
	H. C. Hopman and Mlle. J. Sigart
1933	G. von Cramm and Fraulein H. Krahwinkel
	N. G. Farquharson and Miss M. Heeley
1934	R. Miki and Miss D. E. Round
	H. W. Austin and Mrs D. C. Shepherd-Barron
1935	F. J. Perry and Miss D. E. Round
	H. C. Hopman and Mrs. H. C. Hopman
1936	F. J. Perry and Miss D. E. Round
	J. D. Budge and Mrs. S. P. Fabyan
1937	J. D. Budge and Miss A. Marble
	Y. Petra and Mme. R. Mathieu
1938	J. D. Budge and Miss A. Marble
	H. Henkel and Mrs. S. P. Fabyan
1939	R. L. Riggs and Miss A. Marble
	F. H. D. Wilde and Miss N. B. Brown
1946	T. Brown and Miss L. Brough
	G. E. Brown and Miss D. Bundy
1947	J. E. Bromwich and Miss L. Brough
	C. F. Long and Mrs. N. M. Bolton
1948	J. E. Bromwich and Miss L. Brough

	F. A. Sedgman and Miss D. Hart
1949	E. W. Sturgess and Mrs. S. P. Summers
	J. E. Bromwich and Miss L. Brough
1950	E. W. Sturgess and Miss L. Brough
	G. E. Brown and Mrs. P. C. Todd
1951	F. A. Sedgman and Miss D. Hart
	M. G. Rose and Miss N. M. Bolton
1952	F. A. Sedgman and Miss D. Hart
	E. Morea and Mrs. T. D. Long
1953	V. Seixas and Miss D. Hart
	E. Morea and Miss S. Fry
1954	V. Seixas and Miss D. Hart
	K. R. Rosewall and Mrs. W. du Pont
1955	V. Seixas and Miss D. Hart
	E. Morea and Miss L. Brough
1956	V. Seixas and Miss S. Fry
	G. Mulloy and Miss A. Gibson
1957	M. G. Rose and Miss D. R. Hard
	N. A. Fraser and Miss A. Gibson
1958	R. N. Howe and Miss L. Coghlan
	K. Nielsen and Miss A. Gibson
1959	R. Laver and Miss D. R. Hard
	N. A. Fraser and Miss M. E. Bueno
1960	R. Laver and Miss D. R. Hard
	R. N. Howe and Miss M. E. Bueno
1961	F. S. Stolle and Miss L. R. Turner
	R. N. Howe and Miss E. Buding
1962	N. A. Fraser and Mrs. W. du Pont
	R. D. Ralston and Miss A. S. Haydon
1963	K. N. Fletcher and Miss M. Smith
	R. A. J. Hewitt and Miss D. R. Hard
1964	F. S. Stolle and Miss L. R. Turner
	K. N. Fletcher and Miss M. Smith
1965	K. N. Fletcher and Miss M. Smith
	A. D. Roche and Miss J. A. M. Tegart
1966	K. N. Fletcher and Miss M. Smith
	R. D. Ralston amd Mrs. L. W. King
1967	O. K. Davidson and Mrs. L. W. King
	K. N. Fletcher and Miss M. E. Bueno
1968	K. N. Fletcher and Mrs. B. M. Court
	A. Metreveli and Miss O. Morozova
1969	F. S. Stolle and Mrs. P. F. Jones
	A. D. Roche and Miss J. A. M. Tegart
1970	I. Nastase and Miss R. Casals
	A. Metreveli and Miss O. Morozova
1971	O. K. Davidson and Mrs. L. W. King
	M. C. Riessen and Mrs. B. M. Court
1972	I. Nastase and Miss R. Casals
	K. G. Warwick and Miss E. F. Goolagong
1973	O. K. Davidson and Mrs. L. W. King
	R. Ramirez and Miss J. S. Newberry

1974	O. K. Davidson and Mrs. L. W. King
	M. J. Farrell and Miss L. J. Charles
1975	M. C. Riessen and Mrs. B. M. Court
	A. J. Stone and Miss B. F. Stove
1976	A. D. Roche and Miss F. Durr
	R. L. Stockton and Miss R. Casals
1977	R. A. J. Hewitt and Miss G. R. Stevens
	F. D. McMillan and Miss B. F. Stove
1978	F. D. McMillan and Miss B. F. Stove
	R. O. Ruffels and Mrs. L. W. King
1979	R. A. J. Hewitt and Miss G. R. Stevens
	F. D. McMillan and Miss B. F. Stove
1980	J. R. Austin and Miss T. Austin
	M. R. Edmondson and Miss D. L. Fromholtz
1981	F. D. McMillan and Miss B. F. Stove
	J. R. Austin and Miss T. Austin
1982	K. Curren and Miss A. E. Smith
	J. M. Lloyd and Miss W. M. Turnbull
1983	J. M. Lloyd and Miss W. M. Turnbull
	S. Denton and Mrs. L. W. King
1984	J. M. Lloyd and Miss W. M. Turnbull
	S. Denton and Miss K. Jordan
1985	P. McNamee and Miss M. Navratilova
	J. B. Fitzgerald and Mrs. P. D. Smylie
1986	K. Flach and Miss K. Jordan
	H. P. Guenthardt and Miss M. Navratilova
1987	M. J. Bates and Miss J. M. Durie
	D. Cahill and Miss N. Provis
1988	S. E. Stewart and Miss Z. L. Garrison
	K. Jones and Mrs. S. W. Magers
1989	J. Pugh and Miss J. Novotna
	M. Kratzmann and Miss J. M. Byrne
1990	R. Leach and Miss Z. L. Garrison
	J. B. Fitzgerald and Mrs P. D. Smylie
1991	J. B. Fitzgerald and Mrs. P. D. Smylie
	J. Pugh and Miss N. Zvereva
1992	C. Suk and Mrs L. Savchenko-Neiland
	J. Eltingh and Miss M. Oremans
1993	M. Woodforde and Miss M. Navratilova
	T. Nijssen and Miss M. M. Bollegraf
1994	T. A. Woodbridge and Miss H. Sukova
	T. J. Middleton and Miss L. M. McNeil
1995	J. Stark and Miss M. Navratilova
	C. Suk and Miss G. Fernandez
1996	C. Suk and Miss H. Sukova
	M. Woodforde and Mrs. L. Neiland
1997	C. Suk and Miss H. Sukova
	A. Olhovskiy and Mrs L. Neiland
1998	M. Mirnyi and Miss S. Williams
	M. Bhupathi and Miss M. Lucic

The Junior Championship Roll

BOYS' SINGLES

1947	K. Nielsen (Denmark)	1960	A. R. Mandelstam (S.A.)	1973	W. Martin (U.S.A.)	1986	E. Velez (Mexico)
1948	S. Stockenberg (Sweden)	1961	C. E. Graebner (U.S.A.)	1974	W. Martin (U.S.A.)	1987	D. Nargiso (Italy)
1949	S. Stockenberg (Sweden)	1962	S. Matthews (G.B.)	1975	C. J. Lewis (N.Z.)	1988	N. Pereira (Venezuela)
1950	J. A. T. Horn (G.B.)	1963	N. Kalogeropoulos (Greece)	1976	H. Guenthardt (Switzerland)	1989	N. Kulti (Sweden)
1951	J. Kupferburger (S.A.)	1964	I. El Shafei (U.A.R.)	1977	V. A. Winitsky (U.S.A.)	1990	L. Paes (India)
1952	R. K. Wilson (G.B.)	1965	V. Korotkov (U.S.S.R.)	1978	I. Lendl (Czechoslovakia)	1991	T. Enquist (Sweden)
1953	W. A. Knight (G.B.)	1966	V. Korotkov (U.S.S.R.)	1979	R. Krishnan (India)	1992	D. Skoch (Czechoslovakia)
1954	R. Krishnan (India)	1967	M. Orantes (Spain)	1980	T. Tulasne (France)	1993	R. Sabau (Romania)
1955	M. P. Hann (G.B.)	1968	J. G. Alexander (Australia)	1981	M. W. Anger (U.S.A.)	1994	S. Humphries (U.S.A.)
1956	R. Holmberg (U.S.A.)	1969	B. Bertram (S.A.)	1982	P. Cash (Australia)	1995	O. Mutis (France)
1957	J. I. Tattersall (G.B.)	1970	B. Bertram (S.A.)	1983	S. Edberg (Sweden)	1996	V. Voltchkov (Belarus)
1958	E. Buchholz (U.S.A.)	1971	R. Kreiss (U.S.A.)	1984	M. Kratzmann (Australia)	1997	W. Whitehouse (South Africa)
1959	T. Lejus (U.S.S.R.)	1972	B. Borg (Sweden)	1985	L. Lavalle (Mexico)	1998	R. Federer (Switzerland)

BOYS' DOUBLES

1982	P. Cash and J. Frawley	1988	J. Stoltenberg and T. Woodbridge	1994	B. Ellwood and M. Philippoussis
1983	M. Kratzmann and S. Youl	1989	J. Palmer and J. Stark	1995	M. Lee and J. M. Trotman
1984	R. Brown and R. Weiss	1990	S. Lareau and S. Leblanc	1996	D. Bracciali and J. Robichaud
1985	A. Moreno and J. Yzaga	1991	K. Alami and G. Rusedski	1997	L. Horna and N. Massu
1986	T. Carbonell and P. Korda	1992	S. Baldas and S. Draper	1998	R. Federer and O. Rochus
1987	J. Stoltenberg and T. Woodbridge	1993	S. Downs and J. Greenhalgh		

GIRLS' SINGLES

1947	Miss B. Domken (Belgium)	1960	Miss K. Hantze (U.S.A.)	1973	Miss A. Kiyomura (U.S.A.)	1986	Miss N. Zvereva (U.S.S.R.)
1948	Miss O. Miskova (Czechoslovakia)	1961	Miss G. Baksheeva (U.S.S.R.)	1974	Miss M. Jausovec (Yugoslavia)	1987	Miss N. Zvereva (U.S.S.R.)
1949	Miss C. Mercelis (Belgium)	1962	Miss G. Baksheeva (U.S.S.R.)	1975	Miss N. Y. Chmyreva (U.S.S.R.)	1988	Miss B. Schultz (Netherlands)
1950	Miss L. Cornell (G.B.)	1963	Miss D. M. Salfati (France)	1976	Miss N. Y. Chmyreva (U.S.S.R.)	1989	Miss A. Strnadova (Czechoslovakia)
1951	Miss L. Cornell (G.B.)	1964	Miss P. Bartkowicz (U.S.A.)	1977	Miss L. Antonoplis (U.S.A.)	1990	Miss A. Strnadova (Czechoslovakia)
1952	Miss ten Bosch (Netherlands)	1965	Miss O. Morozova (U.S.S.R.)	1978	Miss T. Austin (U.S.A.)	1991	Miss B. Rittner (Germany)
1953	Miss D. Kilian (S.A.)	1966	Miss B. Lindstrom (Finland)	1979	Miss M. L. Piatek (U.S.A.)	1992	Miss C. Rubin (U.S.A.)
1954	Miss V. A. Pitt (G.B.)	1967	Miss J. Salome (Netherlands)	1980	Miss D. Freeman (Australia)	1993	Miss N. Feber (Belgium)
1955	Miss S. M. Armstrong (G.B.)	1968	Miss K. Pigeon (U.S.A.)	1981	Miss Z. Garrison (U.S.A.)	1994	Miss M. Hingis (Switzerland)
1956	Miss A. S. Haydon (G.B.)	1969	Miss K. Sawamatsu (Japan)	1982	Miss C. Tanvier (France)	1995	Miss A. Olsza (Poland)
1957	Miss M. Arnold (U.S.A.)	1970	Miss S. Walsh (U.S.A.)	1983	Miss P. Paradis (France)	1996	Miss A. Mauresmo (France)
1958	Miss S. M. Moore (U.S.A.)	1971	Miss M. Kroschina (U.S.S.R.)	1984	Miss A. N. Croft (G.B.)	1997	Miss C. Black (Zimbabwe)
1959	Miss J. Cross (S.A.)	1972	Miss I. Kloss (S.A.)	1985	Miss A. Holikova (Czechoslovakia)	1998	Miss K. Srebotnik (Slovenia)

GIRLS' DOUBLES

1982	Miss B. Herr and Miss P. Barg	1988	Miss J. A. Faull and Miss R. McQuillan	1994	Miss E. De Villiers and Miss E. E. Jelfs
1983	Miss P. Fendick and Miss P. Hy	1989	Miss J. Capriati and Miss M. McGrath	1995	Miss C. Black and Miss A. Olsza
1984	Miss C. Kuhlman and Miss S. Rehe	1990	Miss K. Habsudova and Miss A. Strnadova	1996	Miss O. Barabanschikova and Miss A. Mauresmo
1985	Miss L. Field and Miss J. Thompson	1991	Miss C. Barclay and Miss L. Zaltz	1997	Miss C. Black and Miss I. Selyutina
1986	Miss M. Jaggard and Miss L. O'Neill	1992	Miss M. Avotins and Miss L. McShea	1998	Miss E. Dyrberg and Miss J. Kostanic
1987	Miss N. Medvedeva and Miss N. Zvereva	1993	Miss L. Courtois and Miss N. Feber		

The Gentlemen's Singles Championship 1998
Holder: P. Sampras

The Winner became the holder, for the year only, of the CHALLENGE CUP presented by The All England Lawn Tennis and Croquet Club. The Winner received a silver replica of the Challenge Cup.
A Silver Salver was presented to the Runner-up and a Bronze Medal to each defeated Semi-finalist. The matches were the best of five sets.

First Round	Second Round	Third Round	Fourth Round	Quarter-Finals	Semi-Finals	Final
1. **P.Sampras [1]** ....(USA)	**P.Sampras [1]** 6/3 6/3 6/2	**P.Sampras [1]**				
2. D.Hrbaty ....(SVK)						
3. M.Tillstrom ....(SWE)	M.Tillstrom ....6/4 6/7(5) 7/5 6/3	...............6/4 6/4 7/6(5)				
(Q) 4. A.Radulescu ....(GER)			**P.Sampras [1]**			
5. D.Nestor ....(CAN)	T.Enqvist ....6/7(2) 6/7(8) 6/4 6/0 6/0	T.Enqvist				
6. T.Enqvist ....(SWE)			...............6/3 7/6(4) 7/6(3)			
7. S.Draper ....(AUS)	S.Draper 6/3 7/5 3/6 6/3					
8. R.Schuttler ....(GER)				**P.Sampras [1]**		
9. K.Alami ....(MAR)	B.MacPhie 4/6 6/3 6/4 3/6 7/5	S.Grosjean				
(Q) 10. B.MacPhie ....(USA)						
11. M.Damm ....(CZE)	S.Grosjean ....6/3 7/6(8) 6/3	...............6/4 3/6 6/1 6/4		...............6/3 6/4 6/4		
(Q) 12. S.Grosjean ....(FRA)			S.Grosjean			
13. R.Vasek ....(CZE)	R.Vasek ....7/6(4) 6/3 6/1					
14. O.Gross ....(GER)						
(L) 15. C.Van Garsse ....(BEL)	**F.Mantilla [16]** 6/2 6/2 1/6 4/6 6/2	**F.Mantilla [16]**	...............6/0 7/6(8) 6/2			
16. **F.Mantilla [16]** ....(ESP)		...............7/6(4) 3/6 6/3 6/4				
17. **A.Corretja [10]** ....(ESP)	J.Gimelstob ....7/6(3) 6/2 6/3	M.Woodforde			**P.Sampras [1]**	
18. J.Gimelstob ....(USA)					7/6(5) 6/4 6/4	
19. J.Knippschild ....(GER)	M.Woodforde ....4/6 6/3 7/6(7) 6/1	...............2/6 6/1 6/4 6/4				
20. M.Woodforde ....(AUS)			J.Stoltenberg			
21. P.Haarhuis ....(NED)	J.Tarango 1/6 6/3 6/3 6/0	J.Stoltenberg				
22. J.Tarango ....(USA)			...............6/1 3/6 6/3 3/6 6/3			
23. G.Kuerten ....(BRA)	J.Stoltenberg 4/6 6/3 6/1 4/6 10/8	...............6/4 2/6 6/2 6/7(3) 6/3				
24. J.Stoltenberg ....(AUS)				M.Philippoussis		
25. L.Arnold ....(ARG)	B.Ulihrach ....2/6 7/6(6) 6/3 6/3	D.Bracciali		...............5/7 6/1 6/3 6/3		
26. B.Ulihrach ....(CZE)						
(Q) 27. D.Bracciali ....(ITA)	D.Bracciali ....4/6 6/7(6) 7/6(6) 6/2 6/2	...............6/4 6/4 3/6 6/2				
(W) 28. M.Lee ....(GBR)			D.Bracciali			
(Q) 29. A.O'Brien ....(USA)	A.O'Brien 4/6 4/6 6/4 6/3 6/4	M.Philippoussis				
30. K.Carlsen ....(DEN)			...............6/3 6/4 6/4			
31. M.Philippoussis ....(AUS)	M.Philippoussis .....6/7(5) 7/6(1) 6/4 6/2	...............6/7(3) 6/4 7/6(2) 6/3	M.Philippoussis			
32. **Y.Kafelnikov [7]** ....(RUS)						
33. **P.Korda [3]** ....(CZE)	**P.Korda [3]** 6/3 6/4 6/3	**P.Korda [3]**				
34. J.Sanchez ....(ESP)						
35. S.Campbell ....(USA)	F.Dewulf 6/3 2/6 6/1 6/0	...............6/4 6/3 6/2				
36. F.Dewulf ....(BEL)			**P.Korda [3]**			
(W) 37. D.E.Sapsford ....(GBR)	J.Golmard ....7/6(6) 6/2 6/3	J.Golmard				
38. J.Golmard ....(FRA)			...............6/3 6/4 4/6 7/6(6)			
(W) 39. D.Wheaton ....(USA)	N.Escude ....6/1 7/6(3) 6/4		...............4/6 7/5 7/5 7/5			
40. N.Escude ....(FRA)				P.Korda [3]		
41. S.Lareau ....(CAN)	S.Lareau 6/4 6/3 6/2	J.Van Lottum		...............6/3 6/4 7/6(4)		
42. R.A.Reneberg ....(USA)						
43. J.Van Lottum ....(NED)	J.Van Lottum ....7/6(1) 4/6 3/6 4/6 7/6(3)	...............6/2 5/7 6/4 6/3				
44. G.Raoux ....(FRA)			J.Van Lottum			
45. T.Haas ....(GER)	T.Haas ....6/7(4) 6/3 6/3 6/3	T.Haas				
46. R.Delgado ....(PAR)			...............4/6 6/1 7/6(4) 6/4	...............6/3 6/3 6/3		
47. A.Calatrava ....(ESP)	**A.Agassi [13]** 6/2 6/4 6/3					
48. **A.Agassi [13]** ....(USA)						
49. **T.Henman [12]** ....(GBR)	**T.Henman [12]** ....7/6(4) 7/5 5/7 4/6 6/2	**T.Henman [12]**				
50. J.Novak ....(CZE)						
(Q) 51. T.Ketola ....(FIN)	D.Nainkin ....6/1 7/6(4) 6/4	...............6/3 5/7 6/4 6/2				
(Q) 52. D.Nainkin ....(RSA)			**T.Henman [12]**			
53. J.Gambill ....(USA)	J.Gambill ....7/6(6) 6/4 6/7(5) 4/6 8/6	B.Black				
54. S.Schalken ....(NED)			...............7/5 6/4 7/5			
55. B.Black ....(ZIM)	B.Black ....7/5 3/6 3/6 7/6(7) 6/2	...............6/4 6/4 3/6 7/5				
56. R.Fromberg ....(AUS)				T.Henman [12]		
(W) 57. M.R.J.Petchey ....(GBR)	M.Gustafsson 6/2 1/6 6/3 6/2	M.Gustafsson		...............6/3 6/7(3) 6/3 6/2		
58. M.Gustafsson ....(SWE)						
59. J.Viloca ....(ESP)	M.Chang 6/4 6/3 3/6 3/6 6/2	...............6/2 5/7 6/2 1/6 6/2				
60. M.Chang ....(USA)			P.Rafter [6]			
61. T.Nydahl ....(SWE)	T.Nydahl ....7/5 6/2 7/6(6)	P.Rafter [6]				
62. H.Gumy ....(ARG)			...............7/6(3) 6/2 7/6(3)	...............6/3 6/7(7) 6/2 6/1		
(Q) 63. I.Heuberger ....(SUI)	**P.Rafter [6]** 6/1 6/2 4/6 6/1					
64. **P.Rafter [6]** ....(AUS)						
65. **C.Moya [5]** ....(ESP)	**C.Moya [5]** 6/4 4/6 6/4 2/6 6/3	H.Arazi			**T.Henman [12]**	
(Q) 66. M.Bhupathi ....(IND)					6/3 6/4 6/2	
(W) 67. A.L.Richardson ....(GBR)	H.Arazi 6/4 2/6 6/3 6/2	...............4/6 6/4 6/3 6/4				
68. H.Arazi ....(MAR)			M.Larsson			
69. S.Sargsian ....(ARM)	S.Sargsian 6/0 7/5 6/2	M.Larsson				
70. A.Portas ....(ESP)			...............6/3 6/3 6/2			
71. M.Filippini ....(URU)	M.Larsson 7/5 6/1 6/4	...............6/3 6/7(5) 6/3 7/5	M.Larsson			
72. M.Larsson ....(SWE)						
73. N.Lapentti ....(ECU)	D.Prinosil 4/6 6/3 6/4 6/3	J.Siemerink		J.Siemerink		
74. D.Prinosil ....(GER)				...............4/6 6/3 6/3 6/2		
75. J.Siemerink ....(NED)	J.Siemerink ....6/1 4/6 7/6(3)	...............6/4 6/7(3) 6/4 6/2				
76. S.Dosedel ....(CZE)						
(Q) 77. S.Pescosolido ....(ITA)	S.Pescosolido 6/2 6/1 6/1	**J.Bjorkman [11]**	J.Siemerink			
78. J.A.Marin ....(CRC)				...............7/6(6) 5/7 2/6 6/4 7/5		
(Q) 79. D.Dilucia ....(USA)	**J.Bjorkman [11]** 6/4 3/6 6/3 6/2	...............4/6 6/4 6/4 6/2				
80. **J.Bjorkman [11]** ....(SWE)						
81. **G.Ivanisevic [14]** ....(CRO)	**G.Ivanisevic [14]** 6/3 6/3 6/2	**G.Ivanisevic [14]**				
82. G.Stafford ....(RSA)						
(W) 83. M.Safin ....(RUS)	A.Medvedev 6/3 6/4 3/6 6/4	...............6/3 7/6(4) 4/6 6/0				
84. A.Medvedev ....(UKR)			**G.Ivanisevic [14]**			
85. G.Pozzi ....(ITA)	D.Vacek ....7/6(1) 7/6(4) 6/3	D.Vacek				
86. D.Vacek ....(CZE)			...............6/7(6) 7/6(4) 6/3 6/4			
87. J.Burillo ....(ESP)	M-K.Goellner 4/6 5/7 6/3 6/1 6/2	...............6/4 7/5 6/3			**G.Ivanisevic [14]**	
88. M-K.Goellner ....(GER)					7/6(5) 6/3 3/6 7/6(2)	
89. T.A.Woodbridge ....(AUS)	T.A.Woodbridge 6/1 6/2 6/1	T.A.Woodbridge		**G.Ivanisevic [14]**		
90. G.Blanco ....(ESP)						
91. W.Black ....(ZIM)	W.Black 6/4 7/5 6/4	...............6/1 3/6 6/3 6/2				
92. L.Paes ....(IND)						
93. T.Martin ....(USA)	T.Martin 6/3 6/4 6/4	T.Martin	T.Martin			
94. A.Sa ....(BRA)			...............6/3 7/5 6/2	...............6/4 4/6 7/6(1) 6/4		
(Q) 95. M.Draper ....(AUS)	M.Draper ....4/6 6/2 5/4 Ret'd					
96. **G.Rusedski [4]** ....(GBR)						
97. **C.Pioline [8]** ....(FRA)	M.Rosset ....6/4 3/6 4/6 7/6(5) 13/11	C.Wilkinson				
98. M.Rosset ....(SUI)						
(Q) 99. M.Knowles ....(BAH)	C.Wilkinson 6/4 6/0 6/1	...............6/4 6/4 7/6(3)				
(W)100. C.Wilkinson ....(GBR)			W.Ferreira			
101. M.Norman ....(SWE)	A.Costa ....7/5 7/5 7/6(5)	W.Ferreira				
102. A.Costa ....(ESP)			...............3/6 7/5 6/3 6/3	...............6/2 4/6 6/3 6/1		
103. A.Clement ....(FRA)	W.Ferreira 4/6 6/3 6/4 6/2					
104. W.Ferreira ....(RSA)						
105. J.Alonso ....(ESP)	N.Kiefer 6/2 6/2 6/3	N.Kiefer			**G.Ivanisevic [14]**	
106. N.Kiefer ....(GER)					6/3 6/4 5/7 6/7(5) 15/13	
107. H.Dreekmann ....(GER)	H.Dreekmann ......6/7(3) 7/6(10) 6/3 3/6 6/3	...............6/4 6/3 1/6 6/4				
(W)108. B.Cowan ....(GBR)			R.Krajicek [9]			
(Q)109. N.Godwin ....(RSA)	D.Pescariu 6/4 6/2 6/3	R.Krajicek [9]				
110. D.Pescariu ....(ROM)			...............6/1 6/3 6/2	...............6/4 7/6(2) 7/6(4)		
111. B.Steven ....(NZL)	**R.Krajicek [9]** ....6/3 7/6(7) 4/6 6/2					
112. **R.Krajicek [9]** ....(NED)						
113. **K.Kucera [15]** ....(SVK)	V.Voltchkov ....7/6(6) 6/3 6/4	V.Voltchkov		**R.Krajicek [9]**		
(Q) 114. V.Voltchkov ....(BLR)				...............6/3 6/3 7/5		
(Q) 115. W.McGuire ....(USA)	M.Tebbutt 6/3 6/0 7/5	...............6/4 6/3 7/6(4)				
116. M.Tebbutt ....(AUS)						
117. M.Puerta ....(ARG)	F.Squillari ....6/7(5) 6/3 7/5 6/4	D.Sanguinetti			**R.Krajicek [9]**	
118. F.Squillari ....(ARG)				D.Sanguinetti	6/2 6/3 6/4	
119. D.Sanguinetti ....(ITA)	D.Sanguinetti ....6/7(0) 6/1 6/1 2/0 Ret'd	...............6/1 6/3 6/2	...............3/6 6/1 5/7 6/2 6/1			
120. J.Van Herck ....(BEL)						
121. A.Pavel ....(ROM)	V.Spadea 6/3 6/3 6/3					
122. V.Spadea ....(USA)			T.Johansson			
123. J.Courier ....(USA)	T.Johansson ....6/4 7/6(6) 6/4	...............7/5 6/1 6/3		D.Sanguinetti		
124. T.Johansson ....(SWE)				...............7/6(3) 6/1 6/4		
125. M.Sinner ....(GER)	G.Canas 6/2 6/2 6/4	F.Clavet				
126. G.Canas ....(ARG)			...............6/7(2) 2/6 7/6(4) 6/1 6/4			
127. F.Clavet ....(ESP)	F.Clavet 6/3 3/6 7/5 3/6 6/3		...............7/6(4) 3/6 6/3			
128. **M.Rios [2]** ....(CHI)						

Final: P.Sampras [1] 6/7(2) 7/6(9) 6/4 3/6 6/2

P.Sampras [1] 6/3 4/6 7/5 6/3

P.Sampras [1]

116

Heavy type denotes seeded players. The figure in brackets against names denotes the order in which they have been seeded. (W)=Wild card. (Q)=Qualifier. (L)=Lucky loser.

The Ladies' Singles Championship 1998
Holder: Miss M. Hingis

The Winner became the holder, for the year only, of the CHALLENGE TROPHY presented by The All England Lawn Tennis and Croquet Club. The Winner will received a silver replica of the Trophy.
A Silver Salver was presented to the Runner-up and a Bronze Medal to each defeated Semi-finalist. The matches were the best of three sets.

First Round	Second Round	Third Round	Fourth Round	Quarter-Finals	Semi-Finals	Final
1. Miss M.Hingis [1] ....(SUI)	Miss M.Hingis [1] 7/5 6/3	Miss M.Hingis [1] ....7/6(2) 6/4	Miss M.Hingis [1] 6/2 6/1	Miss M.Hingis [1] 6/3 6/2	Miss M.Hingis [1] 6/3 3/6 6/3	Miss J.Novotna [3] 6/4 7/6(2)
2. Miss L.M.Raymond ....(USA)						
3. Miss E.Makarova ....(RUS)	Miss E.Makarova 6/4 6/2					
(Q) 4. Miss S.Talaja ....(CRO)						
5. Miss F.Perfetti ....(ITA)	Miss F.Perfetti 6/0 6/1	Miss E.Likhovtseva 6/4 6/0				
6. Miss D.Chladkova ....(CZE)						
7. Miss Y.Yoshida ....(JPN)	Miss E.Likhovtseva ......7/6(6) 6/2					
8. Miss E.Likhovtseva ....(RUS)						
(W) 9. Miss K.M.Cross ....(GBR)	Miss K.M.Cross 6/3 6/4	Miss T.Tanasugarn 6/2 7/5	Miss T.Tanasugarn 6/1 6/0			
(W) 10. Miss J.Ward ....(GBR)						
11. Miss T.Tanasugarn ....(THA)	Miss T.Tanasugarn 6/0 7/5					
12. Miss K.Hrdlickova ....(CZE)						
(Q) 13. Miss C.Black ....(ZIM)	Miss C.Black 6/2 6/4	Miss C.Black ....6/7(3) 7/5 6/3				
14. Miss S Jeyaseelan ....(CAN)						
15. Miss H.Sukova ....(CZE)	Miss P.Schnyder [13] 3/6 6/4 6/3					
16. Miss P.Schnyder [13] ....(SUI)						
17. Mrs D.Van Roost [15] ....(BEL)	Mrs D.Van Roost [15] 6/1 6/3	Mrs D.Van Roost [15] 6/1 6/1	Mrs D.Van Roost [15] 6/1 6/2	Miss A.Sanchez Vicario [5] 3/6 6/3 6/2		
18. Miss J.Kruger ....(RSA)						
19. Miss N.Dechy ....(FRA)	Miss A.Miller ....7/6(3) 6/2					
20. Miss A.Miller ....(USA)						
(W) 21. Miss L.Latimer ....(GBR)	Miss L.Latimer 6/4 6/1	Miss S.Appelmans 6/1 6/4				
22. Miss J.Kandarr ....(GER)						
23. Miss S.Appelmans ....(BEL)	Miss S.Appelmans 6/3 6/3					
24. Miss C.Torrens-Valero ....(ESP)						
25. Miss J.Lee ....(TPE)	Miss J.Lee 6/4 6/1	Miss S.Plischke 6/2 6/0	Miss A.Sanchez Vicario [5] 7/5 6/2			
(W) 26. Miss L.A.Woodroffe ......(GBR)						
27. Miss A.Sugiyama ....(JPN)	Miss S.Plischke .....6/4 6/7(2) 6/3					
28. Miss S.Plischke ....(AUT)						
29. Miss M.Grzybowska ....(POL)	Miss M.Grzybowska 6/2 6/4	Miss A.Sanchez Vicario [5] 4/6 6/4 6/3				
30. Miss R.Dragomir ....(ROM)						
31. Miss C.Cristea ....(ROM)	Miss A.Sanchez Vicario [5]5/7 6/2 6/0					
32. Miss A.Sanchez Vicario [5] .....(ESP)						
33. Miss J.Novotna [3] ....(CZE)	Miss J.Novotna [3] 6/2 6/2	Miss J.Novotna [3] 6/3 4/6 6/1	Miss J.Novotna [3] 6/3 6/1	Miss J.Novotna [3] 6/2 6/3	Miss J.Novotna [3] 7/5 7/6(2)	
34. Miss S.Kleinova ....(CZE)						
35. Miss E.Gagliardi ....(SUI)	Miss T.Panova 4/6 7/5 6/4					
36. Miss T.Panova ....(RUS)						
37. Mrs P.Hy-Boulais ....(CAN)	Mrs P.Hy-Boulais 4/6 6/2 6/3	Miss C.Morariu 7/5 6/0				
38. Miss M.Babel ....(GER)						
39. Miss C.Morariu ....(USA)	Miss C.Morariu 4/6 6/1 6/2					
40. Miss M.Maruska ....(AUT)						
(Q) 41. Miss S.De Beer ....(RSA)	Miss S.De Beer 6/4 6/4	Miss S.De Beer 6/2 4/6 6/3	Miss I.Spirlea [10] 6/4 6/4			
42. Miss I.Gorrochategui ....(ARG)						
43. Miss K.Brandi ....(USA)	Miss S-T.Wang ....7/6(4) 7/5					
44. Miss S-T.Wang ....(TPE)						
45. Miss B.Rittner ....(GER)	Miss B.Rittner ....7/6(6) 6/0	Miss I.Spirlea [10] 6/4 6/4				
46. Miss A.Cocheteux ....(FRA)						
47. Miss F.Lubiani ....(ITA)	Miss I.Spirlea [10] 7/5 6/3					
48. Miss I.Spirlea [10] ....(ROM)						
(L) 49. Miss L.Osterloh ....(USA)	Miss K.Po 6/2 2/6 6/1	Miss V.Ruano Pascual 6/2 6/4	Miss V.Ruano Pascual 7/5 4/1	Miss V.Williams [7] 6/3 6/1		
50. Miss K.Po ....(USA)						
51. Miss A.Glass ....(GER)	Miss V.Ruano Pascual....6/1 6/7(4) 6/3					
52. Miss V.Ruano Pascual ....(ESP)						
53. Miss L.Golarsa ....(ITA)	Miss S.Williams 6/4 6/3	Miss S.Williams 6/3 6/0				
54. Miss S.Williams ....(USA)						
55. Miss A.Smashnova ....(ISR)	Miss M.Lucic ....6/4 6/7(5) 6/3					
56. Miss M.Lucic ....(CRO)						
57. Mrs G.Nielsen ....(USA)	Miss C.Rubin 4/6 6/0 6/2	Miss C.Rubin 3/6 7/5 11/9	Miss V.Williams [7] 6/3 6/4			
58. Miss C.Rubin ....(USA)						
59. Miss T.Snyder ....(USA)	Miss T.Snyder 6/3 6/0					
60. Miss L.Nemeckova ....(CZE)						
61. Miss B.Schett ....(AUT)	Miss B.Schett 6/0 6/2	Miss V.Williams [7] 6/1 6/2				
62. Miss P.Stoyanova ....(BUL)						
63. Miss J.Nejedly ....(CAN)	Miss V.Williams [7] 6/3 6/3					
64. Miss V.Williams [7] ....(USA)						
65. Miss M.Seles [6] ....(USA)	Miss M.Seles [6] 6/3 6/3	Miss M.Seles [6] 6/1 6/1	Miss M.Seles [6] 6/2 6/3	Miss M.Seles [6] 6/3 6/2	Miss N.Zvereva 7/6(4) 6/2	
66. Miss M.A.Sanchez Lorenzo......(ESP)						
67. Miss A.Fusai ....(FRA)	Miss A.Fusai 6/3 6/2					
68. Miss K.Studenikova ....(SVK)						
69. Miss Y.Basuki ....(INA)	Miss Y.Basuki 6/4 6/0	Miss Y.Basuki 6/3 6/4				
70. Miss S.Reeves ....(USA)						
71. Miss A.Mauresmo ....(FRA)	Miss A.Mauresmo 6/3 6/4					
(Q) 72. Miss M.Schnitzer ....(GER)						
73. Miss N.J.Pratt ....(AUS)	Miss J.Capriati 6/4 3/6 6/4	Miss L.M.McNeil ...4/6 6/4 6/2	Miss S.Testud [14] ....6/3 7/6(7)			
(W) 74. Miss J.Capriati ....(USA)						
(W) 75. Miss L.M.McNeil ....(USA)	Miss L.M.McNeil ...2/6 6/4 6/4					
(Q) 76. Miss E.S.H.Callens ....(BEL)						
77. Miss S.Noorlander ....(NED)	Miss S.Noorlander 6/3 6/1	Miss S.Testud [14] 6/3 6/1				
78. Miss O.Lugina ....(UKR)						
(Q) 79. Miss R.P.Stubbs ....(AUS)	Miss S.Testud [14] ....7/6(5) 6/0					
80. Miss S.Testud [14] ....(FRA)						
81. Miss M.Pierce [11] ....(FRA)	Miss E.Tatarkova ....7/6(4) 6/3	Miss M.de Swardt ....6/4 7/6(5)	Miss M.Oremans 6/4 7/5	Miss M.Seles [6] 6/3 6/2		
82. Miss E.Tatarkova ....(UKR)						
83. Miss B.Schwartz ....(AUT)	Miss M.de Swardt ....7/6(5) 6/3					
84. Miss M.de Swardt ....(RSA)						
85. Miss A.Gersi ....(CZE)	Miss A.Carlsson 6/1 6/1	Miss M.Oremans 6/2 6/3				
86. Miss A.Carlsson ....(SWE)						
87. Mrs E.Wagner ....(GER)	Miss M.Oremans 2/6 6/3 6/2					
88. Miss M.Oremans ....(NED)						
89. Miss N.Miyagi ....(JPN)	Miss N.Miyagi 6/3 1/6 6/2	Miss N.Zvereva 6/1 6/3	Miss N.Zvereva 6/4 7/5	Miss N.Zvereva 6/4 6/2		
(W) 90. Miss J.M.Pullin ....(GBR)						
91. Miss N.Zvereva ....(BLR)	Miss N.Zvereva 7/5 6/4					
92. Miss R.McQuillan ....(AUS)						
93. Miss H.Nagyova ....(SVK)	Miss H.Nagyova .....6/7(3) 6/2 6/4	Miss S.Graf [4] 6/0 6/4				
94. Miss A.Frazier ....(USA)						
95. Miss G.Leon Garcia ....(ESP)	Miss S.Graf [4] 6/4 6/1					
96. Miss S.Graf [4] ....(GER)						
97. Miss C.Martinez [8] ....(ESP)	Miss C.Martinez [8] 6/1 6/0	Miss C.Martinez [8] 7/5 7/5	Miss S.Smith 2/6 6/3 7/5	Miss N.Tauziat [16] 6/3 6/1	Miss N.Tauziat [16] 1/6 7/6(1) 6/3	
98. Miss S.Farina ....(ITA)						
99. Miss K.Boogert ....(NED)	Miss K.Boogert 3/6 6/2 6/1					
100. Miss M.Saeki ....(JPN)						
101. Miss M.Diaz Oliva ....(ARG)	Miss M.Diaz Oliva 6/3 6/2	Miss S.Smith 6/1 6/3				
102. Miss P.Suarez ....(ARG)						
103. Miss A-G.Sidot ....(FRA)	Miss S.Smith 6/3 4/6 6/2					
(W) 104. Miss S.Smith ....(GBR)						
105. Miss S-H.Park ....(KOR)	Mrs J.Halard-Decugis 6/2 6/4	Mrs J.Halard-Decugis ....6/4 7/6(6)	Miss N.Tauziat [16] ....7/6(5) 3/6 6/4			
106. Mrs J.Halard-Decugis ....(FRA)						
107. Miss O.Barabanschikova ....(BLR)	Mrs A.Dechaume-Balleret..6/4 6/7(5) 11/9					
108. Mrs A.Dechaume-Balleret ......(FRA)						
109. Miss I.Majoli ....(CRO)	Miss I.Majoli 6/2 6/3	Miss N.Tauziat [16] 6/0 6/1				
110. Miss K.Habsudova ....(SVK)						
(Q) 111. Miss H.Inoue ....(JPN)	Miss N.Tauziat [16] 2/6 6/1 6/3					
112. Miss N.Tauziat [16] ....(FRA)						
113. Miss A.J.Coetzer [9] ....(RSA)	Miss A.J.Coetzer [9] 6/2 6/2	Miss N.Sawamatsu 3/6 6/3 6/2	Miss M.Serna 6/3 5/7 6/0	Miss L.A.Davenport [2] 6/1 6/0	Miss N.Tauziat [16] 6/3 6/3	
114. Miss K-A.Guse ....(AUS)						
115. Miss N.Sawamatsu ....(JPN)	Miss N.Sawamatsu 2/6 6/3 6/2					
116. Miss B.Paulus ....(AUT)						
117. Miss F.Li ....(CHN)	Miss R.Grande 6/1 6/4	Miss M.Serna 6/4 6/1				
118. Miss R.Grande ....(ITA)						
119. Miss M.Serna ....(ESP)	Miss M.Serna 7/5 4/6 6/1					
(Q) 120. Miss R.Bobkova ....(CZE)						
(L) 121. Miss K.Miller ....(USA)	Miss N.Kijimuta 3/6 6/3 6/4	Miss M.A.Vento 6/0 7/5	Miss L.A.Davenport [2] 6/3 1/6 6/2			
122. Miss N.Kijimuta ....(JPN)						
123. Miss M.A.Vento ....(VEN)	Miss M.A.Vento ....7/6(1) 4/6 6/3					
124. Miss S.Cacic ....(USA)						
125. Miss S.Pitkowski ....(FRA)	Mrs L.Neiland 6/1 5/7 6/3	Miss L.A.Davenport [2] 6/1 7/5				
126. Mrs L.Neiland ....(LAT)						
127. Miss F.Labat ....(ARG)	Miss L.A.Davenport [2] 6/2 6/2					
128. Miss L.A.Davenport [2] ....(USA)						

Heavy type denotes seeded players. The figure in brackets against names denotes the order in which they have been seeded. (W)=Wild card. (Q)=Qualifier. (L)=Lucky loser.

ACKNOWLEDGEMENTS

The Committee of Management wish to thank the following for their assistance during The Championships:

ASSOCIATION OF HONORARY STEWARDS

SERVICE AND LONDON FIRE BRIGADE STEWARDS

BRITISH TENNIS UMPIRES ASSOCIATION

BRITISH WOMEN'S TENNIS ASSOCIATION
who staff the Players' Information Desk

MERTON EDUCATION COMMITTEE & THE GOVERNORS OF THE BEACON SCHOOL, BANSTEAD
from whose schools the ball boys and girls are chosen

THE POLICE

ST JOHN AMBULANCE & THE LONDON AMBULANCE SERVICE
who staff the first aid posts and the ambulances

WOMEN'S ROYAL VOLUNTARY SERVICE
who staff the information desks

CANON
OFFICIAL SUPPLIER OF CAMERAS, COPIERS & FACSIMILES

DIET COKE
OFFICIAL CARBONATED SOFT DRINK

HERTZ
OFFICIAL CAR

IBM
OFFICIAL SUPPLIER OF INFORMATION TECHNOLOGY

NESCAFÉ
OFFICIAL COFFEE

PERRIER
OFFICIAL MINERAL WATER

PHILIPS
OFFICIAL SUPPLIER OF TELEVISIONS & VIDEO RECORDERS

ROBINSONS
OFFICIAL STILL SOFT DRINK

ROLEX
OFFICIAL TIMEKEEPER

SECURICOR
OFFICIAL SECURITY SERVICES PROVIDER

SLAZENGER
OFFICIAL BALL

BARCLAYS
who provide banking facilities

BOW BRAND
*who provide racket stringing
for the competitors*

BRONNLEY
*who provide soap to the dressing rooms,
Members and Debenture Holders*

CARTERS
who provide the grass seed

CHRISTY
*who provide Championship towels
to the dressing rooms*

HI-TEC
*who provide footwear for the
ball boys and girls*

JACOB'S CREEK
*who are the exclusive
Australian wine supplier*

THE SCOTTS COMPANY
who provide turfcare products

LLOYDS PHARMACY
*who provide the Chemist Shop
in conjunction with*
SMITHKLINE BEECHAM

THE WIMBLEDON PROGRAMME

PRODUCTION, DISTRIBUTION AND SALE OF ADVERTISING SPACE

The Programme Publications Group, Bradford House, 39A East Street, Epsom, Surrey KT17 1BL

Telephone 01372 743377, Facsimile 01372 743399

email: lynn@programmepubs.demon.co.uk   website: www.eventprogrammes.com

DESIGN

Jules Akel, Oak View, Brickhouse Lane, Godstone, Surrey RH9 8JW

Telephone 01342 843703

PHOTOGRAPHY

Allsport, Prosport, Michael Cole Camerawork

REPRODUCTION

Speedgraphics Ltd., 1 Westwood Court, Clayhill Industrial Park, Neston, South Wirral L64 3UG